INSIGHT ◎ GUIDES

CALIFORNIA

◉ Walking Eye App

YOUR FREE DESTINATION CONTENT AND EBOOK AVAILABLE THROUGH THE WALKING EYE APP

Your guide now includes a free eBook and destination content for your chosen destination, all for the same great price as before. Simply download the Walking Eye App from the App Store or Google Play to access your free eBook and destination content.

HOW THE WALKING EYE APP WORKS

Through the Walking Eye App, you can purchase a range of eBooks and destination content. However, when you buy this book, you can download the corresponding eBook and destination content for free. Just see below in the grey panels where to find your free content and then scan the QR code at the bottom of this page.

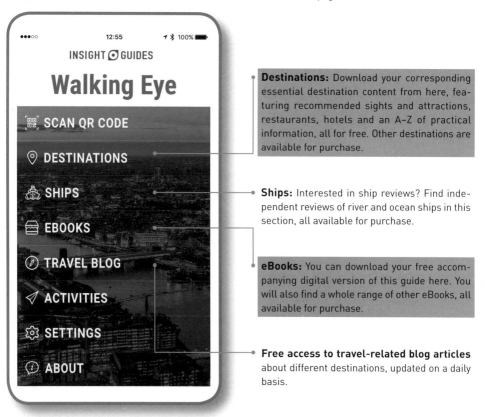

Destinations: Download your corresponding essential destination content from here, featuring recommended sights and attractions, restaurants, hotels and an A–Z of practical information, all for free. Other destinations are available for purchase.

Ships: Interested in ship reviews? Find independent reviews of river and ocean ships in this section, all available for purchase.

eBooks: You can download your free accompanying digital version of this guide here. You will also find a whole range of other eBooks, all available for purchase.

Free access to travel-related blog articles about different destinations, updated on a daily basis.

HOW THE DESTINATION CONTENT WORKS

Each destination includes a short introduction, an A–Z of practical information and recommended points of interest, split into 4 different categories:

- Highlights
- Accommodation
- Eating out
- What to do

You can view the location of every point of interest and save it by adding it to your Favourites. In the 'Around Me' section you can view all the points of interest within 5km.

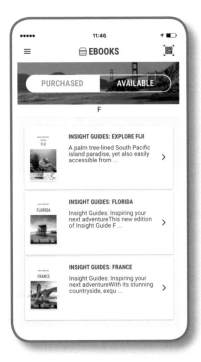

HOW THE EBOOKS WORK

The eBooks are provided in EPUB file format. Please note that you will need an eBook reader installed on your device to open the file. Many devices come with this as standard, but you may still need to install one manually from Google Play.

The eBook content is identical to the content in the printed guide.

HOW TO DOWNLOAD THE WALKING EYE APP

1. Download the Walking Eye App from the App Store or Google Play.
2. Open the app and select the scanning function from the main menu.
3. Scan the QR code on this page – you will then be asked a security question to verify ownership of the book.
4. Once this has been verified, you will see your eBook and destination content in the purchased ebook and destination sections, where you will be able to download them.

Other destination apps and eBooks are available for purchase separately or are free with the purchase of the Insight Guide book.

CONTENTS

Travel tips

TRANSPORTATION

A – Z

FURTHER READING

Maps

Inside front cover California
Inside back cover California National
  Parks and Reserves

LEGEND
📍 Insight on
📷 Photo story

THE BEST OF CALIFORNIA: TOP ATTRACTIONS

△ **Yosemite National Park**. From the sheer granite cliffs of El Capitan to waterfalls and green meadows, the crown jewel of America's national parks is heaven for adventurous types. See page 183.

△ **Golden Gate Bridge**. San Francisco's famous bridge opened in 1937, four years after construction began. Painted not gold but "international orange," the bridge is one of the world's favorite icons. See page 121.

▽ **Wine Country**. The emerald vineyards, lush red wines, warm sunshine, and fresh California cuisine of Napa and Sonoma counties make them ideal for a road trip. Or for the best views, take a hot-air balloon ride. See page 141.

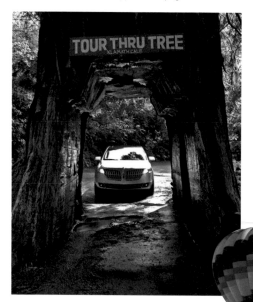

△ **Redwood forests**. Awe-inspiring ancient redwoods tower over visitors in old-growth state parks. Some of these majestic giants, 1,000 years old and reaching 300ft (90 meters), are the largest living things on earth. See page 155.

△ **California cuisine**. Alice Waters changed the restaurant industry forever when she got local farmers to supply her with the freshest seasonal ingredients for her daily changing menus. See page 67.

▽ **Monterey**. Coastal Monterey offers something for everyone: Steinbeck's Cannery Row, the Monterey Bay Aquarium (arguably the world's finest), plus diving in kelp forests and swimming with sea otters. See page 195.

△ **PCH**. In the Los Angeles area, Highway 1 is also known as the Pacific Coast Highway, or the PCH. The road twists and turns along SoCal's breathtaking coast, offering gorgeous views of both land and sea. See page 230.

△ **SoCal beaches**. There's a reason Southern Californians sport tans year-round – from Santa Barbara to Santa Monica, and Huntington Beach to San Diego, the state's southern coast is packed with miles of sunny beaches. See page 232.

△ **Death Valley**. The lowest point on the North American continent, Death Valley can be insanely hot in summer, but is awash with colorful desert wild-flowers and cactus blooms in spring. See page 272.

▽ **Hollywood**. Synonymous with the movie industry, Hollywood today pays homage to its cinematic history with attractions like the Hollywood Walk of Fame and opulent old movie houses. See page 221.

THE BEST OF CALIFORNIA: EDITOR'S CHOICE

An aerial view of the notorious Alcatraz.

ONLY IN CALIFORNIA

Alcatraz. Haunting yet fascinating, "the Rock" is a former high-security prison on an island in the San Francisco Bay that once housed some of America's most notorious criminals. See page 109.

Cable cars. Wonderfully old-fashioned cable cars creakily lumber up and roll down San Francisco's hills, ringing their bells as passengers hang out the sides. See page 113.

TCL's Chinese Theatre. This 1920s-era LA movie palace in Hollywood has a forecourt of illustriousis hand and footprints. See page 221.

La Brea Tar Pits. One of the world's most famous fossil locations, these bubbling pools of asphalt have been revealing prehistoric remains since the 1900s. See page 227.

Santa Catalina Island. With two-thirds of its interior protected land, beautiful Catalina is calm, practically car free, and ideal for a day trip. See page 253.

Hollywood Walk of Fame. One of Los Angeles' most famous attractions, where over 2,400 star-shaped plaques are emblazoned with celebrities' names. See page 222.

Bay to Breakers. A crazy annual footrace involving thousands of people in outrageous costumes – or nothing at all – filling the streets of San Francisco. See page 294.

CULTURAL HIGHLIGHTS

Getty Center. This stunning LA cliff-top complex combines art, architecture, and delightful gardens, all of which you can explore for free. See page 236.

LACMA. With a collection of nearly 130,000 objects spanning from antiquity to the present, the Los Angeles County Museum of Art is the largest art museum in the western United States. See page 224.

Hollywood Bowl. Instantly recognizable by its dome shape, this classic performance amphitheater in Los Angeles attracts music lovers who come to hear classical music and jazz concerts. See page 222.

San Diego Museum of Contemporary Art. A world-class modern art museum in two locations, one in downtown San Diego, and the other in a fabulous ocean-front setting in La Jolla. See page 282.

San Jose Museum of Art. Nearly 12,500 works of art are housed here, including glittering blown-glass sculptures by Dale Chihuly. See page 138.

SF MoMA. Housing Northern California's premier art collection, the distinctive San Francisco Museum of Modern Art, designed by Swiss architect Mario Botta, was recently expanded showcasing three times more gallery space in 10 breathtaking floors and features a five-story glass roofed staircase . See page 116.

Civic Center. San Francisco's Asian Art Museum, Main Library, War Memorial, and Performing Arts Center, including Opera House, and Davies Symphony Hall are all clustered together near City Hall. See page 117.

Exhibit in San Jose Museum of Art.

Lake Tahoe.

BEST FOR KIDS

Disneyland. Mickey Mouse isn't the only attraction: families flock here for Space Mountain, the Fantasmic! fireworks show, and the rides at California Adventure. See page 246.

Universal Studios. Attractions based on Harry Potter, Jurassic Park, The Walking Dead and King Kong are winners for kids – and adults too. See page 242.

San Diego Zoo. Looking for giant pandas? Visit lush Balboa Park for one of the world's most impressive zoos, with a more natural setting that uses moats instead of cages. See page 281.

SeaWorld. Watch irresistible dolphins, killer whales, sea lions, and a vast array of fish, then hit the rides at this over-the-top San Diego water park. See page 278.

Pier 39 Fisherman's Wharf's. Pier 39 has an aquarium, street performers, sea lions, an arcade, and the San Francisco Carousel. Ice cream sundaes at Ghirardelli Square aren't far away. See page 108.

Monterey Bay Aquarium. Don't miss feeding time at this spectacular seaside sanctuary with around 350,000 specimens. See page 195.

Knott's Berry Farm. America's first theme park delights with gunfights, Wild West stunt shows, Camp Snoopy musicals, and fried chicken dinners. See page 249.

Calico Ghost Town. Not far from the Mojave Desert, an 1880s silver-mining town is now a theme park. See page 268.

Exploratorium. Kids and science come together for a day of fun and learning with hands-on exhibits involving light, color, sounds, and other sensory thrills. See page 115.

MOST SPECTACULAR SCENERY

Avenue of the Giants. Surrounded by Humboldt Redwoods State Park, this 31-mile (50km) stretch of highway offers a jaw-dropping display of giant redwoods. See page 154.

Big Sur. Hugging the rugged coast in a series of switchbacks, Highway 1 south of San Francisco through the Monterey Peninsula to Big Sur may be the most spectacular route in America. See page 198.

Lake Tahoe. The sparkling blue lake is stunning in summer as well as winter, when skiers come to tackle surrounding mountains. Nearby is Devils Postpile National Monument, the gigantic, geometrically fractured core of an ancient volcano. See page 181.

Joshua Tree National Park. Joshua Tree is a strange, other-worldly place, with huge sand-stone boulders the color of sunsets and rust, interspersed with oddly shaped and often very old Joshua and yucca trees. See page 265.

Yosemite Valley. Look in awe upon the giant Half Dome, sheer-faced El Capitan, and gushing waterfalls. It's not surpri-sing that millions visit each year. See page 184.

The High North. A remote and stunning domain of mountains, valleys, volcanoes, rivers, canyons, and basins. See page 159.

Roller coaster ride at Knott's Berry Farm.

Ferris wheel on Santa Monica Pier.

BEST BEACHES

Huntington Beach. Ever wonder where "Surf City USA" is? You just found it. See page 255.
Cabrillo Beach. Cabrillo has windsurfing, scuba diving, whale watching, a good aquarium, and views of Santa Catalina Island. See page 252.
Malibu's Zuma and Surfrider beaches. Popular with surfers, sunbathers, and bird-watchers, Malibu's beaches have wetlands, flower gardens, tide pools, and terrific bird-watching perches. You can spot celebrities' houses from the sand too. See page 231.
Venice Beach. There's terrific people-watching potential here, from hippie artists to muscle-bound men. See page 234.
Santa Cruz. This stylish town has three beaches: Main Beach has the boardwalk, Cowell Beach is for learner surfers, and Steamer Lane is for experts and their boards. See page 193.
Santa Monica Beach. The soft white sand flanking Santa Monica Pier is a wonderful place to enjoy Pacific sunsets. See page 232.
Stinson Beach. Despite the chilly water, Stinson is the most popular beach in the San Francisco Bay Area. See page 132.

WINE COUNTRY HIGHLIGHTS

Calistoga spas. With thermal hot springs feeding warm pools, and volcanic mud treatments, Calistoga's luxurious spas are world-renowned. See page 145.
Hot-air ballooning. Get a bird's eye view of the Wine Country with a morning hot-air balloon ride, followed by a champagne breakfast. See page 145.
Dining with a view. Dine with panoramic views on Auberge du Soleil's terrace, one of the prettiest outdoor dining spots in the Wine Country. See page 146.
Napa Valley Wine Train. Take a tour of Napa Valley in lavishly restored 1915 Pullman dining and lounge cars, while feasting on seasonal fare and local wines. See page 143.
Oxbow Public Market. Taste everything from oysters to organic ice cream at the colorful stalls, and check out the many varied events like unique happy hours, cooking demos, and music performances. See page 143.
Relaxed wine tasting. Have a patio picnic lunch at affordable Louis M. Martini, followed by another tasting or two at wineries like Paraduxx or Frog's Leap. See pages 143 and 144.

OUTDOOR FUN

Diving in Monterey. Explore thick kelp forests in Monterey Bay, a popular place to get scuba certified in Northern California. See page 196.
Hiking Half Dome. Brave souls make the steep climb up Half Dome (the last part with cables to hold onto) for magnificent Yosemite views. Make reservations in advance. See page 185.
Hiking in Muir Woods. San Francisco in the morning; redwoods in the afternoon. Take a stroll under grand trees and stop at the Pelican Inn at Muir Beach for a spot of tea or a cold mug of mead. See page 131.
River rafting. Complete beginners take float trips through Coloma Valley, while experienced rafters can tackle Class IV rapids south of Sacramento. See page 170.
Winter weekends in Lake Tahoe. Hit the slopes for skiing or snowboarding, cross-country skiing or snowshoeing, in the lovely setting of the Sierra Nevada mountain range. See page 90.

ARCHITECTURAL HIGHLIGHTS

Academy of Sciences. The award-winning Renzo Piano-designed eco-house in San Francisco's Golden Gate Park boasts a living roof. See page 124.

Balboa Park. Originally built for the 1915–16 Panama-California Exhibition, ornate Spanish Colonial Revival-style buildings now fill San Diego's museum-filled park. See page 280.

California State Capitol Building. The state's domed capitol building (which is gorgeous from the inside too) has dominated the Sacramento cityscape since 1869. See page 169.

Hearst Castle. This castle in the sky was built by William Randolph Hearst, the media magnate who was the subject of Orson Welles's Citizen Kane. See page 200.

Mission Dolores. The only mission chapel that is still intact, Mission Dolores is also the oldest building in San Francisco. Immortalized in the Hitchcock film Vertigo, a serene cemetery holds the remains of some of the city's first leaders. See page 121.

Painted ladies. These tall, stately Victorian homes can be found all over San Francisco, but some of the brightest, most renowned, and most colorful border Alamo Square. See page 123.

Transamerica Pyramid. Once likened to an upside-down ice-cream cone, or a dunce cap, the 48-floor building built in 1970 by William L. Pereira is now one of San Francisco's favorite icons. See page 115.

Walt Disney Concert Hall. The home of the LA Philharmonic is a gleaming modern design by noted architect Frank Gehry. See page 219.

Winchester Mystery House. Full of staircases that lead nowhere and doors that open into walls, the spooky Winchester Mystery House is a building like no other. See page 138.

ICONIC HOTELS

Mission Inn Hotel and Spa. Utterly breathtaking architecture – from intricate spiral staircases to flower-topped balconies – and grand vistas make this riverside hotel one of the most beautiful and historic in the state. See page 261.

Majestic Yosemite Hotel. The grande dame of Yosemite's hotels, this elegant historic lodge, built in the 1920s, is the most luxurious way to enjoy Yosemite Valley. See page 185.

Hotel del Coronado. Built in 1888, the Coronado's red turrets and Victorian style make it unmissable on the San Diego beachfront. It's unforgettable, too. See page 282.

The Beverly Hills Hotel. Affectionately known as the "Pink Palace," this old celebrity haunt has recorded John F. Kennedy, Elizabeth Taylor and Richard Burton, Charlie Chaplin, Spencer Tracy, Marilyn Monroe, John Wayne, and the Duke of Windsor among its guests. See page 229.

The Palace Hotel. A fine tea or lunch in San Francisco's first hotel is an utterly opulent reminder of the city's past. See page 117.

Madonna Inn. With imaginative interiors and bizarre themed rooms, this landmark hotel seems pure kitsch to some, and a creative wonder to others. See page 209.

Bumpass Hell in Mount Lassen Volcanic National Park.

MONEY-SAVING TIPS

National parks pass. Frequent visitors to California's national parks should buy an "America the Beautiful" pass ($80) which covers entrance fees for the holder, a vehicle, plus any passengers at more than 2,000 federal recreation sites in the country. www.nps.gov/findapark/passes.htm

CityPass. Offers visitor cards for San Francisco or Southern California that provide discounts to major attractions, and cuts down on waiting in lines. Go to CityPass.com. Alternatively, try the Go Cards (www.smartdestinations.com), which offer access to a long list of key attractions, or you can customize a pass for the sites you plan to visit.

Groupon. If you're planning your trip at least a month in advance, register at offer sites like www.groupon.com or , www. livingsocial.com, to receive emails with steeply disscounted coupons.

Free museums. Many museums in major cities have a free day once a month, or during evening hours. Call or visit individual websites for details. For always-free museums, visit the Getty Center, Getty Villa, and Griffith Observatory in Los Angeles, and the Cable Car Museum and the Musee Mechanique in San Francisco.

Sunset on the South Bay
Bicycle Trail.

Admiring the giant sequoias
in Sequoia National Park.

Sun, sand, and surf
at Ocean Beach.

THE REAL 'GOLDEN STATE'

While it's nicknamed the Golden State, California actually has an incredibly diverse range of destinations, each with its own beautiful natural wonders, impressive cultural attractions, and engaging personality.

Los Angeles.

California is often thought of in north and south halves. In general, the upper half conjures up images of foggy San Francisco, Silicon Valley tech nerds, great wine, a cold and rugged coast, redwood forests, Tahoe for snow sport aficionados, and Yosemite for backpackers. The south is about sunshine and warmth, with blonde surfers catching waves along its coast, celebrities and image-obsessed wannabes flocking to Los Angeles, families enjoying Disneyland, and chic Palm Springs, the gateway to miles and miles of inland desert.

Of course the reality is a much more complex picture. In the north, liberal San Francisco boasts cultural landmarks like the Golden Gate Bridge and historic cable cars, plus world-class museums and an innovative food scene. Just an hour and a half away is Napa Valley, where you can sip Cabernet while gazing at miles of lush vineyards, followed by the meal of a lifetime at French Laundry.

A breathtaking drive south for a few hours along the rugged coast brings you to Big Sur for great hiking, while a drive north connects to the Marin Headlands and Muir Woods, then quiet coastal towns like Mendocino. Head inland and you're taken back to Gold Rush days in Old Town Sacramento.

Head further into nature to find Northern California's 3,000-year-old redwood trees in old-growth state parks and Yosemite National Park's stunning granite peaks and waterfalls. The park's miles and miles of trails could take a lifetime to explore, as could skiing or snowboarding the snowy peaks of sparkling blue Lake Tahoe.

Casino in Avalon, Santa Catalina Island.

The South can hold its own in the nature department: inland are massive deserts, Anza-Borrego Desert State Park's wildflowers, and Joshua Tree National Park's twisted trees. The coastline south of Big Sur leads to Pismo Beach's giant sand dunes and clouds of Monarch butterflies. Further along are Paso Robles vineyards, the Channel Islands, and white-sand beaches perfect for surfing and sunbathing.

Chic Santa Barbara, sometimes referred to as the "American Riviera," is quietly upscale, while San Diego draws surfers to the beaches and families to the San Diego Zoo. Sprawling Los Angeles has something for everyone: celebrity-spotting and TV tapings, the Getty Center and LA Museum of Contemporary Art, food trucks and trendy bars, lovely beaches and the canals of Venice. And, of course, Disneyland.

Celebrating the Hispanic Cinco de Mayo festival in Pasadena.

CULTURAL DIVERSITY

Throughout its history, California has seen waves of immigrants attracted by opportunities the state had to offer, with the newcomers bringing new values. California's changing ethnic mix has significant political, social, and artistic implications.

California is the third-largest state in America and ranks highest in number of inhabitants, but perhaps what is less appreciated is that no other part of America can claim such ethnic diversity. From the onset of the industrialized era, the state's population has been melded by boom cycles of immigration: Mexicans, Europeans, the Chinese and Japanese, African-Americans from the South, Russians, Armenians, Asian Indians, Koreans, Salvadoreans, Iranians, Filipinos, Samoans, Vietnamese. Nearly 70 years ago, historian Carey McWilliams was already referring to Southern California as an "archipelago of social and ethnic islands, economically interrelated but culturally disparate." Today, the students of the Los Angeles Unified School District (LAUSD) alone speak more than 90 different languages and dialects.

Horseback riding in Canyon Ranch.

When Los Angeles was founded in 1781, more than half of the settlers were of mixed black, American Indian and Spanish blood. To this day, a large percentage of the Latino population resides in Southern California.

TIDES OF IMMIGRATION

When California joined the Union in 1850, it was considered to be the final frontier, a land promising spiritual and social riches. Boosters furiously sold the fable of the Golden State to the rest of the Union, and pioneers armed with little more than faith came in search of sunshine, fertile soil, and freedom from oppression.

The blending of cultures had begun long before, over two centuries ago when Spanish Franciscan monks arrived to set up missions throughout the state and spread Catholicism to indigenous peoples. Before the end of the 19th century, though, the American Indian population had been decimated and their mestizo (mixed-heritage) descendants found themselves pushed southward by an influx of miners flooding the foothills of the Sierra Nevada mountain range.

The development and growth of California's industries throughout the 19th century brought new tides of immigration. The Chinese initially came as railroad workers on the Central Pacific construction gangs, before branching into agriculture and fishing. African-Americans also came as railroad employees, in smaller numbers at first and then, during World War II, to fill manufacturing and service jobs.

Beverly Hills was once called Rancho Rodeo de Las Aguas. It was owned by Maria Rita Valdez, the granddaughter of black founding settlers.

---

of thousands of Mexicans and Central Americans fleeing civil strife and political persecution immigrated, both legally and illegally, to California.

FAILURES IN MULTICULTURALISM

For much of the 20th century, California was hardly a model of open-mindedness. During the depression in the 1930s, the county of LA "repatriated" thousands of Mexicans on relief, loading them like cattle onto trains. When the need for cheap labor beckoned, Mexicans

Marijuana for sale on Venice Beach boardwalk.

And towards the turn of the century, Japanese immigrants arrived in search of opportunities in the emerging produce industry, which they eventually came to dominate, from packing and shipping the fruit to setting up small stands to sell it.

Nothing, however, compared to the tidal wave of Anglo-Americans who arrived from the Midwest during the 1880s (and then again – fleeing the parched dustbowl farms of the prairies – in the 1920s). Already having established major colonies around the San Francisco and Sacramento areas, they saturated Southern California with visions of manifest destiny.

In the 20th century, the most significant influx occurred in the 1980s, when hundreds

once more became a necessary commodity in the burgeoning economy.

Early in World War II, the notorious Executive Order 9066 authorized the internment of all Japanese on the West Coast – most of whom lost everything they owned. During the same decade, African-Americans who escaped the repression of the Deep South were barred from living in certain neighborhoods by restrictive housing covenants.

As a result of such practices, clusters of ethnic communities formed where people could feel protected and cultures preserved. San Francisco's Chinatown is one such example, developing out of necessity as a refuge from abuse: Until the 1960s, when immigration laws changed, the Chinese had been subjected to severe and continual harassment, and discriminatory legislation had deprived them of eligibility for citizenship, ensuring that they had no legal recourse.

Later, as the job market plummeted in recession-hit California in the 1990s, tensions between ethnic groups amplified. The eruption of civil unrest in Los Angeles in 1992 was a wake-up call to the entire US, an indication that the ethnic stew was boiling over.

THE ARTISTIC FACE OF MULTICULTURALISM

It is perhaps the necessity of asserting one's identity in this Babel-like sea of cultures that has made California the state in which more trends and artistic movements take flight. Rap music, for example, has been linked to the malaise that occurred after the Watts rebellion in 1965. Assembled from the shards of the uprising, the Watts art renaissance delivered up a number of visionaries. Theirs was the poetry of frustration, self-assertion and, unlike some contemporary rap, hope. Bold, bright graffiti art also arrived hard on the heels of disenfranchisement. "Tagging" (initialing) property provided inner-city teens – primarily Latino – with a voice that the larger culture refused to hear. Today, rap's impact on the media and advertising has been palpable.

In California's metropolitan areas, churches often served as the nexus of a community – spiritually, socially, and politically. The first was the African Methodist Episcopal Church in south central Los Angeles, the city's first African-American church.

California also adopted customs of Asian immigrants. Health-conscious Californians submit to strenuous programs of yoga and meditation, and feed on Pad Thai, sushi, and *pho*. Beat Generation writers, who tumbled around San Francisco in the 1950s, derived much of their inspiration from Buddhism, and Japanese and Chinese poetry.

The experience of facing society as "other" in California has produced some of America's finest writers and artists since the 1940s, including playwright William Saroyan, who grew up in an Armenian enclave of grape growers and farmers in Fresno; poet and novelist Alice Walker, best known for *The Color Purple*; essayist Richard Rodriguez, who writes about gay and Latino assimilation and the politics of multi-culturalism; Filipino-born artist Manuel Ocampo, whose paintings often depict symbols of racism and the brutish

Mexican farmworker in San Joaquin Valley.

⊘ LATINO COMMUNITY ACTIVISM

Although Latinos in California are heavily involved in community activism, they are generally underrepresented in the political arena. One reason is that the number of Latinos who are citizens – and therefore capable of voting – is much smaller than the actual population, and few of these register or turn up to vote. For many years the only notable Latino leader was the late Cesar Chavez, president of the United Farm Workers of America. However, more recently Kevin de León and Ricardo Lara have both been active in improving immigrant rights and increasing access to education and economic mobility for all.

imperialism of the colonials; theater artist Anna Deavere Smith, whose performance piece *Twilight: Los Angeles, 1992* concerned the riots that devastated the city, told through the voices of the people who experienced it; and novelist Amy Tan, who found the characters of her widely acclaimed *Joy Luck Club* in the Chinatown (San Francisco) of her childhood.

MULTI-ETHNIC STYLE

California epitomizes the best and worst of what being a truly multi-ethnic society can mean. There are some who believe that the obsession with tribalism is a leading factor in causing the sometimes bitter divisiveness throughout the state. Others say recognizing California's many ethnic groups is the

In 2015, the number of people of Latino or Hispanic descent officially outnumbered non-Hispanic Caucasians in California.

Ukulele players in San Diego.

⊘ FESTIVALS

There are celebrations up and down the state that reflect California's multi-ethnic population. San Francisco's Chinese New Year celebration is one of the biggest in America, while Vietnamese New Year has devotees in San Jose. Oakland has a Greek cultural festival in May and San Diego a Pacific Islander's festival in summer. Cinco de Mayo, the Mexican holiday, is celebrated in all major cities, while Brazilians, Scots, Irish, and Germans all have their own street parties. For a list of monthly festivities, consult the "Calendar" section of the *LA Times* at www.latimes.com/about/la-events-listings or check the *San Francisco Chronicle* at www.sfgate.com/events.

first step towards peaceful coexistence. What has become more and more evident, though, is that the people of California have slowly absorbed each other's habits and styles, tastes, and mannerisms.

While many California towns and suburbs are relatively homogeneous, others are home to diverse pockets of cultures that border one another, highlighting differences in religions and customs. California is hip-hop and cha-cha-cha wrapped in a dazzling gold-flecked sari. And now, more than any time in the history of the state, multiculturalism is reflected in the offices of elected and appointed officials: mayors and congressional representatives, city council members, and police chiefs.

One of the murals on the Great Wall of Los Angeles, depicting Californian history.

& PROPERTY

DECISIVE DATES

Pre-1500s
The Miwok, Ohlone, and Wituk tribes occupy much of the land now known as Northern California.

1579
Sir Francis Drake lands at Point Reyes, reporting to Europe that California is an island.

1770s
The Spanish found a *presidio* and mission near San Francisco Bay.

1781
Don Felipe de Neve founds what will become Los Angeles.

1769–1823
Spanish padres found 21 missions between San Diego and Sonoma.

1846
The US declares war on Mexico and captures California.

1848
Gold is discovered in the Sierra foothills.

1850s
Native Americans sign away up to 90 percent of their lands in treaties.

1858
The Butterfield Stage Line delivers Los Angeles' first overland mail.

1859
The Comstock Lode discovery turns San Francisco into a prosperous metropolis.

1869
The transcontinental railroad is completed, terminating at Oakland.

1873
The world's first cable car runs in San Francisco.

1876
The Southern Pacific Railway arrives in Los Angeles.

1886
Harvey H. Wilcox opens a subdivision that his wife names Hollywood.

1892
Oil is struck near what is now Los Angeles' MacArthur Park.

1905
Abbott Kinney opens his Venetian-style resort near Santa Monica.

1906
A massive earthquake (8.25 on the Richter scale) rocks San Francisco.

Exhibits at Columbia State Historic Park, a restored Gold Rush town.

1932
LA's Coliseum, then the world's largest stadium, hosts the Olympics.

1933
A Los Angeles earthquake (6.3 on the Richter scale) kills 120 people.

1937
The Golden Gate Bridge is opened to an uproarious reception.

1939
LA's Union Station, the last of the great railroad terminals, opens.

1945
The United Nations Organization is born in San Francisco.

1947
California passes a law against smog.

1950s
The "Beats," a bohemian literary group, hang out in San Francisco's North Beach.

1955
Disneyland opens in Anaheim.

1960s
Hippies flock to San Francisco's Haight-Ashbury district, celebrating the Summer of Love in 1967.

1965
Rioting in Los Angeles' Watts area kills 34 people.

1968
Presidential candidate Robert F. Kennedy is shot and killed in Los Angeles.

San Francisco's Golden Gate Bridge.

1971
An earthquake (6.6 on the Richter scale) kills 64 Southern Californians.

1974
Oil tycoon J. Paul Getty donates his Los Angeles home as a museum. BART (Bay Area Rapid Transit System) starts a regular transportation service.

1978
San Francisco mayor George Moscone and supervisor Harvey Milk are assassinated by a former Supervisor.

1980
Former governor of California Ronald Reagan becomes the 39th US president.

1980s
The computer industry's phenomenal growth puts Silicon Valley on the map.

1989
An earthquake (7.1 on the Richter scale) collapses a freeway and causes destruction in the San Francisco Bay Area.

1991
Berkeley Hills fire kills 25 people and destroys over 3,000 homes.

1992
LA police officers are acquitted of beating a black motorist, starting riots that kill 50 people.

1995
The new Museum of Modern Art in San Francisco's SoMa district spearheads a downtown building boom.

1995–97
The murder trial of football star O.J. Simpson enthrals the nation.

2003
Movie star Arnold Schwarzenegger becomes California's governor in an historic recall election.

2005
George Lucas moves his movie studio to San Francisco's Presidio.

2006
The Amgen Tour bicycling race, from San Francisco to LA, makes its debut.

2007
Wildfires from Santa Barbara to San Diego kill 12 people and destroy 1,500 buildings.

2008
The Writers Guild of America goes on strike, delaying TV broadcasts.

2012
Construction begins on a high-speed rail line connecting San Francisco and Sacramento to Los Angeles and San Diego.

2014
In the third year of one of the worst droughts in the past century, California State Governor Jerry Brown declares a drought state of emergency. The drought continues to persist. The San Francisco Giants win World Series for the third time in five seasons.

2015
The Golden State Warriors, a member of the National Basketball Association (NBA) based in Oakland, win the championship title for the first time in 40 years and break numerous records on the way to victory. A mass shooting and attempted bomb attack in San Bernardino kills 14 people and injures 22.

2016
Massive wildfires rage throughout the drought-ravaged state. A lengthy and divisive presidential election process culminates with the election of Donald Trump as the 45th President of the United States, despite California voting in favour of Democrat candidate Hillary Clinton.

2017
Over 9,000 wildfires ravage vast areas of California killing at least 44 people and destroying over 10,000 buildings.

2018
Recreational marihuana is made legal across the state for over 21s. Mudslides kill 20 people in Santa Barbara County.

NATIVE TRIBES AND EUROPEANS

For 10,000 years, a network of California tribes thrived and prospered, harvesting the riches from land, lakes, and sea. Then the white man brought disease and religion, decimating and subjugating the Native American population.

The first tenants of the rich land that became California were the prehistoric tribes that, through the centuries, crossed the land bridge of the Bering Strait and slowly filtered down into the North American continent. By the time the Europeans arrived, it is thought that some 230,000 Native Americans were living in the northern region of the continent. However, so many native people died soon after Europeans arrived that anthropologists have had to rely on patchy mission records to estimate the population's size.

THE EARLY TRIBES

Customs, talents, and preoccupations varied from tribe to tribe, each with separate identities and distinct languages. The Miwoks and Ohlones around what is now San Francisco Bay were nomads, sometimes trekking from coastal shell mounds up to the oak groves on what are now the Berkeley Hills, or to meadowland and its rich harvest of deer and elk. It is thought the two tribes socialized a little, but warily.

Map of California and Mexico dating from 1676.

California has the largest native American population in the US. The temperature, climate and easy access to food sources meant that around one third of all indigenous peoples lived in California.

The land around the bay probably supported more humans than any other California locale, but the area where the city of San Francisco now stands was not much frequented. It was a sandy, windy, desolate place compared to the lushness of the Berkeley Hills, the mild slopes of Mount Tamalpais, or the woods of the southern peninsula. In fact, San Francisco today has more trees and wildlife than at any other time in its history.

In the south, the Chumash tribe, living in what is now Santa Barbara, were adept fishermen who used seashell hooks, basket traps, nets, and vegetable poisons, even catching fish with their bare hands. The tons of shellfish eaten over centuries have left us with mounds of discarded shells that can now reach 20ft (7 meters) deep.

The Chumash in particular were expert boat builders. Canoes were made with easily worked timbers such as red cedar and red-wood, and were distinguished by their symmetry, neatness of finish, and frequent decoration. All of this was achieved with limited tools, the principal ones being chisels, curved knives, abrasive stones, wedges, and sharkskin. One of their elegant vessels can be admired today at the Santa Barbara Museum of Natural History.

The California tribes' lifestyle prospered for 10,000 years with few major changes and, by our standards, few possessions. The arrival of America in 1534. Stumbling upon a peninsula (known today as Baja California) which stretched down between the sea and a gulf, he believed he'd found a long-lost fabled island, and he named it "California." But the discovery of the state of California is officially credited to Juan Rodríguez Cabrillo, the Portuguese commander of two Spanish caravels, who is thought to have embarked from the Mexican port of Navidad in June 1542. He explored most of California's coast, entering San Diego's "enclosed and very good" harbor in September 1542.

Members of a native tribe dancing near the San Francisco Mission, 1822.

white people bewildered them and radically changed the culture of all Native Americans. Their acquisition of manufactured articles such as guns, metal utensils, axes, knives, blankets, and cloth led inevitably to a decline of native arts and crafts. With the encroachment of white settlements, warfare became a unifying force and tribes that had been enemies united against the intruders. But even this did not save them: They had survived regular earthquakes and droughts, but the white man proved too strong for them.

THE AGE OF EXPLORATION

Hernando Cortés, the Spaniard who conquered Mexico, sailed up the west coast of North

Sir Francis Drake, sailing around the world in 1579 in the Golden Hind, passed by the entrance to the bay of San Francisco without noticing an opening. His log shows that he anchored just north and sent several landing parties ashore.

Then, 23 years later, Sebastian Vizcaíno arrived in the south, searching for suitable ports of call for his Manila galleon on its annual return to the Philippines, which was part of the Spanish Empire at the time. What Spain most needed was a safe haven from marauding Dutch and British pirates for the treasure ships en route to Spain, which were laden with riches from across its empire. But the pirates weren't the only people the Spanish needed protection from. The canny and ambitious Spanish king, Charles III, was also keenly aware that Russian fur traders from the north posed a risk to Spain's land claims, as the traders were increasingly hunting farther and farther south, even coming down as far south as Bodega Bay.

Vizcaíno gave lasting names to several California sites, such as San Clemente Island, San Diego, and Santa Catalina Island. Of more importance was his glowing report on the virtues of the California coast, which urged Spain to colonize the state.

important were the numerous able-bodied, alert, and amiable Indians because Spanish policy looked towards preserving, Christianizing, hispanizing, and engrossing the natives as a major element in the Spanish colony now to be established." Over the centuries, Spain had developed a standard method for settling new territory: using the sword to cut down any opposition from the native peoples, and pacifying the area with the introduction of Christianity. This was the approach used in California, where between 1769 and early in

Oil painting of Hernando Cortés.

Engraving of Sir Francis Drake, published in 1628.

CONVERTING THE NATIVE PEOPLES

What followed was another 150 years of lassitude until the overland arrival in 1769 of Gaspar de Portolá from Baja. Crossing the Santa Ana river and exchanging gifts with friendly tribes, de Portolá's band passed by the bubbling tar pits of La Brea, through the mountains at Sepulveda Pass to Lake Encino, and headed northwards to open up the route to Monterey.

"The three diarists in the party agree that the practical discovery of most significance was the advantageous site on the Los Angeles river," noted John Caughey in a volume published by the California Historical Society to mark the city's bicentennial. "Equally

the following century a chain of 21 Franciscan missions was established between San Diego and Sonoma. These missions enslaved hundreds of coastal Indians into an endless round of work and prayer.

MISSION LIFE

As early as 1775 the native peoples rebelled: In an uprising at the San Diego mission one of the Franciscans was killed. But abolishing age-old tribal customs and introducing a complex religious structure centered on endless work eventually converted the native Americans into obedient servants. The object of every mission was to become self-sufficient, to which end the Indian men became farmers, blacksmiths, tanners, home builders, vintners, and other types of useful laborers. Meanwhile the Indian women focused on cooking, sewing, and laundering.

"White" diseases such as measles and chicken pox killed thousands of Native Americans and as a result they developed a mortal fear of mission life. Nevertheless, benevolent despotism kept thousands in the missions and it was their labor that made the system successful. Not until the Mexican government's secularization decrees of 1834 (following its independence from Spain and acquisition of the province of Alta Califor-

For over 65 years it was believed that one of Drake's landing parties may have left behind a small brass plate that was discovered in 1936 near Drake's Bay. But in 2003 it was declared an elaborate hoax.

or ploughed under, and the missions – the so-called "string of pearls" – were transformed into a patchwork quilt of ranches.

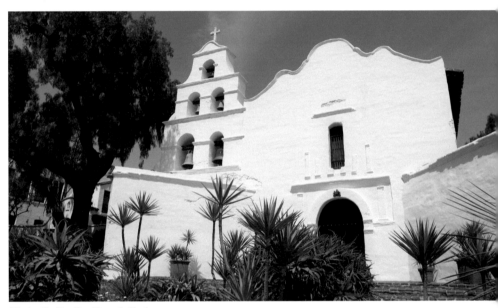

Mission Basilica San Diego de Alcala.

nia in 1821) were the native people freed – only to exchange their status for that of underpaid peons on the vast ranches.

In theory, the Secularization Act of 1834 gave lay administrators and Native Americans the right to ownership of the missions and their property; a potential ranchero could ask for as many as 50,000 acres (20,200 hectares). In practice, the acts were barely observed: tribes were driven out into the world of poverty and helplessness, ill-equipped to deal with white men's laws.

Some returned to the hills, others indentured themselves as ranch hands or turned to drinking and gambling. Meanwhile, the orange groves and the productive gardens were cleared

⊘ NATIVE AMERICAN CUSTOMS

California tribes led a simple life, their igloo-shaped homes of reed providing breezy shelter in summer, while deer-skin roofs afforded protection during the rainy season. When it grew cool, open fires were built in the homes, with holes in the roof allowing the smoke to escape. In warm weather, the men and children were naked except for ornamental jewelry such as necklaces, earrings, bracelets, and anklets. They kept warm when needed with robes of yellow cedar bark or crudely tanned pelts. Some groups practiced tattooing. The women wore two-piece aprons made of deer skins or reeds.

📷 THE MISSIONS OF OLD CALIFORNIA

The 21 historic Franciscan missions spread out along the coast offer a fascinating insight into California's Spanish Colonial period.

California's chain of Spanish missions that runs from San Diego to Sonoma marks a significant chapter in the state's history. Under pressure in the mid-18th century to establish a presence in its Alta California territories, Spain charged Father Junípero Serra and his Franciscan missionaries with the task of establishing a network of missions to be situated along the coast, following the successful missions that Spain had built in its colony of Mexico.

The first settlement was in San Diego, where Father Serra raised a flag in 1769. Over the next 54 years, another 20 missions would be established between San Diego and Sonoma, with missions roughly a day's journey apart along the El Camino Real ("The Royal Road").

At each of the timber and adobe missions – which all feature the thick walls, small windows, and elegant bell towers usually associated with Mexican churches – the Europeans introduced livestock, grains, agriculture, industry, and the Catholic religion to Native Americans. The missions were also the repository of some of the state's most treasured murals and art.

Following the Secularization Act of 1834, the missions fell into disuse and were abandoned until interest in them was sparked again in the 1880s by Helen Hunt Jackson's magazine articles that brought attention to the plight of former mission Indians. Now, despite the ravages of time, revolt, and neglect, most of the missions still operate as active Catholic parishes.

For more information on missions, see the relevant chapter: ie, San Francisco (see page 121), Santa Barbara (see page 212), San Juan Capistrano (see page 257), and San Diego (see page 278).

Statue of Father Serra at the Mission San Diego de Alcala, California's first church.

Mission San Gabriel Arcángel.

Mission Santa Clara de Asís was founded in 1777. Although ruined and rebuilt six times, the settlement was never abandoned.

Inside Mission San Juan Capistrano, in Orange County, which has extensive grounds containing gardens, fountains, and adobe buildings.

The Mission of San Juan Capistrano

Orange County's Mission San Juan Capistrano has several interesting legends associated with it. The first is very much tied to reality: for at least two centuries, cliff swallows have been visiting the church each spring, building their nests out of mud in the tiled roof. They historically arrived each year on or around March 19 – St Joseph's Day – flying north from their winter vacation in Argentina. Legend says the influx began back in the mists of time when the original brood took refuge in the mission's eaves after a local innkeeper destroyed their nests. More recently, the swallows have been finding other places to nest, but the mission continues to try to woo them back.

Another legend that is associated with the mission – described as "an American Acropolis" – is that of a woman named Magdalena whose penance was to walk up and down the church aisle with a lighted candle, to atone for disobeying her father by courting a man of whom he disapproved. On occasion, it is said, her candle can still be seen shining among the ruins of the cruciform Great Stone Church in which the poor unfortunate perished during an earthquake. The Great Stone Church, one of the oldest sections of the mission still standing, has recently been restored to its former glory.

For more information on Mission San Juan Capistrano, see page 257.

Nests at Mission San Juan Capistrano.

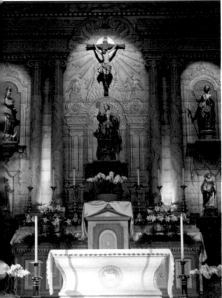

e beautiful Old Mission Santa Barbara, known as the ueen of the Missions," was established in 1786 and is nted by attractive gardens.

PULL AWAY CHEERILY!

(THE GOLD DIGGER'S SONG.)

WRITTEN AND SUNG BY **HARRY LEE CARTER,** IN HIS ENTERTAINMENT OF

"The Two Lands of Gold."

ALSO SUNG BY

GEORGE HENRY RUSSELL,

IN M.R PAYNE'S POPULAR ENTERTAINMENT,

"A Night in the Lands of Gold."

MUSIC COMPOSED BY

HENRY RUSSELL.

LONDON: MUSICAL BOUQUET OFFICE, 192, HIGH HOLBORN;
& J. ALLEN, 20, WARWICK LANE, PATERNOSTER ROW.

691 & 692. MUSICAL BOUQUET.   COPYRIGHT.

FROM RANCHOS TO STATEHOOD

It started as a simple war with Mexico over territory that Americans thought should be theirs. But it ended by transforming a wild and savage wilderness into the 31st state of the Union.

After three centuries of Spanish rule, Mexico finally broke away and declared itself a republic on September 27, 1821. Coincidentally, secularization of the missions was then sought by Spanish-Mexican settlers, known as Californios, who complained that the Catholic Church owned too much of the land. Eight million acres (3.2 million hectares) of mission land were fragmented into 800 privately owned ranches, with some governors handing out land to their cronies for only a few pennies per acre.

The vaquero's sports were violent, including calf branding, wild-horse roundups, bear hunts, and cock- and bullfights. His entertainment included dances, and at his fiestas he was bedecked in gold-braided clothes dripping with silver.

An 1842 portrait of Richard Henry Dana, author of the influential Two Years Before the Mast.

LIFE UNDER THE CALIFORNIOS

Orange orchards were cleared for firewood, herds were given to private hands, and the predominant lifestyle quickly changed to that of an untamed frontier-style cattle range. Cattle ranching in this part of the world, however, made few demands upon its owners. With no line fences to patrol and repair on the open range, and no need for vigilance because of branded stock, the *vaquero* had little to do but practice feats of horsemanship to prove his masculinity and impress the *señoritas*.

Author Richard Henry Dana, who visited the state in 1835, called the Californians "an idle thriftless people," an observation lent considerable weight by the lifestyle of so many of the rancheros, who found it a simple matter to maintain and increase their wealth. The sudden influx of prospectors to the north created an immense demand for beef, which the southerners were readily able to supply.

Yankee trading ships plied up and down the coast, operating like floating department stores offering mahogany furniture, gleaming copperware, framed mirrors, Irish linen, silver candlesticks, and cashmere shawls. These trading ships were the first opportunity for many native-born Spanish settlers to obtain jewelry, furniture, and other goods from the old world. Sometimes the trading ships, which had survived the precarious Straits of Magellan, would stay an entire year.

A genteel contraband soon developed. To reduce import taxes, ships worked in pairs to transfer cargo from one to the other on the open seas. The partially emptied ship would then make port and submit to customs inspection. With duties paid, it would rejoin its consort and reverse the transfer. Sometimes the Yankee traders used lonely coves to unload their cargoes, which were eventually smuggled ashore. The weather remained temperate except for the occasional hot, dry, gale-force wind the Native Americans called

After the Battle of Monterey, Mexican General de Ampudia surrenders to American General Taylor during the Mexican-American War of 1846–8.

"wind of the evil spirits." The Spaniards called them *santanas*, a name which today has become corrupted to Santa Ana winds. Now and again an earthquake rumbled down the San Andreas fault. The rancheros spent their energy rebuilding damaged haciendas, made from red-tile roofing set on white-painted adobe brick walls. The missions, meanwhile, fell into ruins: restoration of the missions began only in the 20th century after they were declared historical landmarks.

In 1834, Governor Figueroa issued the first of the Secularization Acts, which in theory gave lay administrators and Indian neophytes

the right to ownership of the missions and their property. Having been first introduced to the "civilized" world and then enslaved, the native peoples were disoriented. At the height of the mission era, as many as 20,000 Indians had been tied to the system as unpaid laborers, and were now psychologically ill-prepared to cope with freedom.

THE MEXICAN-AMERICAN WAR

Official Washington soon became aware of this land of milk and honey on the Pacific coast. President Andrew Jackson sent an emissary to Mexico City in the 1830s to buy California for the sum of $500,000. The plan failed.

When James K. Polk took office in 1845, he pledged to acquire California by any means. Pressured by English financial interests that plotted to exchange $26 million of defaulted Mexican bonds for the rich land of California, he declared war on Mexico on May 13, 1846, which surprised no one.

News of the war had not yet reached California, however, when a group of settlers stormed General Mariano Vallejo's Sonoma

> *Soldiers who'd finished in the army often stayed in California rather than return to Spain or Mexico. Under Mexican law, a ranchero could ask for up to 50,000 acres (20,200 hectares); native slave labor became part of the plunder.*

estate. Vallejo soothed the men with brandy and watched as they raised their hastily sewn Bear Flag over Sonoma. The Bear Flag Revolt is sanctified in California history – the flag now being the official state flag – but for all its drama, it was immaterial. Within a few weeks Commodore John Sloat arrived to usher California into the Union.

Most of the fighting in the War of American Conquest took place in the south. The war in the north effectively ended on July 9, 1846, when 70 hearty sailors and marines from the ship *Portsmouth* marched ashore in Yerba Buena village and raised the American flag

In addition to being denied legality and having their labor exploited and their culture destroyed, the Native Americans had been fatally exposed to alcoholism and all manner of foreign diseases to which they had little natural resistance.

in the village's central plaza, now Portsmouth Square in San Francisco.

California was rushed into the Union on September 9, 1850, as the 31st state, only 10 months after convening a formal government. But it had already drafted a constitution that guaranteed the right to "enjoying and defending life and liberty, acquiring, possessing and protecting property, and pursuing and obtaining happiness," with hindsight a typically Californian mix of the sublime and the practical.

The bloodiest battle on California soil took place in the Valley of San Pasqual, near Escondido. The Army of the West, commanded by General Stephen W. Kearney, fought a brief battle during which 18 Americans were killed.

Kearney's aide-de-camp was US naval officer Robert F. Stockton. Together they skirmished with Mexican–Californians at Paso de Bartolo on the San Gabriel River. The Californios, however, soon readily capitulated to the Americans, and California's participation in the Mexican–American War finally ended with the Treaty of Cahuenga, signed by John Fremont and General Pico.

⊘ THE PONY EXPRESS

When California gained statehood in 1850, mail from the East took six months to deliver. Overland stagecoaches cut this to less than a month, but in 1860, the sinewy riders of the Pony Express brought San Francisco much closer to the rest of the nation. Mail traveled over hostile territory from St Joseph, Missouri, to the young city of San Francisco in only 10 days. Riders had just a revolver, water sack, and a mail pouch, the most famous of them being 15-year-old William "Buffalo Bill" Cody. Just as quickly, though, came the Transcontinental Telegraph, and on October 26, 1861, the Pony Express closed its doors.

The treaty came into force on July 4 (US Independence Day), 1848, and made California a territory of the United States of America. Only through fierce negotiation was San Diego placed on the north side of the Mexico–California border.

For three decades after America had acquired Alta California in 1848, Los Angeles remained a predominantly Mexican city infused with a Latino culture and traditions. But the arrival of the Southern Pacific Railroad triggered a series of land booms with the

The California flag.

subsequent influx of Anglo-American, Asian, and European immigrants eventually outnumbering Mexicans 10 to 1.

Meanwhile the Native American population continued to suffer. From 1850 onwards the Federal government signed treaties (never ratified by the Senate) under which more than 7 million acres (2.8 million hectares) of tribal land dwindled to less than 10 percent of that total.

Next to suffer from marginalization and racist attitudes were the Chinese, thousands of whom had poured into Northern California from the gold fields and, later into Los Angeles after the railroads had been completed.

Miners in the Sierras (1851–52) by German artists Charles Christian Nahl and August Wenderoth.

THE CALIFORNIA GOLD RUSH

Gold and silver were the stuff of dreams, making millionaires out of ordinary men and, sometimes, paupers out of millionaires. Gold fever grabbed the nation and California's population exploded.

Gold was discovered in California's Placeritas Canyon, north of Mission San Fernando, in 1842. Francisco Lopez, rounding up stray horses, stopped to rest beneath an oak tree. He opened his knife to uproot some wild onions, and their roots came out attached to something gleaming bright in the sun – a nugget of gold. Six years later, gold was discovered in quantity at Sutter's Mill, near Sacramento. Word quickly spread east and the stampede began. Soon a torrent of gold-dazzled prospectors gushed west through the Sierras to California.

GOLD IS DISCOVERED

The first big discovery of gold took place in the Sierra Nevada foothills, at a sawmill beside the American River. The mill belonged to John Augustus Sutter – a man, one contemporary wrote, with a disastrous "mania for undertaking too much." Born in Switzerland in 1803, Sutter arrived in San Francisco in 1839. Despite a disorderly career as a Swiss Army officer and dry-goods merchant, he somehow impressed Alta California's authorities enough to receive a Central Valley land grant of nearly 50,000 acres (about 20,000 hectares). Naming his land "New Helvetia" and using Native Americans as serf labor, Sutter set out to create his own semi-independent barony.

Sutter's Fort, at what is now Sacramento, was often the first stop for bedraggled pioneers after their harrowing Sierra crossing. Sutter gloried in providing comfort and goods (at a price) to California's new settlers. He planted wheat and fruit orchards, bought out the Russians at Fort Ross, and, in 1847, decided to build the sawmill that was his ultimate undoing.

Pony Express Rider Leaving Station, artist unknown.

James Marshall, who had been hired to oversee the mill's construction, peered into the millrace on January 24, 1848, and noticed a bit of shiny material. It was, of course, one of the millions of smithereens of gold that had been tumbling down the streams of the Sierra for millennia.

After applying "every test of their ingenuity and the *American Encyclopaedia*," and deciding that it was indeed gold, Marshall and Sutter raced back to the sawmill and found quite a bit more.

Realizing his New Helvetia would be over-run if word of the discovery leaked out prematurely, Sutter swore his mill hands to secrecy.

But nuggets kept popping up in bars and stores all over the region. Soon shopkeeper Sam

Brannan would break the news in San Francisco, and the secret would be well and truly out.

GOLD FEVER TAKES HOLD

When Sam Brannan ambled down Montgomery Street with a vial of recently prospected gold, San Francisco's population numbered less than 1,000. By early 1850, when the madness was in full swing, the population topped 30,000.

The word quickly spread all over California: stores closed, city officials left their offices, soldiers deserted, sailors jumped ship, and the

"As a lumber enterprise, the mill was a failure, but as a gold discovery, it was a grand success," said a later report of Sutter's Mill.

back to Washington, DC, where it was exhibited at the War Office, increasing greed in the capital. On December 2 1848, President Polk told Congress that the "extraordinary accounts" were true. A few days later, the *New York Herald* summed it up: "The El Dorado of the old

The Monitor, by Henry Sandham, published in 1883, shows hydraulic mining for gold.

exasperated editor of the *Californian* announced the suspension of his daily newspaper because the staff had walked out. San Francisco was left nearly deserted, its shops stripped of axes, pans, tents, beans, soda crackers, picks, and whatever else might conceivably be of use. Monterey, San Jose, all of Northern California's mission towns and farms joined in the scramble.

Gold fever worked its way to the states of Utah and Oregon, where two-thirds of the able-bodied men were on their way to the diggings. Entire caravans of covered wagons made their way west. Ships in the Pacific spread the word to Peru, Chile, Hawaii, and Australia. Lieutenant L. Loeser carried a "small chest... containing $3,000-worth of gold in lumps and scales"

Spaniards is discovered at last."

HOW CLAIMS WERE STAKED

Hundreds of thousands of reveries were fixed on the fabled Mother Lode region, which ran for 120 miles (190 km) from north of Sutter's Mill to Mariposa in the south. Forty-niners (as the Gold Rush miners were known) first worked the streams of the Klamath Mountains in the far north: later, the southern deserts had their share of boom towns. But the Mother Lode's wooded hills and deep valleys were the great centers of the raucous, short-lived argonaut civilization.

Gold Rush mining, especially in the early days before the streams were panned out, was a simple affair. The Mother Lode was owned by the federal government, and claims were limited to the ground a man and his fellows could work. Stockpiling claims was impossible and hiring a workforce was unlikely. There was scant reason to make another man rich when one's own wealth-spouting claim was so easily achieved.

There was money to be wrung out of those hills. The problem lay in keeping it. In 1849, $10 million of gold was mined in California; the next year, four times that amount. In 1852, at the pinnacle of the Gold Rush, $80 million wound up in prospectors' pockets.

The Sierra streams did much of the miner's work for him. The rushing waters eroded the hillsides and sent placer gold (from dust to nugget size) rushing downstream. A miner crouched by the streambank scooped up a panful of gravel, shifting and turning his pan as the debris washed out and the gold sank to the bottom. Later, sluices were built and holes were dug. Finally hydraulic mining took over, although this was banned in 1884 after causing dramatic ecological damage to the foothills.

WATER RIGHTS

The endless disputes over water rights, which continue to this day, mostly date to the days of the gold prospectors when miners, whose claims were far from stream beds, collaborated to build ditches funnelling water from sources whose "riparian rights" (that is, owning the adjoining land) were in conflict with "appropriation rights." The introduction of hydraulic mining, bringing streams of water to bear on hillsides, intensified the problem. The extensive network of canals and flumes which eventually brought water a long way from its original source came to be worth more than the claims it served, but the conflicting arguments over who had a prior right to the water were never entirely solved. (However, as the mines petered out, the agribusinesses of the state's central valleys gained the lions' share.)

As easy as it was to find, the Mother Lode's gold was easier to lose – to rapacious traders, in the gambling halls and bawdy-houses, and to the simple foolishness of young men. But for most prospectors it was a grand adventure. Many returned home sheepishly, but full of stories for their grandchildren.

SAN FRANCISCO IN THE GOLD RUSH

California as It Is and as It May Be, Or, A Guide to the Goldfields was the title of the first book to be published in San Francisco (in 1849). In it, the author F.B. Wierzbicki wrote that the city looked like it had been built to endure for only a day, so fast had been its growth and so flimsy its construction.

"The town has led the van in growth... there is nothing like it on record. From eight to 10 thousand may be afloat on the streets and hundreds arrive daily; many live in shanties, many in tents, and many the best way they can... The freaks of

Gold was first found on John Sutter's property.

"The whole country," wrote the Californian editor, "resounds with the sordid cry of gold! gold! gold! – while the field is left half-planted, the house half-built, and everything neglected but the manufacture of shovels and pickaxes."

fortune are equally as remarkable in this place as everything else connected with it; some men who two years ago had not a cent in their pockets, count by thousands now..."

Truly, nowhere was the Gold Rush's magic more powerful than in San Francisco. Bayard Taylor, a reporter for the *New York Tribune*, described the atmosphere as a "perpetual carnival." What he found when he returned from four months at the diggings was not the town

> None of California's new towns, much less San Francisco, were built with care or foresight. Pre-Gold Rush street plans, based on tight grids, were expanded out from flat Yerba Buena Cove without paying attention to the city's hills.

Prospectors with shovels and pickaxes.

of "tents and canvas houses with a show of frame buildings" that he had left but "an actual metropolis, displaying street after street of well-built edifices... lofty hotels, gaudy with verandas and balconies... finished with home luxury and aristocratic restaurants presenting daily their long bills of fare, rich with the choicest technicalities of Parisian cuisine."

For most of the '49ers, the city was rough and expensive. Eggs from the Farallone Islands sold for $1 apiece. Real-estate speculation was epidemic. Each boatload of '49ers represented another batch of customers. As the city burst from the boundaries of Yerba Buena Cove, "water lots" sold for crazy prices on the expectation they could be made habitable with

landfill, and, indeed, much of today's downtown San Francisco is built on landfill.

Most of California's new tenants had little desire to lay the foundation for the orderly society that would surely follow the Gold Rush. The popular conception was that the foothills were crammed with gold. "Ages will not exhaust the supply," Bayard Taylor wrote. In the end, the winners in the great money-scramble were those who took the time to sink roots by establishing businesses and buying land, taking advantage of the '49ers' disdain for tomorrow. In 1853, the Gold Rush began to wind down. Real-estate values fell 20 to 30 percent. Immigration slowed to a trickle, and merchants were cornered by massive over-supplies ordered during the heady days. The men who started the Gold Rush, John Sutter and James Marshall, were only two of the many losers in the great game. Marshall ended his days in 1885 near the site of his discovery, broken-down, weepy, shaking his fist at fate. Sutter, whose barony was overrun just as he'd feared, kept a brave front for some years. But history had swept him aside, too, and he died in 1880 after years of futile petitions to Congress for restitution.

THE SILVER RUSH

Whatever chance California had of becoming placid was swept away in 1859 by yet another flood of riches flowing down the Sierra slope. This time it was silver, not gold, that geared up the rush. One of the most comfortless outposts of the Gold Rush had been centered around Nevada's Sun Mountain, on the dry eastern slope of the Sierra near Lake Tahoe. There was a little gold up in the Virginia Range, but eking a living out of the area's irritating bluish clay was wicked work. In June 1859, a sample of that "blue stuff" found its way to Melville Atwood, an assayer in Grass Valley. Examining it closely, Atwood found an astounding $3,876 worth of silver in that sample of ore.

At first it appeared that the Silver Rush would mimic the Gold Rush of a decade earlier. "Our towns are near depleted," wrote one spectator. "They look as languid as a consumptive girl. What has become of our sinewy and athletic fellow citizens? They are coursing through ravines and over mountaintops" looking for silver.

One of the athletic young men who rushed up to the Virginia Range was Mark Twain. In his marvelous book, *Roughing It*, he describes how he and his fellow almost-millionaires "expected to find masses of silver lying all about the ground." The problem for Twain and the thousands like him was that the silver was in, not on, the steep and rugged mountains, and getting it out was no simple matter of poking and panning.

The Silver Rush, it turned out, was a game for capitalists, men who possessed the money to dig tunnels, purchase claims, and install the expensive machinery and mills that transformed the "blue stuff" into cash. They were men like William Ralston of the Bank of California in San Francisco, and the four legendary "Bonanza Kings" – James Flood and William O'Brien, former saloon-keepers; and James Fair and John W. Mackay, old miners whose Consolidated Virginia Mining Company regularly disgorged $6 million a month.

The treasures of the Comstock Lode flowed from the boomtown of Virginia City to San Francisco. By 1863, $40 million of silver had been wrestled out of the tunnels, and 2,000 mining companies traded shares in San Francisco. At one time, more speculative money was wrapped up in Comstock mining shares than actually existed on the whole Pacific Coast.

The Comstock Lode lasted until the 1880s, plumping up California's economy with the $400 million that the Virginia Range yielded. In San Francisco, Billy Ralston, the Comstock's greatest mine owner, had taken over

from Sam Brannan as the city's top booster. (Brannan was going broke trying to make his Calistoga resort "the Saratoga of the West," and died without a dollar to his name in 1889.)

Ralston rebuilt America's largest city hotel; he bought sugar refineries, lumber, and water companies; and as the 1860s drew to a close, he happily made confident preparations for what he and his fellow plutocrats thought would be the capstone to the state's greatness – the long-awaited completion of the Transcontinental Railroad in 1869.

Entrance to the Golden Rule Mine in Tuolumne County.

⊘ VIGILANTE JUSTICE

In San Francisco, hoodlums (a word coined in late-19th-century San Francisco) had organized themselves into gangs like the Sydney Ducks and the Hounds. In addition to setting some of the city's fires, these gangs were known for routine robberies, beatings, and generally ugly behavior. In 1851, the forces of social stability asserted their constitutional right to "acquire, possess and defend property" by warring against the criminal elements in the community.

The robbery and beating in early 1851 of a merchant named C.J. Jensen inflamed the righteous, especially Sam Brannan – a man who, according to

historian Josiah Royce, was "always in love with shedding the blood of the wicked." Newspapers like the *Alta* brought up the specter of lynch law, and Brannan shouted that the time had come to bypass "the quibbles of the law, the insecurity of the prisons, and the laxity of those who pretend to administer justice." A Committee of Vigilance was formed; soon a member of the Sydney Ducks (a gang of criminals from Australia) named John Jenkins was hanged for stealing a safe. Within two weeks Sacramento also had its vigilante corps and other California towns followed its lead. California's first bout of vigilantism put a damper on crime only for a while.

BOOM AND BUST YEARS

After enjoying immense wealth from the discovery of gold and silver, the state was hit by massive unemployment. But California was too rich to suffer for long, thanks especially to the agricultural industry and oil production in the south.

Plans for a railroad linking the coasts had been floating around for many years. When the American Civil War broke out, Congress, intent upon securing California's place in the Union, at last stirred itself. In the winter of 1862, the Pacific Railroad Act granted vast tracts of land out west, low-interest financing, and outright subsidies to two companies – the Central Pacific, building from Sacramento, and the Union Pacific, building from Omaha, Nebraska, in the Midwest. As it happened, the Civil War largely bypassed California, but it nonetheless prompted the building of a railroad that brought unexpected havoc to the residents of the state.

When Frank Norris wrote The Octopus in 1901, no one had to guess at the reference: the Southern Pacific (as it was renamed in 1884) had its greedy tentacles in every corner of the state.

In his regarded and widely read book, *Progress and Poverty*, Henry George, a journeyman printer and passionate theorist, had warned that the increasing dominance of the railroads would prove to be a mixed blessing. He predicted that California's immature factories would be undersold by the eastern manufacturing colossus and that the Central Pacific's ownership of vast parcels of land along its right of way would drive prices of agricultural land shamefully high. George even foresaw the racial tensions that would result from the railroad's importation of thousands of Chinese laborers, who flooded the state's job market in the 1870s.

Officials and workers drive in the last spike of the Pacific Railroad, linking it with the Central Pacific Railroad at Promontory Point, Utah, 1869.

PROBLEMS WITH THE RAILROADS

George's prophecies began arriving with the first train. In San Francisco, real-estate dealing of $3.5 million a month fell to $1.5 million a month within a year. "California's initial enthusiasm soon gave way to distrust and dislike... an echo of the national conviction that the railroads were responsible for most of the country's economic ills," was the assessment of historian John W. Caughey in his book *California*. "The railroad became a monster, the Octopus. It was a target for criticisms by all those made discontented and bitter by the hard times of the Seventies."

The genius of the Central Pacific was a young engineer named Theodore Dehone Judah who had built California's first railroad, the 22-mile (35-km) Sacramento Valley line, in 1856. He spent years crafting the crucial route across the Sierra at Donner Pass. Unfortunately for Judah, the Central Pacific's other partners were uncommonly cunning and grabby men.

Charles Crocker, Mark Hopkins, Collis Huntington, and Leland Stanford, who became known as "The Big Four," had been lured west by the Gold Rush. They were Sacramento shop-

the railroad built, and Stanford's political maneuvering, made the Central Pacific the virtual dictator of California politics for years. Between them, the railroad barons raised private investment, earned government subsidies, acquired bargain-priced land, imported cheap labor from China and by their exploitative and monopolist practices made themselves multi-millionaires.

As the biggest landowners and biggest employers, the immensely rich railroad barons were able to manipulate freight rates, control

Gold seekers en route to California to join the Gold Rush, 1849 or 1850.

With few Americans willing to take part in the hard labor of building the Central Pacific (and the cost of those who did), Charles Crocker hired cheaper Chinese labor: hard-working, they were sometimes derisively called "Crocker's Pets."

keepers when they invested in Judah's scheme. Shortly after Congress dumped its largesse in their laps, they forced Judah out of the Central Pacific. He died, aged 37, in 1863, still trying to wrest back control from his former partners.

The Central Pacific made the Big Four insanely rich. The government's haste to get

water supplies, keep hundreds of thousands of productive land acres for themselves, and subvert politicians and municipalities. It was years before state regulation of the railroads became the norm.

In the beginning, at least, carping at the Big Four's use of the railroad's treasury as a kind of private money preserve was a game for malcontents and socialists. In the mahogany boardrooms of San Francisco's banks, on the editorial pages of its newspapers, in the overheated stock exchange, up and down Montgomery Street, the verdict was the same: the railroad would bring a firm and fabulous prosperity to California.

In April 1868, five years after construction of the First Transcontinental Railroad had begun on Sacramento's Front Street, the first Central Pacific train breached the Sierra at Donner Pass. On May 12, 1869, the ceremonial Golden Spike was driven at Promontory Point, Utah, and the coasts were finally and irrevocably linked. "San Francisco Annexes the Union" read one San Francisco headline. But the rush of prosperity failed utterly to materialize. Only a few deep thinkers – none of them ensconced in boardrooms – had understood the financial calamity the railroad would bring. In the winter of 1869–70, a severe drought crippled the state's agriculture. Between 1873 and 1875 more than a quarter of a million immigrants came to California. Many were factory workers and few could find work. The "Terrible '70s" had arrived, which certainly for William Chapman Ralston were a calamity. As head of San Francisco's Bank of California, he had presided over the boom mentality that was a legacy of the Gold Rush.

The mid-1870s saw the depression at its deepest. On "Black Friday," April 26, 1875, a run on the Bank of California forced it to slam shut its huge oak doors at Sansome and California streets. Driven into debt by Comstock mining losses and by the failure of the railroad to bring prosperity, Bill Ralston drowned while taking his customary morning swim in the Bay.

Ralston's death signalled the end of California's booming affluence. Those hurt most by the great shrinkage of capital in the 1870s were the state's working people. During the Gold and Silver rushes, California's laborers had enjoyed a rare freedom to move easily from job to job and to dictate working conditions. Now, however, with massive unemployment, unionization began to take hold. For the next 60 years California suffered recurrent bouts of labor strife.

AGRICULTURAL GROWTH

The depression was slow to disappear, but California was too rich to suffer permanently. In the next few decades, it slowly built its economic strength up to the point where it could compete with America's prosperous East Coast.

After decades of depending on the land to deliver riches in the form of gold or silver or minerals, the state developed its agricultural lands as never before. In the Central Valley,

wheat, rice, and cotton became major cash crops. In the late 1870s, the fertile Napa Valley began to produce fine wines in earnest.

Sometime between 1873 and 1875, two or three orange trees were sent from the Department of Agriculture in Washington to Eliza and Luther Tibbetts in Riverside, not far from San Diego. The young trees had been budded from a seedless orange whose origin was Bahia, Brazil. The Tibbetts planted the trees, little knowing that a decade later navel oranges would dramatically alter the agricultural, economic, and

Tropical fruit became an early industry in sunny southern California.

social patterns of the entire region. The Washington navel orange, as the seedless and sweet fruit was officially known, became (in the words of Charles F. Lummis, editor of the Los Angeles Times) "not only a fruit but a romance."

Durable enough to survive long-distance shipping, this citrus fruit hit its prime in 1889 when more than 13,000 acres (5,300 hectares) of land in the six southern counties were devoted to its cultivation.

Growers formed a marketing cooperative, the California Fruit Growers Exchange, famed for its ubiquitous trademark, Sunkist. In a mere 18 months, New York Tribune editor Horace Greeley's "Go west, young man" philosophy became a reality. Many boom-towns took root and soon the population of the south equalled that of the north.

This vast semi-tropical, often desert-like land reached its potential. Thousands of acres of good farmland sold by the railroads at low prices were planted with wheat, oranges, grapes, cotton, tea, tobacco, and coffee. Irrigation converted vast tracts of this arid waste to fertile land bearing fruit and field crops.

Agriculture, crucially boosted by rail transportation, became the backbone of Southern

It is hard to imagine what they had against the last-mentioned category, especially in a city growing so sophisticated that by 1897 it boasted the first orchestra to be established west of the Rockies. Eight years later, Abbott Kinney's ambitious reconstruction of Venice on coastal marshland added an international touch, although his initial high-minded attractions soon gave way to motor racing and carnival events.

The pueblo of Los Angeles had become a prosperous community, facing its perennial problem: a shortage of water. To assure

Cartoon on the scandal of 1872–3, when Credit Mobilier, a company formed by Union Pacific Railroad stockholders, was a lucrative but corrupt source of income for congressmen and railroad builders.

California's economy. Well before the new century began, the enterprising Edwin Tobias Earl made a fortune from his invention of the refrigerated railroad car.

THE RISE OF THE SOUTH

Los Angeles, too, was now growing fast: in every decade from 1870 onwards it doubled its population. Before the end of the 19th century, the *Los Angeles Times,* whose editor Charles Lummis had hitchhiked across country from the Midwest, was proclaiming that it was no place for "dudes, loafers, paupers... cheap politicians, business scrubs, impecunious clerks, lawyers and doctors."

a steady water supply, the city fathers made plans for a lengthy trench running from the river and hired a Vermont-born shopkeeper, Ozro W. Childs, to dig this *Zanja Madre* or Mother Ditch, paying him off with land instead of scarce city funds.

The land, a tract bordered by today's 6th & Main streets and Pico Boulevard and Figueroa Street, eventually made Childs so prosperous that, in 1884, he spent $50,000 to build a 1,800-seat opera house. At the ocean, frontage at Santa Monica owned by Southern Pacific Railroad magnate Collis P. Huntington almost became the Port of Los Angeles, but intensive lobbying by rival Santa Fe railroad chiefs won out and San Pedro was chosen instead. Already the region was annually producing almost 5 million barrels of oil, the exporting of which was greatly facilitated by the subsequent opening of the Panama Canal.

CALIFORNIA'S BOUNTY

Southern California's growing reputation as a health resort was responsible for the next big wave of newcomers, enticed by the climate, the abundance of thermal and mineral springs, and the boosterism of such communities as Pasadena, Riverside, Ojai, and Palm Springs. The state was already first in honey production; and vineyards, citrus, and walnut groves blossomed over thousands of acres. "Buy Land in Los Angeles and Wear Diamonds" was typical of the slogans that lured newcomers into the area, where they were met straight from the train with bands, barbecues, and fast-talking salesmen.

In Califiornia's vast deserts and verdant valleys, figs, rice, vegetables, and cotton became profitable crops. The balmy climate encouraged dairy farming, livestock, and poultry raising. And, from the turn of the century, in this already bountiful land, oil production became the most profitable of all.

Due to early huckstering by the big railroads, whose salesmen had gone to such lengths as spiking thorny trees with oranges to sell worthless land, real estate had long been big business. In 1886, Harvey H. Wilcox named his new sub-division Hollywood. After Wilcox's death, his widow sold a plot of land on Cahuenga to a French flower painter named Paul DeLongpre and it was his palatial house and floral gardens that became the area's first major tourist attraction.

A RAPIDLY COALESCING STATE

That same year, ground was broken at Hollywood and Highland for the soon-to-be-famous Hollywood Hotel and for Whitley Heights, an elegant hillside community that became for early movie stars what Beverly Hills would be in later years. Planned as a completely separate community, Hollywood was obliged in 1903 to join the city of Los Angeles, along with many neighboring communities, to obtain an adequate water supply.

Since 1854, California's capital had been Sacramento, but it was San Francisco that ruled a rapidly coalescing state.

Agriculture in the Central Valley had grown in response to the needs of the exploding population; in the decade of the 1850s, California's cattle herds grew from 262,000 to more than 3 million. Towns like Stockton and Monterey were thriving as '49ers set up shops and sank roots. The Gilded Age, with its extravagance and corruption, continued right up to one fateful morning in 1906, after which nothing was the same again.

One of the earliest maps of Hollywood, from 1887.

THE EARLY 20TH CENTURY

The Great Earthquake of 1906 had immediate, devastating consequences for San Francisco. LA was now in the spotlight, gaining wealth from oil production, and renown from Hollywood's movie industry and advertisements proclaiming it "the land of perpetual summer".

The beginning of the 20th century was a hugely transformative period for California's major cities. Propelled by oil discoveries, new water sources, and a new extensive network of electric trains, Los Angeles tripled its population to 300,000 within a decade. Meanwhile, San Francisco struggled to recover and rebuild after a terrible earthquake and fire devastated the city in 1906. Within a decade, however, its Downtown had received a complete makeover, and the city jubilantly hosted a world's fair, the 1915 Panama Pacific International Exposition.

The US government funded the Federal Writers' Project (FWP) in 1935 to help support historians, teachers, writers, and librarians during the Great Depression. The project's goal was to produce American guide books that would promote tourism.

Postcard c.1900 depicting Broadway, Los Angeles.

By the 1930s, "California became that legendary land of perpetual summer," enthused a writer in the Federal Writers Project guide to the state, "of orange groves in sight of snowy peaks, of oil wells spouting wealth, of real-estate promising fortunes, of cinema stars and bathing beauties. It seemed to promise a new start, a kinder providence, a rebirth of soul and body."

THE GROWTH OF THE SOUTH

Spurred by the discovery of oil in 1892 in what is now the Westlake area, Southern California mushroomed from an agricultural community to an industrial complex. Realizing it was sitting on a fat reservoir of wealth, Los Angeles developed the "Salt Lake Field," followed by fields in Huntington Beach, Santa Fe Springs, and Signal Hill. Oil derricks sprouted from the hills to the sea.

The initial unparalleled growth of Southern California was due in large part to the Owens Valley scandal, and additional water brought in by Los Angeles' Water Bureau Superintendent William Mulholland. Today, these aqueducts supply 525 million gallons (nearly 2 billion liters) of water a day. As water problems slowed to a trickle, the flood of newcomers to Southern California continued at an astonishing rate.

TRAINS AND TROLLEY CARS

Although downtown LA was linked to Pasadena and Santa Fe by an urban railway, the Southern

Pacific's Collis P. Huntington devised in 1901 a vast interurban network of electric trains to connect the entire area.

Los Angeles, said Collis P. Huntington, was "destined to become the most important city in the country, if not in the world. It can extend in any direction, as far as you like." Within a decade his trolley cars stretched everywhere.

Collis P. Huntington.

"The whole area within a radius of 70 miles of the city took on a new life," wrote Huntington's biographer, Isaac Marcosson, in 1914. "Villages became towns; towns blossomed into miniature cities." When the author Henry James came by on a lecture tour in 1905, he said he'd never seen such an efficient transit system in all his worldwide travels.

Within five years, however, traffic had become problematic. When Los Angeles held its second annual motor show in 1909, it had more cars on its streets than any other city in the world, and the population was still soaring.

MOVIE MADNESS

It was the film industry that really shot Los Angeles to fame and, unwittingly, it was Leland Stanford whose wager about a galloping horse helped launch it. With its origins in the nickelodeon, the movie industry began to emerge around the turn of the 20th century and headed west partly to escape the stranglehold patents held by the New York-based Edison company and partly because of California's superb climate, which made outdoor filming cheaper and easier.

Within a dozen years, the streets of Harvey Wilcox's sedate town of Hollywood were filled with intruders bearing cameras and megaphones, roping off streets, crashing cars, and staging pretend shoot-outs. Some prolific directors were turning out one-reel Westerns or comedies almost daily. The locals didn't like it at all. "They thought we were tramps," recalled screenwriter Anita Loos. "They saw themselves as being invaded and supplanted as elegant ladies and gentlemen so they ganged up on us."

From 1926, the Pickford-Fairbanks Studio immortalized such luminaries as actor Charlie Chaplin and directors D.W. Griffith and Cecil B. de Mille. Comedy became king. Mack Sennett's Keystone Kops had the whole nation laughing. Before long, studios sprang up in Culver City and Universal City, as well as in Hollywood. The latter name had by now become more or less synonymous with the word "movies."

Silent movies accompanied by organ music gave way to the "talkies." Hundreds of movie houses sprang up, and instant fortunes came to stars, directors, and producers, while novelists earned more from film rights than from their original novels. Studios wielded great power, starting instant fads, and shaping tastes and ideas the world over.

The 1906 earthquake – measuring 8.25 on the Richter scale – and subsequent fire in San Francisco killed more than 300 people and destroyed 500 square blocks and 28,000 buildings.

In the summer of 1920, the population of Los Angeles reached 576,000, for the first time surpassing that of San Francisco, and LA became the 10th most populous city in the country. The southern portion of the state was "the world's closest approach to bedlam and babel," sneered journalist and politician, George Creel, with columnist Westbrook Pegler urging that the same territory "be declared incompetent and placed in charge of a guardian."

THE SAN FRANCISCO EARTHQUAKE

While LA spent much of the early 20th century expanding, San Francisco spent it rebuilding: an earthquake measuring 8.25 on the Richter scale shook Northern Californians from their beds at 5.12am on April 18, 1906. When the deadly San Andreas fault lurched that morning, it sent terrifying jolts through an area 210 miles (338km) long and 30 miles (48km) wide, from San Juan Bautista in the south to Fort Bragg in the north. Other towns, like San Jose and Point Reyes Station near Drake's Bay, suffered more from the initial shock than San Francisco. Church bells jangled chaotically, dishes fell, windows shattered, dogs barked, Enrico Caruso (appearing locally in the opera *Carmen*) was scared voiceless, and San Francisco's new City Hall crumbled. In just 48 seconds, it was all over, but the city lay in ruins.

The subsequent fire destroyed 28,000 buildings over an area of more than 4 sq miles (10 sq km). It killed 315 people; the bodies of 352 more were never found. The city had experienced many earthquakes before, but none on this scale, and in a city that hosted more than 40 percent of the state's population (compared with around 3 percent today), the effect was cataclysmic. Although the awareness of the mighty

San Andreas fault extended back a dozen years, there had been no prior warning of, or preparations for, this major upheaval. Only an unearthly low rumble preceded fissures opening up and spreading wavelike across the city.

With its alarm system destroyed, the Fire Department lacked coordination, and the commandant of the Presidio, Brigadier General Frederick Funston, leaped in unauthorized to fill the gap in authority. When the brigades did arrive, they found mangled mains lacking any water supply. Hundreds were dead or still trapped in

The Hollywood Bowl, c.1920.

⊘ AIRBORNE LOS ANGELES

Six years after the Wright brothers made their pioneering 59-second flight in North Carolina in 1903, Los Angeles hosted America's first international air show. A half million visitors came to watch Glenn Curtis set a 55mph (88kmh) speed record, including Glenn Martin, who promptly set up a plant that turned out one plane a day by the time World War I was declared. His employee Donald Douglas started his own company; within a few years, Douglas's DC3 was carrying 95 percent of US air traffic. Goodyear began blimp services to Catalina. Western Air Express carried cross-country mail. In 1920, scheduled flights began from Los Angeles to San Francisco.

smoking ruins, 500 city blocks were leveled, and a handful of people had been shot or bayoneted by Funston's inexperienced militia who had poured into the streets to keep order and prevent looting.

> The bank behind the regeneration of San Francisco's small business after the 1906 earthquake and subsequent fire later became the Bank of America, the nation's largest.

in generously, freighting in supplies without charge, offering free passage out of the city, and putting heavy equipment and cranes to work on the enormous task of clearing the debris.

The photographer Arnold Genthe wrote, "While the ruins were still smoking, on top of a heap of collapsed walls, a sign would announce: 'On this site will be erected a six-story office building to be ready for occupancy in the fall.'" San Francisco's renaissance was inevitable. The new, improved, taller buildings of Montgomery Street, the Wall Street of the west, were needed

Aftermath of the San Francisco earthquake of 1906, around Bush Street and Kearny Street.

Golden Gate Park became the home of as many as 300,000 people for at least the next few weeks. Cooking inside the tents was banned, sanitation was rudimentary, water was in very short supply, and rats (and therefore the threat of the bubonic plague) were a dark, lingering menace.

But there was a strong will to recover. A Committee of Forty on the Reconstruction of San Francisco was formed to define the tasks to be undertaken and A.P. Giannini's tiny Bank of Italy, making loans to small businesses intent on rebuilding, was at the forefront of those determined to revive the city's fortunes.

Aid poured in from all over the world, $8 million worth within the first few weeks. Even the much-reviled Southern Pacific Railroad pitched

to process all the money churned out by the state's industries, farms, and banks. The Port of San Francisco was still one of the world's busiest harbors. San Francisco's historic business of making business was unstoppable.

In 1911, San Francisco elected a new mayor, James "Sunny Jim" Rolph, a purveyor of goodwill whose reign encompassed some of San Francisco's giddiest times. The 1915 Panama Pacific International Exposition, which occupied 600 acres (240 hectares) of reclaimed land in what is now the Marina, is still considered one of the greatest of the world's fairs. Today, only one vestige of the flamboyant celebration remains: the Palace of Fine Arts Theatre. It was saved from gradual decay by civic benefactors in the 1960s.

Construction of the
Golden Gate Bridge.

MODERN TIMES

Beatnik bards and happy hippies flocked to find fulfillment in the state where experimentation was encouraged; this ethos went on to pave the way for technological advances in Silicon Valley and the movie industry.

The last half-century saw California's population boom, its movie industry lead the way in modern cinema, its political events impact the nation, and its Silicon Valley produce companies like Facebook and Apple that have not only impacted the state but also become household names around the world.

POPULATION BOOM

In 1940, the population of Los Angeles numbered 1.3 million, of which about 9 percent were Mexican, 3 percent Asian, and 3 percent African-American. By 1950, the City of Angels' 2 million population made it the fourth-largest city in the United States.

The war had plunged California into a frenzy of activity. Twenty-three million tons of war supplies and 1.5 million men and women passed through the Golden Gate during the war's 46 months. The ports of San Francisco, Sausalito, Oakland, Vallejo, and Alameda were busy around the clock building and repairing ships, and loading supplies for the war machine.

In the Bay Area alone, the federal government spent $3 billion on shipbuilding. A new wave of immigration swept into the region as new factories needed new workers – 100,000 at the Kaiser Yards in Richmond, 90,000 more at Sausalito. Within two years of America's entry into the war in December 1941, the number of wage-earners in San Francisco almost tripled. The federal government doled out $83 million in contracts to the California Institute of Technology (Cal Tech) alone.

Even though 750,000 Californians left for military service, the state's wage-earners increased by nearly a million in the first half of the 1940s. After the war, the great suburban sprawl got

1946 poster advertising The Big Sleep, starring Humphrey Bogart and Lauren Bacall.

under way as war workers and their families settled down to post-war prosperity.

World War II gave a tremendous boost to California's aircraft industry, which increased statewide from fewer than 10,000 employees to more than 300,000. When the war was over, a gradual shift in the industry's workers from mainly blue-collar laborers to scientists and technicians meant, as historian Bruce Henstell wrote, that "aeronautics was replaced by something called aerospace."

THE ANTI-CONFORMISTS

As a new, almost instant society, California has always felt free to experiment. Many of its newcomers, from the "Anglo hordes" of the 1840s to

Gold Rush adventurers, to present-day arrivals, have come to the state to escape the burdens of conformity elsewhere. The great majority of Californians have always been settled and to one degree or another, God-fearing. But the anti-conformists – the colorful, freethinking minority – have given California its name for verve and drive.

In the 1950s and 1960s, according to author Mike Davis, Los Angeles became "the capital of youth," but it was in San Francisco that the first stirrings of post-war protest and florid eccentricity were felt. While the American nation

Beat writer Jack Kerouac.

The San Francisco Giants made history in 2010 by defeating the Texas Rangers to win the baseball World Series. The city exploded in Giants pride for their team, who were considered underdogs going into the series. The Giants went on to win the Series again in 2012 and 2014.

settled into a prosperous torpor, the city's historically Italian North Beach area became the haunt of a loosely defined group of poets, writers, declaimers, and sidewalk philosophers – the beatniks.

In the 1950s, they seemed titillating and somehow significant, a tempting combination for the nation's press who ogled at their rambling poetry readings, sniffed at the light marijuana breezes drifting out of the North Beach coffee houses, and wondered if civilization could stand such a limpid assault. The beatniks, it seems, mostly wanted America to go away. But it wouldn't, and before long "beat" had become a fashion and North Beach a tourist attraction.

THE BEAT GENERATION

The beats, however, had struck a nerve of dissatisfaction and alienation in America. Though it was never a coherent movement, it produced juice-stirring literary works like Allen Ginsberg's *Howl* and Jack Kerouac's *On the Road*. That inspired alienation gave rise to two parallel, dissimilar, but oddly congruent movements: the angry politics of the New Left and the woozy love fest of the hippies. The first significant protest of the great, protest-rich 1960s took place in San Francisco in the decade's first year. In mid-May, the House Un-American Activities Committee opened a series of hearings in City Hall. When hundreds of demonstrators met the committee in the rotunda, the police reacted furiously, turning water hoses and billy clubs on the crowds. Dozens of protesters were carted off to jail, but the angry shouts in City Hall were heard around the world.

The locus of dissent was the University of California at Berkeley. There the Free Speech Movement kept up a steady assault against racism, materialism, and the stifling "multiversity" itself. As the horrors of the war in Vietnam grew more apparent, the New Left spread across America and the world, tilting at governments, bombing, marching, and changing the way America looked at itself. The hippies, though, attacked their target with gentler weapons. While the New Left ranted at the evils of an affluent and smug, hypocritical society, the hippies tried to undermine that society with glimmering love and peace, and wearing farfetched clothes.

THE HIPPIES OF HAIGHT-ASHBURY

In the mid-1960s, San Francisco became the mecca of the hippie revolution. It was a natural refuge for spacey idealists, having been created by youthful myth-chasers. Former beatniks slid easily into the free-and-easy hippie style centered around the Haight-Ashbury neighbor-hood, with its funky, cheap Victorian houses, and Golden Gate Park handily nearby for roaming. By 1967, the Haight was thronged with long-haired young men and women, the movement reaching its apogee in the massive Be-In assemblage, and the celebrated Summer of Love.

At first, San Francisco was amused by the hippies. But as altogether too many sons and daughters of wealthy, respected citizens took to marijuana-induced meandering, and as the LSD hysteria took full flight, public sympathy for the nomads gradually began to evaporate.

TENSIONS AND RIOTING

By the mid-1960s, the African-American population in LA had multiplied tenfold and were fed up with discriminatory employment and "unwritten" housing restrictions. On one hot summer evening in 1965, the palm-shaded ghetto of Watts exploded. For six days, the inner city boiled until the National Guard restored order. Almost 30 years later, in April 1992, with conditions in the black and Chicano areas largely unchanged, violence erupted again. The acquittal of four police officers recorded on video beating an African-American man, Rodney King, sparked the worst racial violence in California's history.

By the time the dawn-to-dusk curfew was lifted, there were over 50 dead and 2,500 injured, and 5,200 fires had occurred. South Central LA was devastated. The Rodney King case provided the spark for already existing tension, setting off the intricately connected time bomb of race,

poverty, and the state of the inner city. The seemingly never-ending explosion of gang violence in Los Angeles, for example, has focused national attention on the problem of urban poverty.

SCANDALS AND CELEBRITY THRILLS

Barely a year goes by without major California events making headlines the world over. From 1994 to 1997, TV viewers were glued to their screens by the arrest and trials in Los Angeles of former football hero O.J. Simpson. There was the much publicized 2003 recall of Governor Gray

Beat poet Allen Ginsberg in 1956.

⊘ THE FILM INDUSTRY

Hollywood's film industry eventually shook down into the major studios that dominate the industry today and are household names internationally. The "Big Six" are 20th Century Fox, Paramount, Warner Brothers, Columbia, Universal, and Disney. The Hollywood area is still host to a few smaller, independent production companies such as Lionsgate, and DreamWorks. It is also home to all kinds of ancillary businesses and services such as recording studios, prop houses and talent agencies, lighting equipment companies, and equipment rentals. Also remaining in Hollywood are Eastman Kodak and Technicolor Creative Services, which process millions of feet of film every day.

The entertainment industry is one of the most highly unionized industries in California, with the Screen Actors Guild and American Federation of Television and Radio Artists (SAG-AFTRA) claiming more than 160,000 members nationwide, most of them in Los Angeles. The Directors Guild of America and the Writers Guild of America account for most of the rest of the talent, in addition to all the behind-the-camera workers such as grips, gaffers, film editors, carpenters, plasterers, publicists, costumers, art directors, sound people, and cinematographers, who are represented by the International Alliance of Theatrical Stage Employers (IATSE) and the American Federation of Musicians (AFM). Studio drivers are in the Teamsters.

Davis and the election of mega movie star Arnold Schwarzenegger in his place, plus all the trials and legal woes of Michael Jackson, and starlets like Paris Hilton and Lindsay Lohan. In a crime and trial that sparked mass demonstrations in Oakland, BART Police Officer Johannes Mehserle was sentenced to two years in prison for fatally shooting Oscar Grant on New Year's Day in 2009 – a shooting that was variously labeled involuntary manslaughter and a summary execution.

In 2011 and 2012, the focus shifted from televised trials to live protests, as Occupy Wall

1992's riots over the acquittal of Rodney King's arresting officers left over 50 people dead.

Street protesters filled streets and parks in major cities, from Oakland and San Francisco to Los Angeles.

In 2017 a new scandal erupted when powerful film producer Harvey Weinstein hit the headlines as allegations of sexual harassment and abuse of famous actresses were brought against him. One positive result of the scandal was the global popularity of the #MeToo campaign and the fight against sexual harassment of women in the workplace.

DOT-COM ERA

At the start of the millennium, the future looked bright in San Francisco. Nearby Silicon Valley invigorated established industries and spurred thousands of start-up companies. Venture capitalists threw money at shiny ideas, stock prices soared, and the housing market hit new heights. Recent college graduates earned more money than they could count, but much of the prosperity owed more to innovative book-keeping than real business acumen. The bubble burst on October 9, 2002, and many of these new millionaires were forced to return home to their parents. Today, California's tech fortunes are on the upswing; in 2012 Facebook went public, and Twitter moved to bigger digs in downtown San Francisco. One of the results of so many well-paid young professionals is that the rental prices in the city continue to rise.

DEVASTATING DROUGHT CONDITIONS

The current California drought began in late 2013, with many places in California recording all-time low precipitation records.

On January 17, 2014, State Governor Jerry Brown declared a drought state of emergency. Drought conditions were compounded in 2015 when the Sierra Nevada snowpack (which is counted on to provide 30 percent of the state's water supply when it melts in late spring and summer) hit its lowest recorded levels. As a result of these conditions, in some areas of the Central Valley (where the state's agricultural bounty is grown) the land is sinking by one foot or more per year.

Another consequence is the susceptibility of the land to wildfires. In 2017, nearly 9,000 wildfires ravaged vast areas of California, killing 46 people and destroying over 10,000 buildings across the state.

The drought continues to persist, making it California's longest drought in over a century.

A CONTENTIOUS, DIVIDED ELECTION

On the national front, the U.S. was embroiled in a lengthy electoral battle that pitted former Secretary of State, Hillary Clinton and businessman, Donald Trump against each other in contentious contest.

Victory went to Donald Trump despite the fact that over 61 percent of Californian residents voted for Hillary Clinton. As a result of divisive policies introduced by the current president, petitioners have begun collecting signatures under the California Sovereign and Autonomous Nation Initiative to try and establish an autonomous and independent nation of California.

CALIFORNIA AND THE WORLD STAGE

Whether it's the dramatic rise and fall of the dot-com economy, scandals, or the thrill of celebrity, California will always be on the radar. Over 39 million people live in the state and speak over 90 different languages. Many Californians deeply identify with and prefer one half of the state to the other, inspiring a rivalry – sometimes friendly, sometimes less so. Compared to Southern California's trendy celebrity culture, Northern California considers itself laid-back and authentic. There will always be much excitement in a place with such diverse communities and a high concentration of artists, entrepreneurs, scientists, and trendsetters, who love the fact that California is home.

The pier at Santa Monica.

∅ SAME-SEX MARRIAGE

In 2004, San Francisco's Mayor Newsom authorized the city to begin issuing marriage licenses to same-sex couples inciting a 29-day wedding frenzy during which some 4,000 same-sex couples from all over the US and other countries married. A month later licenses were halted by order of the California Supreme Court and the marriages already made were declared invalid.

The city's gay population and their supporters were undeterred, and filed a lawsuit contending that the revoked legislation violated California's constitutional guarantee for equal treatment. The appeal went to the state Supreme Court in 2006 after the ban against same-sex marriage was upheld.

In May 2008 the court overturned the ban making California the second state to legalize same-sex marriage, but that victory was short-lived. In November 2008, the Proposition 8 ballot measure passed, defining marriage as a union only between a man and a woman. A year later, the state Supreme Court upheld the proposition but ruled that the unions of same-sex couples previously married were to be considered valid. In 2010, a federal court declared the ban unconstitutional, a decision which was upheld in 2012 by the US Court of Appeals for the ninth circuit.

CALIFORNIA CUISINE

California's menu is as varied as the people who live there. From sun-dried tomatoes to sushi, tandoori to tacos, the state is a food-lover's fantasy, bursting with color and flavor.

What are you hungry for? One of California's most quintessential experiences is its food. A multitude of influences and trends have converged in this state, making it an essential destination for foodies from around the world. Walk just a few blocks in most sizeable cities and you will have a choice to whet even the most cosmopolitan of appetites: tacos and burritos, tandoori and curries, noodles and sushi, Mongolian barbecue, pasta and pizza, falafel and bagels, piroshki and baklava, and on through the global menu. It's not only the diversity of food that sets California apart; it's also the innovativeness and quality of food across the board.

SEASONAL INGREDIENTS

The words "California Cuisine" have a dual meaning. Intuitively, they describe the general food of the state, but the term has also come to encapsulate a food movement begun by chef Alice Waters of Chez Panisse in Berkeley that emphasizes using local, seasonal ingredients.

Alice Waters opened Chez Panisse in 1971. Waters set out with no formal training, just a year spent abroad eating her way round Europe. To Waters, freshness was the cardinal virtue, and foods were cooked simply so as to bring out their natural flavors. Chez Panisse opened as a typical French bistro. Frustrated by an inability to get the quality goods that she found in France, Waters began encouraging local purveyors to bring produce to her door. Farmers grew special vegetables to complement a specific dish and hand-reared livestock and poultry to meticulous specifications. Small-time fishermen sold her their

The Napa Valley Barrel Auction draws international wine lovers to bid for (and taste) Napa Valley wines.

catch and, for the first time in years, local oysters were farmed.

Armed with local ingredients, the Chez Panisse kitchen went to work. The result? The strictly French food became less French, and the menu suddenly offered dishes such as ravioli made like gnocchi from potato starch and garlic, and the very English jugged hare.

Waters-trained chefs began to branch out on their own, and the Chez Panisse philosophy spread to other restaurants. The fervor for freshness chimed with the Californian ethos, and in a few short years some chefs have been elevated to celebrity status including Jeremiah Tower.

AN ORGANIC AND SUSTAINABLE APPROACH

With the California Cuisine movement and Californians' generally eco-friendly leanings, consuming organic foods and promoting sustainability in food production have become extremely popular in the state. Restaurant menus credit their suppliers by name – whether by ranch, farm, or cheesemaker. Residents and companies sign up for organic produce boxes to be delivered to their homes or offices, full of fresh, seasonal fruits and

A pumpkin festival is held in Half Moon Bay every fall.

vegetables grown in nearby farms or urban gardens.

Urbanites also buy fresh produce directly from local growers at outdoor farmers markets, a staple in many communities. There you'll find everything from ripe fruits and seasonal vegetables to sustainably raised beef to cheese, jams, honey, nuts, and herbs.

In San Francisco, the Ferry Building Farmers Market has become one of the city's most popular tourist attractions. Large, popular farmers markets are also found in Napa, San Luis Obispo, Santa Monica, and San Diego, along with the Original Farmers Market in Los Angeles.

Of course, it is easy to shop local in California, whether you're looking for almonds, artichokes,

olives, or tomatoes: the state's agricultural industry is the largest in the world, producing more than half of the state's fruits and vegetables.

The focus on produce seen in the state's countless farmers markets is also in line with Californians' generally health-focused attitude. It's no surprise that most restaurants include vegetarian – and often vegan – options predominantly on the menu rather than as a back-up. In major cities, you can expect to find several entirely vegetarian restaurants.

DIVERSE MENUS

California's overall menu is hardly restrictive, however. You name it, it's here – Peruvian, Mexican, Vietnamese, Ethiopian, Thai, Italian, French, Creole, Chinese. To understand what makes this incredible array possible, it helps to consider California's geographic and cultural orientation: the influence of Mexican neighbors to the south and Asian neighbors to the west; the vast tracts of rich soil that make it one of the most fertile and productive places on earth; a climate friendly to growing just about every kind of crop all year round; and local waters that yield a bounty of fish and seafood.

Traditional European fare, especially Italian and French, has long been available in California, particularly prominent among the more expensive restaurants. Today, these upscale restaurants have also become highly regionalized, reflecting Californians' passion for European travel and an increased familiarity with specific regional dishes from, for example, Tuscany and Provence.

But more than these factors, the many people who call themselves Californians define the local food. The vast majority came from other parts of the world (many recently, others a generation or two ago), bringing native regional cuisine with them. Particularly in California's large cities, sizeable ethnic communities support their own specialty food shops and produce markets, as well as an often remarkable number of restaurants (Los Angeles, for example, claims to have around 500 Korean eateries). This results in a vitality, availability, and diversity that, for the curious diner, can make for a fascinating food experience.

LOCAL SPECIALTIES

California hasn't imported everything, though. In addition to huge amounts of produce, the state is famous for more specific local specialties. In San Francisco you can pair tangy sourdough bread with fresh Dungeness crab. Or warm up with a toasty Irish coffee, which was invented at the iconic Buena Vista Café near Fisherman's Wharf. In Los Angeles, Koreatown is a foodie hotspot for ethnic authenticity, and East LA is the place for tacos al pastor (spicy grilled pork and pineapple). Meanwhile San Diego is famous for fish tacos; Drakes Bay, Tomales Bay and Bodega Bay, north of San Francisco, deliver deliciously fresh oysters; the Coachella Valley southeast of Palm Springs farms 95 percent of the nations date crop (celebrated during the annual National Date Festival); the state's Sierras yield honey, wild blackberries, and ollallieberries, chanterelle mushrooms, and venison; while sustainably farmed abalone comes from the North Coast.

Chefs fear him and owners schmooze him. Michael Bauer, San Francisco Chronicle food critc, can make or break a restaurant. Go to: www.sfgate.com and search blogs for "Bauer."

WINE, BEER, AND COFFEE

No discussion of California eating pleasures would be complete without mentioning its world-famous wines, of which locals are justifiably proud. California vintages from the Napa and Sonoma valleys north of San Francisco first achieved world-class status in the 1970s, and along the way have been joined by wines from other parts of the state.

According to the Brewer's Association, California has far more breweries than any other state; popular ones include Sierra Nevada (Chico), Anchor Brewing (San Francisco), Anderson Valley Brewery (Mendocino), and Bear Republic (Healdsburg).

In terms of other beverages, California is serious about coffee too, and offers plenty of alternatives to the worldwide chains. In fact, you can't walk a block in the downtown areas without passing people scurrying along clutching a to-go cup. Coffee has evolved into an art form here. In San Francisco's North Beach are popular family-run establishments like Caffé Trieste; Peet's Coffee & Tea (where the founders of Starbucks used to buy beans) originated across the bay in Berkeley. Meanwhile Blue Bottle Coffee Co. and Ritual Coffee Roasters approach coffee brewing in much the same way winemakers approach wine. Blue Bottle calls their process "artisan micro-roasting" and uses organic, shade-grown beans.

Sushi in a San Francisco restaurant.

⊘ FOOD TRUCKS

One of the most interesting food trends in recent years has been the popularization of food trucks. Serving everything from Korean tacos to gourmet grilled cheese, curries, and cupcakes, these small restaurants on wheels are literally large catering trucks with kitchens. Roving around town, they often broadcast their location for that day's lunch hour on Twitter or their company website. The trend first picked up speed in LA – which now has well over 200 trucks including the popular Kogi BBQ truck (http://kogibbq.com) – and then spread to San Francisco and major cities around the country. Want to try one? Bring cash and be prepared for a 15-minute wait.

FINE WINES OF CALIFORNIA

California's close to 4,000 wineries produce more than 80 percent the country's wine. The quality is just as high as the quantity, with California wines continuing to win awards and worldwide critical acclaim.

In the 18th century, when the Franciscan fathers began winemaking, the grapes were dumped into troughs, trampled into pulp, and hung in cow skins to ferment before leaking into casks. "In those days the flavor was not described with enthusiasm," wrote the Napa Historical Society's Meredie Porterfield, "but that is what passed for wine in early LA."

California wine has come a long way since then, both in terms of quality and quantity. Today, the state accounts for over 80 percent of the total US wine production. The reliably warm weather allows wineries to use very ripe fruit which makes for a fruitier wine, rather than the more earthy flavors of Europe. It also means higher alcohol levels, with some Californian wines having over 13.5 percent.

Napa and Sonoma get the lion's share of publicity, although they produce less than a quarter of the wine. Many more millions of gallons emanate from the San Joaquin Valley, the so-called "jug wines" which are mass-produced and more moderately priced. Other major wine areas are around Mendocino, Lake County, Paso Robles, Livermore, the Santa Ynez Valley near Santa Barbara, and, in the far south, the emerging vineyards of Temecula.

Despite increasing sophistication in bottling and manufacturing, basic winemaking has changed very little over the centuries. Wine is, after all, just fermented grape juice, not manufactured but generated by living yeast cells that ferment grape sugars into grape alcohol.

For more about wine and the Wine Country, see pages 73 and 141.

Detail on the Napa Valley Wine Train. A round-trip journey takes three hours.

Join a tour or tasting class to gain access to the wine cellar

Beringer Winery was established in Napa Valley in 1876 the German Beringer brothers. The estate's Rhine House was built to recreate the family home on Germany's Rhine River, and is on the National Register of Historic Places

The Napa Valley Barrel Auction brings together vintners and wine lovers to taste and bid for Napa Valley wines.

Sustainable winegrowing

Sustainable winegrowing and winemaking practices are a constantly evolving trend in California. Many California wines are now labelled organic, meaning they have no added sulphites to prolong shelf life, no synthetic pesticides or nonorganic chemicals were used, and natural alternatives were used for soil enrichment, pests, weeds, and vine disease management.

Additionally, vintners and growers who represent one-quarter of the state's wine acreage and 40 percent of the annual wine case production currently participate in the voluntary Code of Sustainable Wine Growing program. Introduced in 2003, the code aims to establish environmental standards and practices from ground to glass, including methods minimizing pesticide use, reducing water and energy use, building healthy soil, protecting air and water quality, recycling natural resources, and maintaining surrounding habitats.

Examples of such sustainable winemaking practices include using sheep, bats and beneficial birds to control weeds and pests, using drip irrigation and process ponds to conserve water, and composting and recycling to minimize waste.

In 2012, the California Sustainable Winegrowing Alliance (CCSW) developed a third-party certification program related to the California Sustainable Winegrowing Program (SWP) – essentially like a LEED (Leadership in Energy and Environmental Design) certification program for wineries.

ne tasting at the annual Napa Valley Barrel Auction.

e Napa Valley Wine Train is a smart restaurant serving gional cuisine in a collection of early-20th-century rail rs that convey passengers around the Napa Valley.

Napa contains a greater acreage of Cabernet Sauvignon grapes than any other California county.

Vineyard in Napa Valley.

CALIFORNIA WINE

California wines are world-class, but its winemakers are approachable; from Sonoma to San Luis Obispo, the state's wine regions happily welcome 21 million visitors each year to their wineries.

From breathtaking Napa and Sonoma valleys' concentrated selection of world-class wineries to the quiet vineyards of the Santa Barbara region in the south, California wineries are set up to welcome visitors and dazzle with their offerings. At tucked-away wineries in Monterey and Mendocino you feel like the only guest, while at talked-about vineyards in the Napa Valley you'll feel like you're in on the latest Wine Country buzz.

CALIFORNIA'S WINE HISTORY

The first winemakers in California were 18th-century Spanish missionaries who used wine in religious ceremonies. Large-scale vineyards were established around the Los Angeles area in the 1830s by Jean-Louis Vignes, a French vintner. But the real birthplace of California wine is Sonoma County.

Numerous wineries offer wine tastings and tours of their facilities.

Father Junípero Serra, who founded many of the state's missions, had no taste for California's indigenous wild grapes and instead imported quality vines from his native Spain.

Wine grapes were first planted in Sonoma County around 1812 in Fort Ross. Father Jose Altimira, founder of the Mission San Francisco de Solano at Sonoma, and General Vallejo, who colonized Sonoma and Napa counties by granting land to his relatives and friends, were the first northerners to dabble in winemaking. Then Count Agoston Haraszthy, a flamboyant Hungarian political refugee, pushed the Sonoma region into wine stardom. He began in 1857 at Buena Vista, Northern California's oldest winery, accumulating wine-grape cuttings for California's growers on journeys to Europe. After he died, his protégé Charles Krug, a German political exile, opened Napa Valley's first commercial winery in 1861, and by the 1880s, valley wines were winning medals in Europe.

Prohibition nearly decimated the industry, but following its repeal in 1933, Beaulieu Vineyard's Georges de Latour, the Mondavi family, and others began resurrecting the industry. In the 1960s, a wine boom began as large corporations marketed vintage-dated varietal wines at reasonable prices, and small, privately owned wineries produced more expensive, estatebottled wines at higher costs. Old winemaking families were joined by oil barons, engineers, and actors who revitalized old wineries and opened new ones.

By 1976, California wines were beating French vintages in European tastings. In the most

> *California ranks first in wine consumption in the US, followed by Florida, then New York. There are more than 60,000 registered California wine labels.*

Napa Valley Wine Train takes passengers from Napa to the village of St Helena and back.

famous tasting, the French wine industry's elite gathered in Paris to blind taste four white Burgundies against six California Chardonnays. The winner, to the surprise of the French judges, was Chateau Montelena's 1973 Chardonnay.

THE WINE COUNTRY TODAY

In the years since the 1976 grand tasting, California has become the world's fourth-leading wine producer. In the largest international wine competition, the Decanter World Wine Awards, two California wines received platinum medals in 2017, and 13 received silver. Some 4,000 wineries cover the state, from Napa and Sonoma to the Gold Country and Santa Barbara. Indeed,

grapes are grown in most of California's counties, and some vintners have discovered pockets of land in California that can match the growing conditions of the great north, especially the south central coast of Santa Barbara and San Luis Obispo counties.

NAPA AND SONOMA VALLEYS

North of San Francisco, the valleys of Napa and Sonoma are the heart of California's Wine Country. The collection of small towns and villages are set amid miles of vineyards, whose premier grapes are the result of excellent growing conditions: temperate climate and rich, drainable soil. Napa Valley is especially famous for its Cabernet Sauvignon (Merlot and Sangiovese also do well here) and its high-end foodie scene.

Sonoma Valley has a more relaxed, less polished atmosphere than Napa. So far it remains less trafficked, especially compared to Napa Valley on weekends. Because of the valley's climate and soil variation (the county has more geologically distinct soil types than all of France), numerous varietals thrive in Sonoma County, including Chardonnay, Cabernet Sauvignon, Pinot Noir, Merlot, Zinfandel, Syrah, and Sauvignon Blanc.

MENDOCINO COUNTY

Some 35 miles (56km) long and 15 miles (24km) wide, the Mendocino Ridge Wine Country, within Mendocino Country is a non-contiguous trio of burgundy-hued ridges that produce exceptional

⊘ A WINE PRIMER

Winemaking begins at the crusher, which frees juice from grapes. White wines are made from fermented juice; added yeast converts sugar to alcohol and carbon dioxide, with fermentation occurring in stainless steel tanks. Leaving yeast in creates dry wines; stopping yeast action makes sweeter wines. Sparkling wine begins the same way, then undergoes another fermentation. Carbon dioxide is trapped within the bottle, creating bubbles. For red wines, grape skin and pulp are included in the fermenting tank. After adding yeast, grape skins are pressed, then reds are aged in stainless steel or wooden tanks. The wine is clarified, then aged further before bottling.

Zinfandel at high elevations. In 1988, the Kendall-Jackson Winery said the Mendocino Coastal Ridge was one of the world's greatest Zinfandel regions. The area is now achieving recognition for Pinot Noir and more acidic, less oaky, Chardonnay wines.

MONTEREY

An hour south of Silicon Valley, the Monterey Wine Country has more than 175 vineyards, largely in a 90-mile (145km) -long valley with just eight main viticulture soil types. The northernmost part of Monterey produces Pinot Noir and Chardonnay, while the valley's microclimates help support 42 different varietals. Pick up maps and winery information at Taste of Monterey (700 Cannery Row; www.atasteofmonterey.com), where you can also taste local wines.

SAN JOAQUIN VALLEY AND THE SIERRA FOOTHILLS

California's northern wineries produce just a fraction of the state's total output. Many of the grapes come from the hot, arid San Joaquin Valley, several hundred miles south, and are often used to make modestly priced "jug" wines.

The Sierra Nevada foothills' 10 counties are now home to more than 250 wineries, including Renwood in Plymouth (Amador Country). Many small and family-owned, these wineries excel at full-bodied Zinfandel, Syrah, and Petite Syrah. Rhone-style white varietals are also found here.

SANTA YNEZ VALLEY

Just 35 miles (56km) from Santa Barbara's beaches, the charmingly rustic Santa Inez Valley consists of six distinctive towns: Santa Ynez, Solvang, Los Alamos, Los Olivos, Ballard, and Buellton. Pinot Noir, Chardonnay, and Syrah can be tasted here, along with other varietals. Don't miss the Scandinavian-influenced Solvang either.

SAN LUIS OBISPO

In San Luis Obispo's Edna Valley, Arroyo Grande Valley, and Avila Valley, the rocky volcanic soil and marine influence produce grapes with complex flavors and intense varietal character. Small, family-owned wineries produce primarily Pinot Noir, Chardonnay, Viognier, Syrah,

Grenache, and Zinfandel. In Paso Robles, the three-day Paso Robles Wine Festival in May is the state's largest outdoor wine tasting.

TEMECULA VALLEY

The Temecula Valley (32miles/51km from San Diego) is emerging as California's southernmost wine country. A unique microclimate – with morning mist, cooling ocean air, warm midday sun, and clear nights – and granite-based soil are producing excellent Syrah, Cabernet, and Zinfandel grapes.

Chateau Montelena Winery sits at the base of Mt St Helena.

⊘ WINE-TASTING INFORMATION

Most wineries are open 10am–4pm daily; some are by appointment only. A wine-tasting flight generally costs $10–20, and you may be given anywhere from four to six wines to try. Often, if you purchase bottles your tasting fee will be waived. Additionally, some tours include tastings. The best source for current information is the wineries themselves: call in advance to check on reservations, tasting fees, and discounts. Visitor centers are the best bet for contact details, or try www.winecountry.com. Mix it up with a tour (usually 1–2 hours) and a tasting at one of the larger wineries, then follow up with stops at a few of the smaller wineries.

Gloria Swanson in front of the street sign that immortalized them both.

THE MOVIEMAKERS OF SUNSET BOULEVARD

From such humble beginnings as filming in directors' living rooms, LA's movie industry became both star-maker and style-setter; while its heyday is in the past, the Hollywood neighborhood is still a magnet for people interested in the movie business.

Although its beginnings were elsewhere, Hollywood is what comes to most people's minds when they think of the film industry. In the first half of the 20th century, major changes were made, from silence to sound and from black-and-white to color. The early studios grew up on or around Sunset Boulevard, and the eponymous, quintessential movie about the industry's early days was released in 1950. Meanwhile, the story of California's movie industry has gotten more interesting ever since.

Sound arrives with The Jazz Singer.

William Laurie Dickson is on record at the Library of Congress as producer of the earliest movie: Fred Ott's Sneeze (1890), in which he captured an assistant sneezing.

THE START OF THE MOVIE INDUSTRY

The moving picture was actually invented as the result of a bet. In 1877, English eccentric Eadweard Muybridge helped California governor Leland Stanford win a $25,000 bet by using a series of 12 cameras to film a galloping horse and then printing the individual shots onto a revolving disk, thus proving that a trotting horse has all four hooves off the ground simultaneously. Tripling his battery of cameras, Muybridge devised faster film, mounted his photographs on a wheel combined with light, and called his process Zoopraxiscope.

The Paris inventor Étienne-Jules Marey improved on this by developing a photographic gun with a long barrel for the lens and a circular photographic plate that rotated 12 times in the chamber during the single second the shot was being taken – the first movie camera. By 1888,

George Eastman had produced celluloid film and the Kodak camera in New York, and in New Jersey Thomas Edison (who at first envisioned film as being merely a pictorial addition to his phonograph) added sprockets to synchronize the sound. Eadweard Muybridge died in 1904, unaware of the industry to which he had given birth, an industry that was about to move west.

THE MOVE TO HOLLYWOOD

The first Hollywood census, in 1907, showed that among its population of 3,500 were 103 immigrants from England, 102 from Germany, 86 from Canada, 20 from France, 28 from Ireland, 24 from Scotland, and 158 from New York. Also there was Francis Boggs, a film director visiting from Chicago's Selig

Polyscope Studios, which had been battling over patents with Thomas Edison's movie trust.

A year later, filming the *Count of Monte Cristo* during a severe Illinois winter, Boggs recalled the warmth of Hollywood and moved cast and crew to near Laguna Beach to complete the production, thereby earning his place in the reference books as the first director to shoot at least part of a film in California.

Four years later, Carl Laemmle's Universal Film Manufacturing Company began operations at Sunset and Gower, absorbing the Nestor

The first moving picture machine, Eadweard Muybridge's 1879 Zoopraxiscope.

Charlie Chaplin was not impressed with LA when he first visited in 1910 while touring with one of Fred Karno's variety troupes. It was, he thought, "an ugly city, hot and oppressive, and the people looked sallow and anemic."

Film Company, which had made Hollywood's first studio film, The Law of the Range. Eventually, his company moved through the Cahuenga Pass to found Universal City. Meanwhile, Cecil B. de Mille, Jesse Lasky, Samuel Goldfish (who later changed his name to Goldwyn), and Arthur

Friend formed a company under Lasky's name and planned to make *The Squaw Man*, starring Dustin Farnum, in Arizona, but found the scenery unsuitable. They continued westward to Hollywood and completed the film at a rented barn one block north of Sunset at Vine and Selma.

THE EARLY YEARS

Initially, films were shot quite casually around Hollywood, using private homes for domestic dramas, and banks during weekends for hold-up scenes, and passersby were conscripted on the spot for crowd scenes. But making movies soon became expensive because they were no longer simple. The easy days when sound pioneer Jack Foley was able to simulate galloping horses with coconut shells in a sandbox were giving way to times when the people required to make a film would include visual effects researchers, recording mixers, wranglers, gaffers, dialect coaches, and boom operators, not to mention caterers.

In 1924, both Metro and Goldwyn – studios which had moved onto the former lot on which the Pickford–Fairbanks studio had begun in 1922 – were merged. Mayer was quoted in *Motion Picture Weekly* as saying they aimed to produce 52 films per year, which he hoped would fill the 250,000 seats owned by the Loews theater chain.

This era saw the birth of the new system under which directors virtually ceased to be independent agents and became employees of "a massive, assembly-line organization." So began the great debate about studio versus artist, commercialism versus personal integrity, and "the desecration of great masterpieces and promising careers through the insensitivity of philistine management," wrote Gary Carey in the Mayer biography, *All the Stars in the Heavens*.

THE TALKIES

By 1927, cinema attendances were slumping. The four Warner brothers – Harry, Albert, Sam, and Jack – had added a musical background to their film *Don Juan* (John Barrymore and Mary Astor), which was greeted enthusiastically. Then they had Al Jolson say a few words in *The Jazz Singer*. Although mostly background music with a few songs, the picture made millions and forced the other studios into sound.

In July 1928, Warner released *The Lights of New York*, another instant hit. One month later,

MGM's trademark, Leo the lion, roared from the screen showing a semi-documentary called *White Shadows in the South Seas*. The first MGM

In the early days, Gower Gulch – at Sunset and Gower – was the rendezvous of would-be movie cowboys hoping to work for one of the small companies operating nearby. The formation of Central Casting eliminated this casual approach.

United Artists (which had been set up by Chaplin, Pickford, Fairbanks, and Griffith to distribute their work and that of other independents) played a minor role.

Accelerated by the Depression of the 1930s was the development of color on celluloid, which, by 1934, had progressed enough for Walt Disney to produce his first full-length animated feature, *Snow White and the Seven Dwarfs*, an assemblage of 250,000 individually painted frames. *Ben Hur*, which took around three years in the making, cost about $4 million.

The Birth of a Nation, a controversial movie directed by D.W. Griffith in 1915.

sound film was *Broadway Melody*. One scene was re-shot and MGM experimented with leaving the music as it was and having the players mime the number for the cameras – the beginning of pre-recording. It cost $280,000, grossed $4 million, and won an Oscar for the best picture in the Academy's third year of awards.

THE BIG FIVE

By the 1930s, the industry – one of America's top 10 – was dominated by the "Big Five" majors, all with production studios, large theater chains, and worldwide distribution – Warner Brothers, Loews Theatres (the theater chain that owned MGM), Paramount Pictures, 20th Century Fox, and RKO – while Universal, Columbia, and

⊙ D.W. GRIFFITH

The greatest name in early film, David Wark Griffith – "the teacher of us all," said Charlie Chaplin – started out as an actor and playwright, working in bit parts before becoming a director. Directing hundreds of stylish two-reelers for Biograph, he helped attract middle-class audiences, bringing respectability to an industry that had been largely for the working class who frequented nickelodeons. Boasting a still-impressive grandeur, *The Klansman* (later *Birth of a Nation*), was a sensation, introducing new techniques and sparking controversy with its apparent glorification of the Ku Klux Klan. Griffith is credited with many of the basic stylistic devices that define the modern film.

Developed by David Selznick, *Gone With the Wind* was MGM's top-grossing release of 1939 and 1940. After Selznick borrowed money and Clark Gable from Mayer, Loews got to distribute the movie and MGM received 50 percent of the film's profits.

MOVIES AND POLITICS

By this date, there were almost 100,000 movie houses in the world – a third of them in Russia; only half that number were in the US. Every country's film industry needed foreign sales in order to be viable, which created a touchy situation for the US with the rise of Nazism because Germany was a major market for US films. MGM was cautious and not until Germany had actually declared war on Poland did it start producing anti-Nazi films.

In 1929, the very first American Academy of Motion Pictures awards (more commonly known as the Oscars) were presented in an award show that is now more popular than ever.

Charlie Chaplin and Jackie Coogan in The Kid, 1921.

⊘ CENSORSHIP

From the beginning, there were reformers who wanted to censor the films and keep the industry under some restraints. In 1921 and 1922, such scandals as the Fatty Arbuckle rape case, actor Wallace Reid's drug death, and the (unsolved) murder of director William Desmond Taylor lent them ammunition at the same time as movies were appealing to wider and more middle-class audiences. Lewis Jacobs (author of *The Rise of the American Film*, 1968) wrote that "as the poor became less important as the mainstay of the movies, the ideals and tribulations of the masses lost some of their importance as subject matter."

Hoping to pre-empt the would-be censors, the movie industry invited Will H. Hays, an Indiana crony of President Warren G. Harding, to be its moral watchdog. Only months after taking office, Hays banned Arbuckle from the screen.

Hays's authority as head of the otherwise toothless National Association of the Motion Picture Industry was only moral – a smokescreen, charged some critics – although, for a while, most producers obeyed at least the letter of the law. But, late in the decade, such daring productions as Raoul Walsh's *Sadie Thompson*, in which actress Gloria Swanson portrayed the sad prostitute of W. Somerset Maugham's novel *Rain*, and the MGM filming of another banned title, Michael Arlen's *The Green Hat* as a vehicle for Greta Garbo, reduced the Hays office's credibility.

In 1947, the House Un-American Activities Committee (HUAC) targeted the industry for promoting communist propaganda, and influential columnists urged a boycott of "red" actors. The Hollywood Ten were cited for contempt and denied work. Most top stars escaped attention, although actress Katharine Hepburn, who had addressed a large gathering of people supporting Henry Wallace (a presidential candidate who had been labeled a communist by far-rightists), came in for a good deal of criticism.

> US Courts ruled in 1947 that the film studios' method of production and distribution violated anti-trust laws and that studios must divest themselves of their theater chains. It took Loews 10 years to finalize this move.

Negri, 51. All of them rejected the role as being too close to real life. The final choice, Gloria Swanson, 50, had left Hollywood a decade ear-

Stephen Boyd and Charlton Heston in Ben Hur (1959), which won three Oscars.

THE ULTIMATE HOLLYWOOD MOVIE

When director Billy Wilder and producer Charles Brackett (together with co-writer D.M. Marshman) finished their script for Sunset Boulevard in 1949, they were "acutely conscious of the fact that we lived in a town which had been swept by social change so profound as that brought about in the old South by the Civil War. Overnight the coming of sound brushed gods and goddesses into obscurity. At first we saw [the heroine] as a kind of horror woman... an embodiment of vanity and selfishness. But as we went along, our sympathies became deeply involved with the woman who had been given the brush by 30 million fans."

Several former silent stars were approached: Mae West, then 55; Mary Pickford, 57; and Pola

lier after a 45-movie career that began in Mack Sennett comedies when she was still a teenager. Swanson embraced a lifestyle that typified its time – extravagant parties at which hundreds of the movie elite were presented with gold cigarette cases as party favors.

Sunset Boulevard, which portrayed the pathos of a former silent superstar in her declining years in a broken-down Hollywood mansion, struck a chord with critics as the ultimate inside-Hollywood movie. It garnered 11 Academy Award nominations and won three Oscars (best writing, score, and art direction). But not everybody in the city was pleased by the way the industry was depicted. "You bastard," shouted an outraged Louis B. Mayer to Wilder at a preview screening made on the Paramount lot. "You have disgraced the industry that made and fed you. You should be tarred and feathered and run out of Hollywood." Half a century later, the

> "The public wanted us to live like kings and queens," Swanson recalled. "We were making more money than we ever dreamed existed and there was no reason to believe it would ever stop."

To be sure, Los Angeles still has a thriving industry – it often seems that every other person in Los Angeles is somehow connected to "the industry" also known as the movie business. Inevitably, many struggling actors and actresses find themselves waiting tables and bartending while waiting for their big break. The largest studios are still here, marketing and distributing films made by smaller production companies. Most TV shows are still produced in Los Angeles, and the San Fernando Valley is arguably the pornography capital of the world.

Darth Vader and Wookie provide street entertainment on Hollywood Boulevard.

success of Andrew Lloyd Webber's retelling of the tale in a stage musical demonstrated how timeless the story of Sunset Boulevard and the movies really is.

THE MODERN MOVIE INDUSTRY

Today, the movie industry is much more decentralized. Once controlled by a small number of people, now it's an extremely complex network. Instead of a studio-based industry where the majority of films were shot on lots and film studios, today films are produced all over the world. California's tax code is partly to blame: high taxes for the film-making industry have pushed many producers to states that make it more affordable.

As for Hollywood itself? The neighborhood is mostly now a homage to days of yore, where tourists peruse the Hollywood Walk of Fame and would-be stars flock in hope of finding fame.

Movie stars themselves are a different breed than in the early days of cinema. They Tweet their fans, become entrepreneurs, and often live outside of Los Angeles: it's not likely that you will see any celebrities in Hollywood unless it's Oscars night. The movie stars tend to reside on the coast, in Malibu or Santa Monica, or else exclusive neighborhoods like Bel Air and Beverly Hills. The public has much more access to celebrities than in the past, but some things haven't changed: everyone wants to see one, meet one, or be one.

Rock climbing in Joshua Tree National Park.

THE GREAT OUTDOORS

Like a surfer waiting for a wave, the outdoors enthusiast in California floats on a sea of possibilities: from extreme mountain biking and wilderness backpacking to gentle ocean-front bike trails and fun on the ski slopes.

For many Californians – and visitors, too – the outdoors is synonymous with activity. And here there are endless ways to enjoy the breathtaking outdoor landscape of California, from hiking and climbing, to surfing and diving, to winters sports and whale watching. Whether you're a novice or an expert, California is filled with outdoor adventure schools, clubs, rental shops, outfitters, guides, and resorts to help you get going.

CAMPING

Looking to pitch a tent? Hiking and camping often go hand in hand in California, where many state parks have campgrounds as well. Whether you want to camp with your car nearby and have access to showers and bathrooms, or backpack into the wilderness for a few days, you'll find plenty of options to choose from all over the state. Just be sure to plan ahead; many popular campsites book up a year in advance.

CYCLING AND MOUNTAIN BIKING

Just north of the Golden Gate Bridge, opposite San Francisco, the Marin Headlands and Mount Tamalpais are considered the birthplace of mountain biking. Miles of scenic trails are the perfect routes for this bouncy recreation, though bikers share the trails with hikers and equestrians. Across the bay, road cyclists take long Wine Country tours on the rolling hills that wind through the scores of vineyards. California's central coast also has miles and miles of trails for bikers.

Up in Tahoe, summer adventurers can carry mountain bikes on the lifts of many ski areas to explore the alpine network of trails, some with bird's-eye views of Lake Tahoe. Meanwhile in the northeast corner of the state, bicyclists (of both the road and mountain variety) will find abundant

Corals grow in the kelp forests off Santa Cruz Island.

trails and out-of-the-way roads to explore on two wheels, as long as the bikes are sturdy. (Be sure to have them checked out before you undertake a trip like this; garages are few and far between.)

DIVING AND SNORKELING

Scuba diving is extremely popular in Monterey and along the coast south of the city. Some 65,000 divers from all over the world visit the Monterey Bay Sanctuary each year. Safe conditions and good visibility are part of the draw but it is the kelp forest in an underwater canyon that they all want to experience. The kelp, long and spindly at the base and stretching up to form thick mats at the surface, ranges all along the coast, forming fantastic underwater forests through which divers swim in search of the Garibaldi, ling cod, and many types of rockfish. Bluefish and Whalers Coves at Point Lobos, Lovers Point in Pacific

Sharks are under far more predatorial pressure from man than surfers and windsurfers are from them; many biologists fear that the prehistoric fish are being hunted to extinction out of misplaced fear and misunderstanding.

Diving is also popular among the kelp beds in the San Luis Obispo region, the Santa Catalina Islands, and Channel Islands National Park.

FISHING

At the coast, you can cast from rocks or piers, or embark on a "party boat" to probe the depths for salmon, ling cod, rockfish, and other denizens of the deep. Unusual, chilling sport can be had pursuing surf smelt: the fisherman uses a big triangular net on a frame, plunging the net into oncoming breaking waves, and tends to get soaked com-

Mountain biking in Mount Tamalpais State Park.

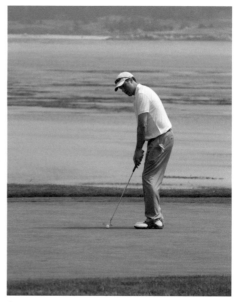

Pebble Beach Golf Links has hosted the US Open Championships five times and overlooks Carmel Bay.

Grove, and Monterey State Beach, San Carlos Beach and McAbee Beach in Monterey are popular beach dives for all levels of divers. For the more advanced, try Monastery Beach and Carmel River State Beach in Carmel. Monterey has been rated as having the best beach dives in the U.S. by Scuba Diving magazine.

Shark-diving (in cages) is also possible out by the Farallon Islands near San Francisco.

On the northwest coast, cold-water diving gear (a 7mm wetsuit, hood, booties, fins, mask, snorkel, and 20lbs/9kg of lead to sink all that neoprene) equips you to hunt for abalone. This giant mollusk is a delicacy, but prying them off the rocks at depth is not for the casual swimmer (and needs a special permit; www.wildlife.ca.gov/Regions/Marine).

pletely. The nets are available for rent; the smelt, sometimes caught by the bucketful, are deep fried for dinner and then eaten whole.

Inland, up near Lassen Volcanic National Park and the surrounding national forest, many alpine lakes dot the area, and children will spend long days paddling driftwood logs like surfboards and watching the big, wary trout cruise slowly below.

Fishermen, particularly fly fishermen who enjoy floating tiny nymphs in the surface film of chalk streams, will find abundant game and frequent caddis and mayfly hatches on the McCloud, Pit, and Fall rivers, as well as within the winding banks of Hat Creek, Hot Creek, Battle Creek, and the many other notorious streams of the area.

GOLF

From Napa Valley to Palm Springs to San Diego, you can play golf all over the Golden State, but a few destinations in particular should move to the top of the list for passionate golfers. First on the list is Pebble Beach, where you'll find the Pebble Beach Golf Links (home to the AT&T Pebble Beach National Pro-Am) and Poppy Hills. In February, the Buick Invitation Tournament takes place at Torrey Pines Golf Course, where two championship courses offer players ocean views.

country, where you can hike for many days without reaching a road (though careful planning and wilderness permits are required).

The Mojave – named after a Southwestern native tribe and pronounced mo-hahv-ee – covers much of the southeast portion of California, floating like a mirage out of Arizona and ending up against the precipice of the Sierras at their southern extreme.

Snorkeling at Laguna Beach, Orange County.

On rainy spring days in the forest slopes above Sonoma, thousands of red-bellied salamanders come out of the woodwork (literally), crawling to the stream beds to spawn.

HIKING

With numerous state parks, national parks, and wilderness areas, California provides superlative opportunities for hiking for all skill levels. Yosemite National Park offers everything from intense climbs with magnificent views of granite cliffs to easy trails along the valley floor. This is some of the Sierra's best backpacking

Kings Canyon, less accessible and more rugged than Yosemite National Park, has both groves of giant sequoias and deep granite-walled canyons that were carved by glaciers. To walk among giant redwoods, visit Sequoia National Park, Muir Woods National Monument north of San Francisco, Redwood National Park, or Prairie Creek Redwoods State Park. Great hiking can also be had in Big Sur, Lake Tahoe, Anzo-Borrego, and parts of the deserts.

For a full list of state parks and information on their hiking trails and campsites, visit www.parks.ca.gov. In general, most parks offer trails with various skill levels, and provide trail maps at visitor centers that help you plan your hikes. Some parks have a small day-use fee or parking fee.

KAYAKING

A popular pastime in Monterey is to rent simple open-topped kayaks, called "scuppers," to paddle out to the local kelp beds. There you're likely to encounter one of California's most delightful wild animals, the winsome and intelligent sea otter, once hunted for its fur but now a favorite of animal lovers. The creatures are often seen floating on their backs with an infant sleeping on their belly, lolling about in the water, fastidiously cleaning their fur or crunching on a just-caught shellfish. Other great places for beginners are Morro Bay,

> The northwest coast is somberly beautiful: gray skies, long, empty beaches littered with driftwood, rugged sea cliffs, sawmills and fishing towns, and forests that end at cliff edges.

Sausalito, and Tomales Bay, while more experienced sea kayakers will love the Channel Islands, Santa Catalina Island, and La Jolla.

ROCK CLIMBING

California has some of the most diverse climbing in the country, with opportunities in both halves of the state. In Southern California, Joshua Tree National Park offers high desert climbing on 8,000 climbing trails, perfect for winter when other areas are too cold.

In April through October, climbers come to Yosemite for sheer granite cliffs, including the famed El Capitan, with its 3,000ft (900-meter) face. In Northern California, Bishop and Lassen national parks are good options, as are Sequoia and Kings Canyon national parks.

SAILING AND WINDSURFING

Sailing is possible in both Northern California – near San Francisco Bay, Santa Cruz, and Monterey – and all along the Southern California coast. On a spring or summer afternoon, you're likely to catch sight of hundreds of windsurfers south of San Francisco, braving the cracking swells and blowing sands of Gazos Creek, Scott Creek, and Waddell Creek. The last is considered one of the best windsurfing spots in the country, where experts are often spotted jumping waves and pulling spectacular aerial maneuvers with names like "killer loop" and "cheese roll."

Windsurfing is also popular at Jalama Beach County Park on the end of Point Conception, the jutting corner of the state where the coast turns east. Wind that whips across the point propels windsurfers up and over the biggest and ugliest of the waves.

SURFING

Both competitive and recreational surfers take the waves along California's coast. San Diego and Los Angeles coasts are particularly popular – the 130-mile (210km) area between the two cities stands

Whitewater rafting on the Truckee River.

⊙ DEATH VALLEY

At 282ft (86 meters) below sea level, Death Valley is the lowest point on the North American continent. At least five million years ago, this deep gap was formed by earthquakes and the folding of the earth's crust, creating what is known as a graben or rift valley. As you hike or camp, you may be lucky enough to spot California's horned lizard, a diamondback rattlesnake, a desert tortoise, or an endangered gila monster (North America's only poisonous lizard). Pack rats and kangaroo rats, bats, hawks, and low-swooping falcons make their home here, too. At night, you'll very probably fall asleep to the melancholy howling of coyotes.

out for the sharp blue line of the ocean. The water is warm here, pushed north by the Japan current, and the swells are manageable in most places,

> *For the most part, coastal swimming is best kept for Southern California. Because of undertows and riptides on the northwest coast, the waves can be powerful and dangerous, and are no place for novices.*

whales. There are numerous spots along the California coast to look for migrating whales. Dana Point, Point Reyes (including from the lighthouse), Redwood National and State parks, and Santa Cruz are all options in Northern California, while Santa Barbara and San Diego (especially Cabrillo National Monument at Point Loma) are good bets in Southern California.

WHITEWATER RAFTING

The California whitewater rafting season runs from April through September.

Hiking in Yosemite National Park.

even for novice surfers. But be aware that surfing has become a rather territorial pastime and has gained a somewhat unfriendly reputation. However, if you're willing to settle for mushy waves, you can paddle out at almost any non-surfing beach and be assured of a good time.

Other popular waves are found at San Luis Obispo's long beaches, which are interspersed with high cliffs. In the north, competitive surfing is found closer to Santa Cruz. Off the coast of Half Moon Bay, an annual surfing competition is held at Mavericks.

WHALE WATCHING

During winter and spring, you can gaze from cliffs or boat cruises to spot migrating gray

The Sacramento area is popular with whitewater rafters of all abilities, while adrenalin junkies seek out the thundering rapids of Burnt Ranch Falls on the Trinity, and the cataracts of Hell's Corner Gorge or the Ikes Falls on the Klamath. The breathtaking forest drops of the California salmon are at once beautiful and thrilling.

Also noteworthy are trips on the American River. Tributary Whitewater Tours (https://whitewatertours.com, tel: 800-672-3846) is one outfit that offers day and overnight tour packages of the south and middle fork of the American River and the Truckee River. Near Yosemite are the Tuolumne and Merced rivers and Cherry Creek.

If thrill seeking isn't your thing, you can float for many days in inflatable kayaks with nary a ripple on the lower Klamath River and parts of the Trinity. Within sight of fertile vineyards and cottage-style wineries, the Russian River and Cache Creek are popular rafting and canoeing streams.

WINTER SPORTS

Tahoe offers California's biggest and best concentration of snow sport opportunities. Attracting the most skiers are Squaw Valley

on the North Shore, and Heavenly Mountain at the South Lake. Both are vast, full-featured resorts: Squaw has a giant hotel, an Olym-

> "Probably more free sunshine falls on this majestic range than on any other... It has the brightest weather, brightest glacier-polished rocks, ... [and] the brightest forests of silver firs and silver pines..." John Muir (1838–1914), founder of the Sierra Club.

Spot whales off the central California coast.

pic history, an ice-skating rink on top of the mountain, a climbing wall, a spa, and several shops. Heavenly is just as good; it's a question of choice. Many smaller areas – Kirkwood, Homewood, Sugar Bowl, Northstar, and Donner Ridge – are more friendly spots to ski, although the sheer vertical drops are not as great. In addition to downhill skiing and snowboarding, you can give cross-country skiing and snowshoeing a try.

On the Sierra's east slope, Mammoth Mountain is central California's premier ski area. Here, the mountains slope down to the desert plain of the Owens River Valley, not far north of the precipitous drop into Death Valley. Resorts generally offer equipment rentals, individual or group lessons (skiing and snowboarding) for all skill levels, and day, weekend, or season passes.

Ⓞ WHALE WATCHING NEAR SAN FRANCISCO

Just 27 miles (43km) from Fisherman's Wharf lie the Farallon Islands, once called the "Devil's Teeth." The islands themselves are off-limits to the public (only a limited part is inhabited, by researchers), but these jagged outcroppings provide a rich sanctuary for 23 species of marine mammals, including 18 types of whales and dolphins, plus seals, seabirds, and great white sharks that migrate here to breed in summer and fall.

A whale-watching excursion allows for the ultimate vantage point to observe these magnificent creatures as they frolic and cavort in their temporary environment. SF Bay Whale Watching (https://sfbaywhalewatching.com) runs full-day expeditions from Fort Mason to the Gulf of the Farallones on weekends from November through June. Get up close to gray, blue, and humpback whales, dolphins, seals, and sea lions as the boat sails from Fisherman's Wharf beneath the Golden Gate Bridge to the roiling waters of the Pacific Ocean. A naturalist expert is on board the motor-catamaran to narrate throughout the trip, point out areas of special interest, and answer questions about local wildlife. They also offer 2.5 hour whale watching tours in the bay. Be sure to dress warmly, and be advised that water outside the Golden Gate can be quite choppy.

Surfing at Ocean Beach, San Diego.

📷 EARTHQUAKES AND OTHER DISASTERS

California is not without its downsides: the state is prone to natural disasters including earthquakes and fires. Still, Californians usually view such risks as a small price to pay for all the advantages.

California is a major earthquake zone. In 1769, Gaspar de Portola's expedition felt the first recorded quake in the state, about 30 miles (48km) southeast of Los Angeles. Today, the southern part of the state alone has about 10,000 earthquakes each year, although only about 15–20 are greater than magnitude 4.0.

The reason is that the southern portion of the state straddles the boundary between the Pacific plate (extending as far west as Japan) and the North American plate (eastwards to Iceland). The former moves northwest at a rate of 1.25 inches (45mm) per year, about as fast as fingernails grow; if this rate continues for the next 15 million years, San Francisco and Los Angeles will become next-door neighbors.

The shift is not gradual and steady but a process where the earth stores up the energy, releasing it with the enormous burst that we know as an earthquake along one or another of the scores of fault lines. One of the state's major faults is the San Andreas fault, which is actually a more than 800-mile-long (1300km) fault zone with many segments, in some parts up to 10 miles (16km) deep. Although there have been recorded earthquakes since the 18th century, it was not until 1935 that Charles F. Richter devised the scale by which seismographs plot today's temblors.

Aftermath of a quake in the San Francisco Bay Area October 1989 that measured 6.9 on the Richter scale causing buildings and part of the two-level Interstate 880 highway to collapse.

Collapsed house in the hills north of Los Angeles, after Northridge earthquake in 1994. It caused around US$7 billion in damage and left thousands of people homeless.

A sudden right slip movement of up to 16ft (4.9 meters) on the San Andreas fault caused the San Francisco quake in 1906 that measured 8.25 on the Richter scale, killing 315 people and causing a fire that took days to extinguish.

Dead palm trees on the shore of Salton Sea, California's biggest lake, which has dried up and refilled numerous times, affected by human changes. Part of the San Andreas fault lies under the lake.

The Big Ones

The most disastrous earthquake in California history was the cataclysmic 8.25-magnitude quake that struck San Francisco on April 18, 1906, at 5:12 am. More than 300 deaths were reported, but today's estimate puts the toll at over 3,000, and 225,000 people lost their homes.

When will the next major earthquake hit? Scientists and California residents have long been anticipating the "Big One," a massive earthquake along the San Andreas fault. Research shows the southern portion of the San Andreas is long overdue for a large quake, leading some scientists to predict an 8.1 magnitude "wall-to-wall" quake running from the Salton Sea, a rift lake sitting directly on the fault line southeast of Palm Springs, to Monterey. Such a quake would release twice the energy of California's 1857 7.9-magnitude earthquake. Northern California's Hayward fault is also overdue for an earthquake. The fault averages a major quake every 140 years, and the last one occurred in 1868, meaning 2008 was the 140-year mark.

If you experience an earthquake, stay indoors and find shelter under something sturdy like a piece of furniture or door frame, and away from glass windows. If outside, avoid trees, power lines, buildings, and bridges.

orest fire crews take drastic measures, fighting fire fire.

ding in the Sacramento delta.

Earthquake drill in a San Francisco school.

The skyline of Downtown Los Angeles at dawn.

Joshua Tree National Park.

Crashing waves on the coast of Ventura County.

California

0   50 miles
0   50 km

Golden Gate Bridge viewed from the Marin County side.

NORTHERN CALIFORNIA

A detailed guide to Northern California, with principal sights clearly cross-referenced by number to the maps.

Grove of redwoods in Northern California.

Towering redwoods, granite cliffs, snowy peaks, picturesque vineyards, cosmopolitan cities... Northern California is home to more natural and social variety than found in any similar-sized territory in the world.

San Francisco is its most famous city, where vintage cable cars crawl up incredibly steep hills, fog rolls eerily around the Golden Gate Bridge, and boisterous sea lions bark at Fisherman's Wharf. Millions of visitors explore this open-minded metropolis every year, perusing farmers' markets and fine art museums, and running, biking, paddleboating, rollerblading, swing dancing, and shooting arrows in Golden Gate Park, or heading to the world-famous Alcatraz island prison on a ferry boat.

A journey of only a few hours in either direction from San Francisco reveals entirely different landscapes. To the south are Monterey's kelp forests and peaceful tide pools, the spectacular Big Sur coast, and grand Hearst Castle; to the north, acres upon acres of rolling vineyards in the serene Napa and Sonoma valleys produce grapes that are used in the production of award-winning wines.

Pacific coastline.

Further inland is the long, fertile Central Valley, the heart of California's agricultural industry. It is also the political heart of the state, home to the pretty state capitol of Sacramento. Sacramento's historic Old Town also is a starting point for exploring California's 1849 Gold Rush history; not far from here in Gold Country's old frontier towns, you can try your luck panning for gold in the rivers of the Sierra Nevada foothills.

Climbing into the Sierra Nevada mountain range you find some of the country's most stunning natural attractions. On the border of California and Nevada, glittering Lake Tahoe draws hikers in summer and hordes of skiers and snowboarders in winter. Sequoia and Kings Canyon national parks protect the tallest redwood trees on earth, and awe-inspiring Yosemite National Park shows off tremendous waterfalls, granite peaks, and woodlands. Even more remote is the northeastern corner of the state, which is dominated by Mount Shasta and Lassen Peak (both active volcanoes) and the town whose name is the state's official motto: Eureka, meaning "I have found it!"

Downtown San Francisco

Cable cars are a fun way to travel around San Francisco.

SAN FRANCISCO

Tony Bennett sang it like it is. The "City by the Bay," long celebrated in lyrics and postcards, wins visitors' hearts straight away despite the city's rather cool temperatures and foggy summers.

San Francisco is without a doubt one of the most beautiful, vibrant, and diverse cities on the planet. Sitting like a thumb at the end of a 32-mile (50km) peninsular finger, this city of seven hills is surrounded by water on three sides and blessed by one of the world's great natural harbors. It is joined to the mainland by two acknowledged masterpieces of bridge design and construction, one of which is the magnificent Golden Gate Bridge that glitters at night however, the lights are sometimes blurred by a blanket of fog.

Beyond the iconic San Francisco – the grand bridges, rattling cable cars, and barking sea lions – the city has far more depth than you might expect from a city only 49 sq miles (127 sq km) in area. It's easy to get caught up in the excitement of Downtown and Union Square, but there are dozens of distinct and wonderfully original neighborhoods to explore, each with its own appeal. And whether it's innovative cuisine, fine art, music and dance, sprawling parks, or boisterous street festivals you're after, you will be sure to find it.

SAN FRANCISCO PEOPLE

This truly endless variety of things to do is in many ways driven by the social and economic diversity of San Franciscans themselves. The more than 870,000 residents of this charmed city, the nation's

13th largest, form an impressive demographic bouillabaisse. The descendants of early Italian, German, and Irish families are still found in snug neighborhood enclaves, but their numbers have fallen as many have moved to the rapidly developing suburbs, replaced by an influx of Asian and Latino people.

Regardless of their heritage, San Franciscans are all known for being left-leaning, environmentally conscious, gay-friendly, and very open-minded – eccentricity rarely raises an eyebrow. Embracing the beautiful

Maps on pages 104, 118

Main attractions
Fisherman's Wharf
Coit Tower
Chinatown
San Francisco Museum of Modern Art
Golden Gate Bridge
Mission Dolores
Golden Gate Park

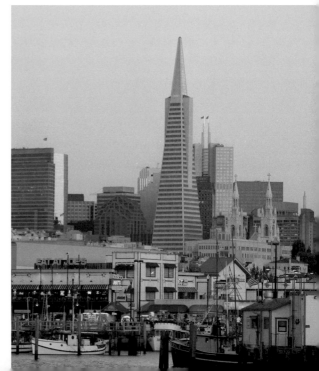

View of the San Francisco skyline from Pier 40.

Mime artist at Fisherman's Wharf.

Fisherman's Wharf.

and eclectic makes San Francisco the vibrant city it is today, and one that draws more than 25 million visitors a year to discover its magic.

FISHERMAN'S WHARF

The city's touristy **Fisherman's Wharf** (www.fishermanswharf.org), is one of the most visited places in San Francisco. A bright, family-oriented carnival of attractions, despite the crowds and occasional tackiness, the Wharf also has tons of seafood restaurants, good little stores tucked between the souvenir stands, and two garden parks with open space for picnicking.

In summer months, the narrow boardwalks are jammed with people and it's easy to forget that this is one of the city's most important historic spots. Along with hundreds of sailboats and yachts and the ferries packed with visitors and commuters, much of San Francisco's maritime past is moored here.

The waterfront retrospective starts at the **Hyde Street Pier**, where a fleet of vintage vessels is docked, including a sidewheel ferry and three schooners that carried heavy freight in the days of sailing ships. The tall masts and rigging at the water's edge belong to the graceful Scottish-built *Balclutha*, a 301ft (81-meter) clipper built in 1886 that made 17 trips around Cape Horn.

These ships are all operated by the **Maritime Museum**, located in the Bath house Building (900 Beach Street; tel 415-561-5000; free), which displays intricate models of boats and muralist Hilaire Hiler's surrealist vision of the Atlantis. It is located in **Aquatic Park**, a terraced greensward that leads out to a small beach and curving municipal pier sometimes dotted with fishermen. Just one block from the museum is the **Cartoon Art Museum** (781 Beach Street; tel: 415 227-8666; www.cartoonart.org; Thu–Tue 11am–5pm). It is located in a refurbished historical, red brick building and offers views over the bay as well as a library, bookstore, and ample gallery space.

South of the Maritime Museum and occupying the entire block bounded by North Point, Polk, Beach, and Larkin streets, Ghirardelli Square (www.ghirardellisq.com) is a shopping center geared owards visitors. Ghirardelli Square was built as a wool mill during the Civil War era and later became a chocolate factory in 1893. Although the working factory has moved, there is still a retail outlet, candy store, and ice cream shop.

If you're in the mood for something warmer, stop at the **Buena Vista Café** (www.thebuenavista.com) on the corner of Hyde and Beach streets for an Irish coffee (it was invented here) and watch the busy cable-car activity at the **Powell-Hyde Cable Car Turnaround**. A short walk east leads to **The Cannery** (2801 Leavenworth Street), once the largest fruit and vegetable cannery in the world, and now a three-story shopping complex.

FISH RESTAURANTS

An appetite for fruits of the sea can be satisfied by strolling down Jefferson Street, the wharf's main drag, where sidewalk vendors boil and steam shellfish all day long. Walk toward the waterfront to Pier 45, which remains as much of a working site as Fisherman's Wharf can offer. Fishermen depart before dawn and return with sand dabs, scallops, Dungeness crabs, and sea bass. Historically, Italians skippered and manned the boats and also ran the restaurants. A glance at the names of the restaurants indicates that not all that much has changed, with most restaurants in the area either serving Italian-inspired fare or some of the freshest fish in the city. Fisherman's Wharf is also a perfect place to try one of San Francisco's proudest legends, its crusty sourdough bread, which pairs perfectly with sweet butter, Dungeness crab, and a glass of crisp Chardonnay.

Moored at Pier 45 is the SS *Jeremiah O'Brien*, a World War II Liberty Ship. Also on Pier 45 at the end of Taylor Street is the **Musée Mecanique**, (tel: 415-346-2000; www.museemecaniquesf.com; daily 10am–8pm), an exercise in nostalgia with its coin-operated pianos, antique slot machines, and a 1910 steam-driven motorcycle.

SEA LIONS AND AN AQUARIUM

To see the city's famous sea lions sunbathe and bark, head to **Pier 39** (www.pier39.com). This 45-acre (18-hectare) collection of shops, arcades, restaurants, and other diversions lures tourists by the thousands to places like the **San Francisco Carousel**, **Players Sports Bar & Arcade, 7D Experience** (http://7dexperience.com) and the **Aquarium of the Bay** (Embarcadero at Beach Street; tel: 415 623 5300; https://bayecotarium.org/about/aquarium-of-the-bay). The oldest thing at Pier 39 is the **Eagle Café** (www.eaglecafe.com), a fixture favored for decades by fishermen and longshoremen before it was moved intact from its original site a couple of blocks away.

ALCATRAZ ISLAND

Set in one of the world's most beautiful harbors and accessible only by ferry, **Alcatraz B** (tel: 415-981-7625; www.alcatrazcruises.com and www.nps.gov/alca; daily tours depart from Pier 33) and its tales of legendary inmates have fascinated visitors since the days of Prohibition and American gangsters.

Row of cells inside Alcatraz; the ones with the doors are for solitary confinement.

⊙ Tip

Less visited than Alcatraz is the larger Angel Island (www.angelisland.com; tel: 415-435-3392); accessible by ferry from several Bay locations. You can climb to the top of Mt Livermore to see all five of the Bay's bridges, or take a Segway tour or hire a bike to explore the perimeter road. There are also picnic sites, music events, and an educational tram tour.

Just over a mile offshore from San Francisco, the hump of rock was sighted in 1775 by Spanish Lieutenant Juan Manuel de Ayala. Back then, the only occupants were pelicans, so Ayala named it Isla de los Alcatraces – the Island of Pelicans. Its strategic location in the bay suited it to military purposes and it was garrisoned with soldiers in the 1850s. Because escape from the island was a remote possibility (requiring a 1.5 mile (2km) swim through the frigid waters and swift currents of the San Francisco Bay), renegade servicemen were incarcerated on Alcatraz, to be followed by Apaches taken prisoner in Arizona during the 1870s Indian wars, and then prisoners from the Spanish-American War.

Alcatraz evolved into a federal prison that housed such hardened criminals as Mafia leader Al Capone and the notorious Machine Gun Kelly. Those few desperate inmates who managed to escape their cells in bids for freedom perished in the cold waters surrounding the island. The prison was finally closed in 1963 when the costs of repairing the constant ravages of wind and weather grew too

The ruined Warden's House on Alcatraz.

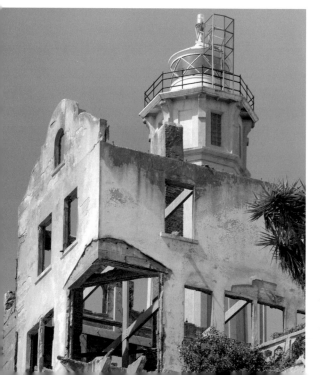

great. It is now part of the Golden Gate National Recreational Area: park rangers give guided tours of safe parts of the island, including a peek at some of the cell blocks, while the evocative, award-winning taped audio tour features voices of some of the original prisoners.

NORTH BEACH

North Beach ❻ is many neighborhoods in one; the Little Italy of San Francisco (though nobody calls it that), the former haunt of Beat poets like Jack Keruoac, the city's strip club hub, and a destination for young nightowls looking to mingle at bars and dance clubs.

The once very tawdry **Broadway** strip has been gentrified a bit, but a number of strip clubs still beckon with promises of lap dances and naked girls. The historic **Condor** (https://condorsf. com) **remains, having** become famous when a waitress named Carol Doda peeled to the waist one night in 1964 and ushered in the topless boom. The venerable Carol Doda used to descend nightly from the ceiling atop a piano, wearing only a G-string.

North Beach is also where several of the city's comedy clubs were located. On Columbus, Woody Allen and Bill Cosby performed at the Hungry I (www.hungryisf.com, now a gentlemen's club), and the likes of Lenny Bruce, Jonathan Winters, and the Smothers Brothers plied their trades at the original Purple Onion which closed in 2012 and now operates as Doc's Lab (www.docslabsf.com).

The neighborhood has also long been congenial to writers, artists, and deep thinkers. A favorite haunt of wordsmiths is the **City Lights** bookstore at 261 Columbus Avenue (www. citylights.com; open late), which has been run since 1953 by poet Lawrence Ferlinghetti, one of the literary luminaries of the 1950s Beat era. Across Kerouac Alley – where quotes from Jack Kerouac, Lawrence Ferlinghetti, Maya Angelou, Confucius, and John Steinbeck are found in the sidewalk is **Vesuvio,** (www.vesuvio.com), an eclectic bar full of Beat nostalgia and intellectuals. Nearby, on Columbus, is the old **Tosca Café,** (http://toscacafesf.com), a bar where opera records play on the jukebox.

Columbus Street, running north from Broadway, is the real heart of North Beach. With the flavor of an old-fashioned Italian neighborhood, it is full of little cafés, Italian restaurants, and a few working-men's bars where elderly Italians sip red wine and muse about life. At the intersection of Columbus and Union is **Washington Square,** a grassy expanse for pick-up sports games, a morning Tai Chi location, and an ideal picnic spot. Overlooking the square is the Romanesque façade of 1924-built **Saints Peter and Paul Church**, where Joe DiMaggio and Marylin Monroe once posed for their wedding pictures.

TELEGRAPH HILL

Above North Beach, at the end of Lombard Street, is **Telegraph Hill,** crowned by the 210ft (55-meter) **Coit Tower** ❹ (tel: 415-249-0995; summer 10am–6pm, winter 10am–5pm; charge to take elevator). Built in 1934 on the site of an early telegraph station and funded by heiress Lillie Hitchcock Coit, it lures visitors with momentous views and WPA frescoes in the style of Diego Rivera. Down the east side of Telegraph Hill are the lovely Filbert and Greenwich street staircases, flanked by attractive and lush private gardens. If you are lucky you will hear and spot the flock of wild red-headed parrots who live there, and who starred in the 2003 documentary *The Wild Parrots of Telegraph Hill.*

The steps end on Sansome Street, directly across from Levi's Plaza, the corporate headquarters of Levi Strauss & Co. A small but interesting visitor center in the main building's lobby chronicles the company's story and the development of the riveted blue denim jeans.

CHINATOWN

The largest outside Asia, this 24-block Chinatown is the quintessential city within in a city. The official entrance is the green pagoda-topped **Chinatown Gate** ❸ at the corner of Bush Street and Grant Avenue, which the Republic of China gifted in 1969. Through the gate, dragon-topped lampposts and crisscrossing lines of red lanterns run the length of Grant Avenue, Chinatown's main tourist street, and shop windows beckon with crowded displays of silk, porcelain, hand-painted vases, teak furniture, and plenty of cheap tchotchkes. Food ranges from tiny cafés and obscure eateries to popular dim sum lunches, for which waitresses push carts of dumplings and pastries from table to table like peddlers.

Two blocks north along Grant Avenue is **Old St Mary's Church**, the city's main Catholic cathedral from 1853 to 1891 and today a parish church. In the past this area was known for its seedy array of brothels, gambling houses, and opium dens; all attempts at clean-up failed until

◉ Tip

Parking is very scarce near Coit Tower. To avoid the steep climb by foot, catch the No. 39 bus near St Peter and Paul's Church, and ride it all the way to the tower.

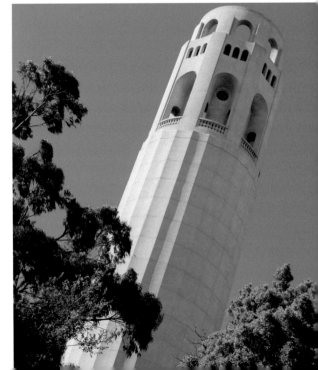

Coit Tower on Telegraph Hill.

the 1906 fire destroyed most of the commercial establishments.

It's on the narrow streets intersecting Grant that Chinatown truly comes to life. Turn left on Clay Street to find **Waverly Place** , a colorful alley that lent its name to one of Amy Tan's characters in *The Joy Luck Club*. After admiring the bright curved roofs and ornate balconies, you can climb three flights of stairs at No. 125 to visit the Tin Hou temple, dedicated in 1852 to the Goddess of the Seven Seas, where hundreds of red-and-gold paper lanterns flood the ceiling and incense fills the air. Waverly is just one of dozens of quiet alleys in Chinatown. Other alleys include Spofford Alley – notable for its cameo in *The Maltese Falcon* – and Ross Alley, home to an erhu-playing barber and a tiny one-room fortune cookie "factory" where you can see fresh fortune cookies being made and pick up a bag to take home.

On Washington Street, tiny, cluttered herb shops offer powders and poultices promising everything from rheumatism relief to the restoration of sexual powers. Outdoor produce and pastry shops also

One of the frescoes in Coit Tower.

vie for your nose. A little farther west is **Stockton Street**, where all of Chinatown comes to grocery shop. Diminutive Chinese women clutch plastic bags in both hands as they go about their errands while the old men smoke cigarettes and read Chinese-language newspapers.

When you're done exploring, head south of Grant on Washington or Clay Street to reach **Portsmouth Square**, Chinatown's small urban park, where Tai Chi devotees practice their balletic movements in the morning, children clamber on play structures, and men gather to bet over mahjong and Chinese cards. Here Robert Louis Stevenson used to watch the ships come in, biding his time until the married woman he loved would divorce her husband. Across Kearny Street and inside the Hilton Hotel is the **Chinese Cultural Center** (www.cccsf.us; Tue–Sat 10am–4pm), which offers art shows, cultural events, and guided tours.

UNION SQUARE

Considered the city's geographical center in pioneer days, **Union Square** and the surrounding blocks today comprise San Francisco's downtown hub for shopping, entertainment, and tourism. The land was set aside for public use in 1850 and received its name a decade later when pro-Union sympathizers rallied here before the Civil War. In the center of the square, a 90ft (27-meter) Corinthian column with a bronze winged *Victory* statue in the square commemorates another conflict – Commodore George Dewey's naval victory over the Spanish in 1898.

Just west of the square is the **Westin St Francis** (www.westinstfrancis.com), the city's second-oldest hotel and a majestic reminder of the past. For a spectacular view, take a ride in its glass elevators up to the 32nd floor. The St Francis' neighbors in Union Square are upscale department stores, including **Neiman Marcus** (www.neimanmarcus.com) with its glorious rotunda, Saks Fifth Avenue (www.saks fifthavenue.com), Barney's (www.barneys

com), and Macy's (www.macys.com). Weave down Powell through the crowds of shoppers to the cable car turnaround. Two of the three cable car lines begin and end here, leading towards Fisherman's Wharf via slightly different routes.

VISITOR CENTER AND THEATER DISTRICT

Down the nearby stairs you'll find the **San Francisco Visitor Information Center** (900 Market Street; tel: 415-391-2000; www.sftravel.com; Mon–Fri 9am–5pm, Sat–Sun 9am–3pm, Nov–Apr closed Sun), offering maps, brochures, transportation passes, and advice in several languages. Cross Market Street to explore the elaborate Westfield Shopping Center (www.westfield.com/sanfrancisco), anchored on either end by Bloomingdales (www.bloomingdales.com) and Nordstrom (www.nordstrom.com) department stores.

Just west of the Union Square area, San Francisco's theater (mostly spelled theatre here) district begins along Geary and Sutter streets. The Geary Theatre is the home of the **American Conservatory Theater**, (www.act-sf.org), one of the nation's best repertory companies and winner of several Tony awards. Next door, the Curran (https://sfcurran.com) offers big hits and stars from New York. Theatres on Sutter Street include the **Lorraine Hansberry Theatre** (www.lhtsf.org); the nearby **Marines' Memorial Theatre**, (www.marinesmemorialtheatre.com) which specializes in Broadway musicals; and the **Actors Theatre**, which performs classics by luminaries like John Steinbeck.

In the other direction from Union Square, you can cross Stockton Street and wander down chic **Maiden Lane**, a quiet pedestrianized street of high-end boutiques that was named in the Gold Rush for the female company men found here during the tough Gold Rush era. At No. 140 is the only Frank Lloyd Wright-designed building in the city.

NOB HILL AND RUSSIAN HILL

The cable cars from Fisherman's Wharf and Union Square climb one of the city's best-known slopes, **Nob Hill**. Called the "Hill of Palaces" by writer Robert Louis

Lombard Street.

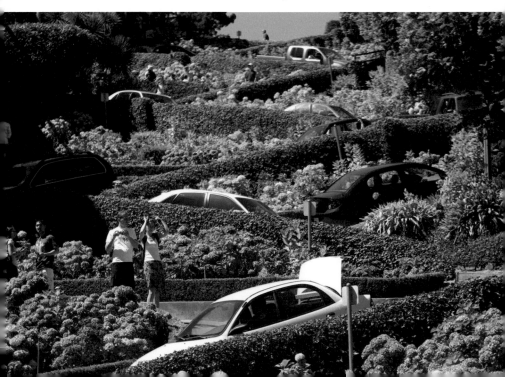

⊙ Tip

The CityPass ($89, $66 ages 5–11; www.citypass. com/san-francisco) is sold at the Visitor Information Center near Union Square. It includes a 3-day Cable Car and Muni Bus Passport, plus admission to California Academy of Sciences, Aquarium of the Bay, Exploratorium OR de Young + Legion of Honor, and a Blue and Gold Fleet Bay Cruise Adventure. It saves you 42 percent of the full cost and is valid nine days.

One of the city's iconic, rattling cable cars.

Stevenson, the hill is celebrated mostly for the size and elegance of the mansions and hotels built there a century ago.

Here, the **Intercontinental Mark Hopkins Hotel** (www.intercontinentalmark hopkins.com) occupies the site of the former Mark Hopkins mansion, where the **Top of the Mark** bar (tel: 415-616-6916) on the 19th floor is a romantic and time-honored custom for visitors, offering a 100-martini menu and spectacular views of the city and bay. The lovely **Stanford Court** (www.stanfordcourt.com) and **Scarlet Huntington** hotels (www.thescarlethotels.com) were also built on the ashes of mansions, and the **Fairmont Hotel** (www.fairmont.com) retains an aura of (rebuilt) splendor, having been open only two days before being burned down in the fires that raged after the 1906 earthquake. It reopened for business just one year later. Across the street, the private Pacific Union Club is housed in the only Nob Hill mansion to survive the 1906 earthquake and fire, a sturdy brownstone built for silver magnate James Flood in 1855.

All these lavish structures encircle and provide the perfect setting for the grand neo-Gothic **Grace Cathedral**, inspired by Paris' Notre Dame. The doors are cast from Lorenzo Ghiberti's original *Doors of Paradise* in Florence, while the rose window was inspired by the blue glass of Chartres Cathedral. The acoustics are superb when the organ is played and the church's boys' choir sings. Northeast at the corner of Washington and Mason streets, is the **Cable Car Museum** (tel 415-474-1887; www.cablecarmuseum.org daily 10am–6pm, until 5pm in winter) which exhibits the city's transit history as well as the massive machinery and cables that still pull the glamorous transportation through the town.

Next to Nob Hill, Russian Hill is known for magnificent views, stately homes, hidden bistros, and a labyrinth of secret streets, stairways, and alleys like **Macondray Lane**, which connects Taylor and Jones streets and was the setting for writer Armistead Maupin's popular Tales of the City. Russian Hill is home to **Lombard Street** Ⓗ, known as "the crookedest street in the world." Located

⊙ THE BARBARY COAST

During the California Gold Rush from 1848 to 1855, modern-day Jackson Square was a place of unparalleled vice. The Barbary Coast (as it was then named) was a vast marketplace of flesh and liquor. Sailors and miners found fleeting pleasures, fast money, and, just as likely, a violent end. Gambling and shoot-outs were favored sports, and fortunes rode on the wink of an eye. Barbary Coast businessmen trafficked in human bodies, selling sex to miners and kidnapped sailors to the captains of hell ships. Both enterprises returned high profits, and local politicians turned a blind eye for a piece of the action. Red lights burned on almost every block from both high-class "parlors" and squalid "cribs," where prostitutes worked in rooms barely big enough to hold a bed.

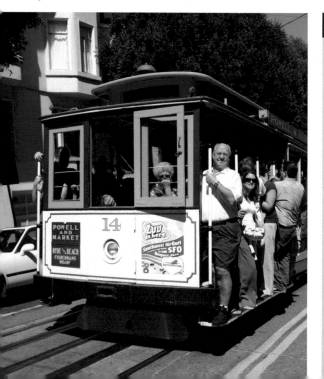

between Hyde and Leavenworth streets, this one block takes cars on eight hairpin turns along a cobblestone roadway.

THE FINANCIAL DISTRICT

The original '49ers sailed into San Francisco Bay, dropped anchor, and set off north to pursue their dream of striking gold. It wasn't long before the city's original shoreline began to burgeon, contributing to the birth of today's soaring Financial District. Brokers, bankers, marketers, and software engineers now pursue wealth on several acres of landfill on and around Montgomery Street.

The most obvious attraction in this neighborhood is the **Transamerica Pyramid ❶** on Montgomery Street. When it was completed in 1972, a lot of people were appalled by its pointed, unorthodox appearance, but now almost everyone has come to appreciate its architectural eccentricity. Unfortunately visitors cannot enter the tower.

A little farther north on Montgomery is Jackson Square, in the beautiful brick-lined Barbary Coast neighborhood. Here you'll find some acclaimed and expensive restaurants, architectural shops, and a few remaining high-end antique dealers.

South on Montgomery is the Wells Fargo History Museum (420 Montgomery Street; tel: 415-396-2619; www.wellsfargohistory.com; Mon–Fri 9am–5pm), which displays Gold Rush relics alongside the history of the Wells Fargo company.

The sprawling Embarcadero Center (http://embarcaderocenter.com) takes up four-square-blocks; connected by bridges are numerous shops, restaurants and high-rise apartments, as well as the Hyatt Regency Hotel, which boasts a spectacular 20-story atrium lobby. Noticeable from any part of town is the Bank of America building (555 California Street or Triple Five), which is so tall its roof sometimes disappears in the fog.

Where Market Street ends, the bay begins with the **Ferry Building ❶**, whose design was influenced by the Cathedral tower in Seville, Spain. It's still the gateway for ferry riders from all over the bay, as well as the site of an outrageously popular farmers' market and upscale food esplanade. On Saturday mornings, foodies converge here for breakfast at one of the many mobile kitchens, or to buy fresh produce, artisan cheese, bread, and chocolates. The ferries are especially convenient for commuters who need only to cross the Embarcadero intersection to reach the **Financial District**.

North from the Ferry Building is the **Exploratorium** (Pier 15; tel: 415-561-0360; www.exploratorium.edu; Tue–Sun 10am–5pm, also Thu 6–10pm), an interactive children's museum with more than 600 exhibits to awaken even the most dormant interest in science. This was founded by Frank Oppenheimer, brother of the inventor of the atomic bomb.

SOUTH OF MARKET (SOMA)

Stretching in wide blocks south of Market Street to the bay, **SoMa** is one of the

⊘ Tip

The SF Museum and Historical Society sponsors a self-guided walk called the Barbary Coast Trail, indicated by bronze medallions set in the sidewalk linking 20 historic sites. For more information, go to www.sfhistory.org.

⊘ THE FERRY BUILDING

Once a thriving terminal, the Ferry Building is now an upscale emporium designed to satisfy the local passion for food.

Before the rise of the automobile and the construction of bridges over San Francisco Bay, the Ferry Building was one of the world's most active transit terminals. Built in 1898 on the site of the original wooden ferry house at the foot of Market Street, the long and graceful building with its distinctive clock tower received thousands of daily ferry commuters from Marin County and the East Bay.

When speedier alternatives came on the scene in the 1930s, passengers abandoned the ferries. By the mid-1950s, the once-airy Grand Nave was clogged with offices, sealing out the natural light. Next, the building was walled off by the Embarcadero freeway. But after the freeway was damaged by the 1989 earthquake, it was demolished in 1991 and the Ferry Building, now in full view, inspired plans for the structure's regeneration. Meticulously restored, it now has a food hall that is open daily with artisan shops, restaurants, and cafes, and a farmers' market twice a week. The ferries with their cross-bay commuters have returned, too.

Free walking tours are conducted at noon on most Saturdays, and Tuesdays. For more information, visit www.sfcityguides.org.

city's most forward-looking districts, fueled by artistic and entrepreneurial energy. As well as the locale for some of the city's best nightclubs, restaurants, and museums, it emerged as the high-tech district, with many innovative Internet, design, and programming firms in residence. The bold **San Francisco Museum of Modern Art** Ⓚ (151 Third Street; tel: 415-357-4000; www.sfmoma.org; Fri–Tue 10am–5pm, Thu 10am–9pm) is the neighborhood's biggest attraction.

Across the street are the **Yerba Buena Gardens**, which started out as a lovely public park with a waterfall monument honoring Martin Luther King, Jr, and has now become a mecca for art and entertainment. Buildings around it house, for instance, the **Yerba Buena Center for the Arts** (www.ybca.org), where plays, modern art exhibitions, and experimental multimedia performances are staged.

One of Yerba Buena's most innovative venues is the Children's Creative Museum, (https://creativity.org), a visual arts facility geared toward young people. It includes an animation studio

San Francisco Museum of Modern Art.

and a production studio where kids can make and star in their own music videos.

Next to the Esplanade is the **Metreon** complex (www.shoppingmetreon.com), with a 15-screen movie theater, an IMAX theater (www.amctheatres.com), a food court, and a Target store. Not far away is the largest structure in the heart of SoMa, the **Moscone Convention Center**, (www.moscone.com), which hosts most of the major conventions held in the city.

MUSEUMS AND MINT

Down on Mission Street are the **museum of the California Historical Society** (No. 678; 415-357-1848; www. californiahistoricalsociety.org; Tue–Sun 11am–5pm), and the Museum of the African Diaspora (No. 685; tel: 415-358-7200; www.moadsf.org; Sun noon–5pm, Wed–Sat 11am–6pm), which explores the culture, history, and art of people of African descent.

Another signature building is the new home of the **Contemporary Jewish Museum** (736 Mission Street; tel: 415-655-7800; www.thecjm.org; Fri–Tue

11am–5pm, Thu 11am–8pm). It has three program spaces, designed by internationally renowned architect Daniel Liebeskind, and houses one of the world's leading collections of Jewish art and artifacts.

A couple of blocks away on 5th Street is another fine old building (c. 1875), San Francisco's **Old Mint** (http://thesan franciscomint.com). Dating from the days when the city was still a Wild West town, it was in this massive building that silver from Nevada was first converted into dollars and then stored in huge safes in the cellar.

PALACE HOTEL

To the east bordering Market Street and New Montgomery Street is the venerable **Palace Hotel** (www.sfpalace.com). Opened in 1875, it is San Francisco's oldest and still one of its premier luxury hotels, notable for its 150ft (46-meter) Palm Garden, with a leaded-glass dome roof that bathes diners in light, and the Pied Piper bar with its beautiful Maxfield Parrish mural. Seven American presidents have stayed here, including Ulysses S. Grant, Franklin Roosevelt, and Warren G. Harding, who died at the Palace in 1923 while still in office.

CIVIC CENTER

San Francisco's collection of historic buildings is centered in the Civic Center, bisected by Van Ness Avenue, the city's widest street. West of the large central square is **City Hall** ◑ (tel: 415- 554-6139 for tours; http://sfgov.org/cityhall; Mon–Fri 10am, noon, and 2pm), one of the most beautiful public buildings in the United States. It was designed by Arthur Brown, an architect so young and so unknown that he figured he might as well shoot for the moon in the early-20th-century competition to select the building design. To his surprise, Brown and his partner, John Bakewell, won with a design that called for the lavish use of costly marble, and a neoclassical dome that was influenced by Brown's time spent in Paris studying at the Ecole des Beaux-Arts. Built in 1914, City Hall is honeycombed with municipal offices, and both civil and criminal courts. The full effect is best experienced from its Polk Street entrance, which

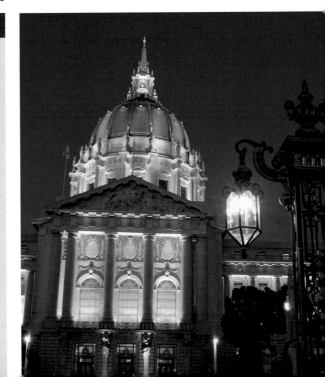

City Hall.

⊘ THE NEXT QUAKE

No one can predict when the next earthquake will come and lay waste to the great beauty of San Francisco as it did in 1906 and, more recently, in October 1989. This last quake, which lasted only 15 seconds, caused billions of dollars of damage to the city (although most of the downtown remained intact) and cost many people their lives. More people were not killed during the quake because the Bay Area's two home baseball teams were competing in the World Series, and most people were either at the stadium or at home glued to the television. Although the 1989 quake was a major one, and there have been smaller "shivers" since, thankfully none has proven to be "the big one" Californians talk of someday facing.

⊘ Tip

East of Civic Center to Union Square and bordered by Market and Sutter streets is the gritty Tenderloin neighborhood, which can be dangerous and is notorious for drugs, crime, and homelessness. There are several different stories as to how the Tenderloin got its name; one stems from the eponymous cut of meat, the "soft underbelly" of the city, relating to the vice, corruption, and harsh realities of street life found there.

faces the plaza. The magnificent stairway inside leads to the second-floor Board of Supervisors' chambers.

This is the building in which supervisor Dan White shot and killed Mayor George Moscone in 1978 for refusing to reappoint him to the seat White had resigned. White then shot and killed gay supervisor Harvey Milk. After White was convicted of manslaughter and given a remarkably lenient sentence, mobs descended on City Hall. The episode made headlines around the country and became a rallying cry for gay activists. Since then, the building has undergone sensitive retro-fitting and restoration in order to showcase its architecture and make the building earthquake-proof.

Opposite City Hall on Van Ness Avenue is a series of distinguished buildings. The **War Memorial Veterans Building** at the corner of Van Ness and McAllister streets was built in 1932 and houses the **Herbst Theatre**. Next to it is the **Opera House**, one of the country's greatest, and built in the same year as the Veterans Building. It has a summer opera festival and a regular season running from September to December. The opera company, which draws the foremost artists of the day to its stage, shares quarters with the highly regarded San Francisco Ballet. Across the street from the Opera House is the lavish **Louise M. Davies Symphony Hall** which has a separate wing containing Harold L. Zellerbach Rehearsal Hall. All the venues make up the War Memorial and Performing Arts Center (SFWMPAC; www.sfwmpac.org; tours Mon 10am–2pm on the hour).

ASIAN ART MUSEUM

The **Asian Art Museum** moved from Golden Gate Park to occupy the 1917 Beaux-Arts style premises that once housed the old public library (the main branch of the **Public Library** is nearby). The museum (200 Larkin Street; tel: 415-581-3500; www.asianart.org; Tue–Sun 10am–5pm, Thu 10am–9pm) houses the Avery Brundage Collection and is one of the largest museums of its kind outside Asia, replete with Japanese paintings, ceramics, and lacquer; Chinese bronzes and jade;

and sculpture from Korea and India. At the south end of the plaza is the **Bill Graham Civic Auditorium**, (www.billgrahamcivicauditorium.com), built in 1913 and renamed in honor of the city's late, great rock entrepreneur.

The north side of the plaza has the **State Office Building**, constructed in 1926. Together, they present an appearance of order and harmony. The brutal federal building standing behind the state building on Golden Gate Avenue is a reminder of how badly the Civic Center could have turned out had it been planned less carefully.

PACIFIC HEIGHTS

South of Union Street, the massive hills of one of the city's wealthiest neighborhoods, **Pacific Heights**, provide unparalleled views of the bay and are home to local luminaries like romance novelist Danielle Steele and the prestigious Getty oil family. Stunning mansions line every steep-and-wide street whose integrity is maintained by the upkeep of underground telephone lines. A stellar example of Victorian Queen Anne

architecture that is also open to the public is the beautiful **Haas-Lilienthal House** (2007 Franklin Street; tel: 415-441-3000; www.haas-lilienthalhouse.org Wed and Sat noon–2.30pm, Sun 11am–3.30pm; one-hour guided tours).

JAPANTOWN

Farther south, the hill crests at Jackson Street to mark the beginning of **Fillmore Street**. Further south of Fillmore itself at Post Street is the heart of **Japantown**. The **Japan Center** (https://japancentersf.com), the neighborhood's focal point, is an Asian-oriented shopping center that stretches three blocks and is filled with affordable Japanese restaurants and little stores featuring everything from kimonos to bonsai trees: a concentrated expression of Japanese culture in the middle of San Francisco. The handsome, distinctive five-tiered Peace Pagoda, designed by the Japanese architect Yoshiro Taniguchi, stands as a monument of goodwill between the Japanese people and those of the United States.

The Golden Gate Bridge spans the bay separating San Francisco and Marin County to the north.

At the Museum of Asian Art.

⊙ Where

The Mission district is full of colorful murals and street art. One of the best examples is Balmy Alley, located five blocks east of Mission Street, between 24th and 25th streets, and at the Women's Building on 18th Street. Precita Eyes Arts and Visitors Center runs tours on weekends (tel: 415-285-2287; www.precitaeyes.org).

Walk or cycle across the bridge, then take the ferry back across the bay from Sausalito.

THE MARINA

The waterfront Marina District is popular with young urban dwellers, and encompasses the area all the way from Fort Mason to the Presidio, and inland to Chestnut and Union streets.

By day, Chestnut acts as one big outdoor café where the next generation of yuppies congregates in workout gear, when they're not shopping in the trendy boutiques. After dark, the same crowd meets in the plethora of tasty and inexpensive restaurants, then heads to the post-collegiate-type bars. Union Street is a more chic stretch of boutiques, antiques stores, gourmet shops, delicatessens, and classy restaurants.

On the waterfront, **Fort Mason** Ⓜ (https://fortmason.org) is a decommissioned military base whose long huts now house art galleries, ethnic museums, workshops, and a gourmet vegetarian restaurant called Greens (www.greensrestaurant.com) that overlooks the harbor. The yachts in the harbor belong to the members of the **San Francisco Yacht Club** (www.sfyc.org), whose clubhouse looks out on the bay, which is often alive with windsurfers. A little bit west is **Marina Green**, beloved by kite flyers and joggers.

PALACE OF FINE ARTS

For a walk toward the bridge, follow the waterfront Golden Gate Promenade. One of the most beautiful man-made sights stands a few blocks inland from the promenade: the "Plaster Palace," across Marina Boulevard to the south, is the classic rococo rotunda of the **Palace of Fine Arts** Ⓝ (https://palaceoffinearts.com). Designed by Bernard Maybeck, the palace was originally built of plaster of Paris for the Panama-Pacific Exposition of 1915. It wasn't meant to last, but somehow it did. Not until 1967 was it strengthened and made permanent.

Just west of the Palace on the waterfront is **Crissy Field**, an airfield-turned-picnic area belonging to the 1,480-acre (599-hectare) **Presidio**. Established by the Spanish in 1776 and once owned by the US Army, the Presidio is a very unwarlike military installation. Decommissioned in 1992, its manicured grounds, which include

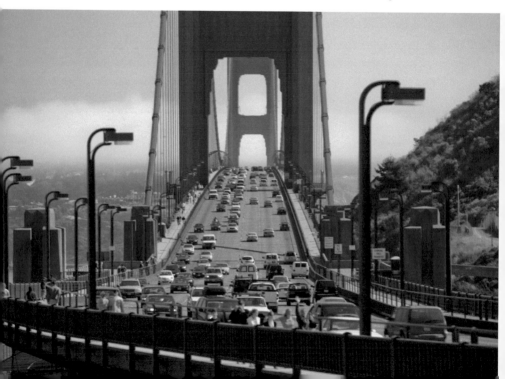

tands of pine and eucalyptus and even lake, are currently overseen by the ational Park Service (www.presidio.gov). fter fierce debate concerning its fate, lm director George Lucas was allowed o build a $300 million, 900,000-sq-ft 34,000-sq-meter) film studio in the ark. The headquarters of Industrial ight & Magic and LucasArts, the Letterman Digital Arts Center, was opened n 2005 (www.onelettermandrive.com).

GOLDEN GATE BRIDGE

Vhether sailing under the **Golden Gate ridge ⊙** or taking in its enormity from ne Marina's shore, it is interesting to onsider that at one time many reputable engineers argued that it would be npossible to build a span at this point ecause of the depth of the water and the owerful tidal rush in and out. The city uthorized the first studies in 1918, but it as 1937 before the bridge was finished t a cost of $35 million and the lives of 11 onstruction workers. The full splendor f this vast, reddish-gold structure can e appreciated from a viewpoint near the ccess road on the south of the bridge. A

bronze memorial of Joseph B. Strauss, the bridge's Chief Engineer, looks down on the throngs of visitors.

THE MISSION

The Mission is San Francisco's great melting pot of Latin American cultures. In the latter part of the 20th century, thanks to accessibility and lower rents, artists and musicians moved in too, earning the Mission its easy-going reputation for being the city's new bohemia. Now, with a wealth of trendy restaurants and hip nightspots, the neighborhood attracts an eclectic mix of people.

The district gets its name from **Mission Dolores ⊙** (3321 16th Street; tel: 415-621-8203; www.missiondolores. org; daily, 9am–4pm, May–Oct until 4.30pm), the sixth mission in the chain of Spanish settlements that stretched 650 miles (1,050km) from San Diego to northern California. Mission Dolores was founded less than a week before the American Declaration of Independence was signed in 1776, and its thick adobe walls still form what is the oldest building in San Francisco. The

Mural on Mission Street.

⊘ GOLDEN GATE BRIDGE

On opening day in 1937, the *San Francisco Chronicle* described the bridge as "a thirty-five million dollar steel harp." In the 75 years since, the bridge has weathered political detractors, powerful wind, and an earthquake.

Romantic as the bridge is, the hard facts are undeniably impressive. Including its freeway approaches, the Golden Gate Bridge is 1.7 miles (2.7km) long, with the main suspended span stretching for 4,200ft (1,280 meters). When completed, the bridge was celebrated as being the longest suspension bridge in the world. The Art Deco towers stand 746ft (227 meters) above the water; when first built, they were the highest structures in the West. Its distinctive vermillion color, called International Orange, was chosen to stand out in the famous Bay fog.

Café in the Castro area.

graves of many early pioneers, and thousands of native Costonoan Indians, can be found in the mission cemetery.

Valencia Street is full of popular boutiques, and hip restaurants and bars, while just a block east, Mission Street has an entirely different feel with discount shops, pawnbrokers, and produce stands. At the vast Dolores Park, families gather for birthday celebrations, gay sunbathers lie shirtless, and twentysomethings camp out on weekend afternoons.

In a town as condensed as this one, you need only go a few blocks to find yourself in an entirely different community. To the west of Mission, near Dolores, the sunny districts of **Noe Valley** and the **Castro** are comprised of many well-kept Victorian homes and shopping streets.

THE CASTRO

The **Castro** neighborhood is the world's most celebrated gay community. The streets are filled with same-sex couples, rainbow flags, hopping bars, and whimsical novelty shops,

especially on Castro Street between 17th and 19th streets.

The **Castro Theatre** (www.castrotheatre.com) is a beautiful work of Spanish Baroque design. This Revival house features classic and cult films (including sing-along versions of *The Sound of Music, Mary Poppins, and Grease*) and film festivals, and sometimes a live organist plays on an ascending platform for a bit of nostalgia.

Another testament to the gay community is **Harvey Milk Plaza**, the plaza in front of a Muni bus stop that's been dedicated to celebrated gay resident Supervisor Harvey Milk who was shot and killed in 1978, along with Mayor Moscone, by anti-homosexual Supervisor Dan White.

The Charles M. Holmes Campus at The Center, known locally as "The SF LGBT Center" (1800 Market Street; tel 415-865-5555; www.sfcenter.org), is closer to the Mission than the Castro but has become the nexus for community events, classes, support groups, and information regarding the local LGBT community. Here, it's possible to attend a Mensa

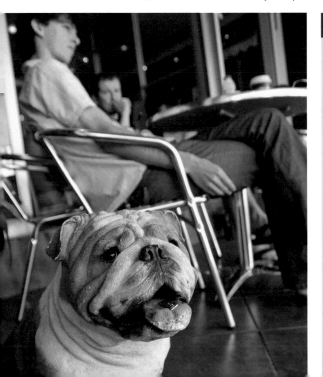

sexual support group, view a show of bert Rauschenberg, or obtain personized legal services all in one place.

The westernmost section of the Caso leads into the Twin Peaks area, full elegant homes. The neighborhood is amed after the two 900ft (274-meter) lls that provide stunning views of the ntire city, and are well worth the short scent to the top.

HE HAIGHT

eading north, back towards Downwn via Stanyan Street, is lively aight-Ashbury **Q** and tranquil Golden ate Park. Stanyan Street borders the astern edge of the park and intersects aight Street, a world-famous thorughfare in the 1960s, when long hair, e-dyed fabrics, hallucinogens, and a elief in the power of love and peace ersuaded a generation that they uld create an alternative lifestyle. hey were called "hippies," openly noked marijuana, took up forms of astern mysticism, declined to fight foreign wars, and otherwise were a orn in the sides of their elders, who

sometimes sent police in riot gear to the middle of the **Haight-Ashbury** district to clean it up.

Haight Street was once so gaudy and bizarre that tour buses full of goggle-eyed tourists ran up and down it. Like most such radical departures from the social norm, the hippie experiment fell victim to time and fashion. The neighborhood still retains its anti-establishment roots, but today flower power has been replaced by piercing shops and tattoo parlors. It's still a vibrant, colorful stretch, however, with great shopping and a wide range of good, inexpensive restaurants and cafés.

ALAMO SQUARE

Nine blocks south, at the corner of Fulton and Steiner streets, a very different history is preserved. The "postcard rows" of perfectly maintained Victorian houses surrounding a grassy square with skyscrapers peeping over the top is called **Alamo Square Q** and the location of thousands of photographs of the streets of San Francisco. The harmonious beauties, called "Painted

Eat

Inside the Japanese Tea Garden there is a beautiful Tea House where you can enjoy a refreshing cup of green tea and some rice cookies. You might also catch one of the authentic Japanese tea ceremony demonstrations.

Painting the Conservatory of Flowers, Golden Gate Park.

HIPPIES IN THE HAIGHT

For several hot months in the first Summer of Love, 1967, life became a costume party in a wonderland setting of brightly painted Victorian buildings. The neighborhood was a swirl of colors as flower children painted storefronts, sidewalks, posters, cars, vans, and, of course, themselves, with Day-Glo. The days and nights were filled with sex, drugs, and a pot-laced breeze, with a soundtrack provided by Janis Joplin, Jefferson Airplane, and the Grateful Dead, who all lived in Haight-Ashbury pads.

Things change, of course. Half a century later, tourists still snatch up Summer of Love T-shirts, but today there are more families and homeless youngsters than hippies on the streets. Nevertheless, vintage boutiques, music stores, restaurants, and cocktail bars mean the neighborhood is happening again.

⊙ Kids

The San Francisco Zoo (1 Zoo Road; tel: 415-753-7080; www.sfzoo.org; daily 10am–4pm), the largest and oldest in California, anchors the southern end of the Great Highway, the road that parallels Ocean Beach on one side and the Sunset district on the other. There are 250 species living there, and also a children's zoo.

"Painted Ladies" at Alamo Square.

Ladies," are characterized by pointed gables and tiny oriel windows.

GOLDEN GATE PARK

Golden Gate Park (https://goldengate park.com) is 3 miles (5km) long and half a mile (1km) wide, and consists of groves of redwoods, eucalyptus, pine, and countless varieties of other trees from all over the world. It is dotted with lakes, grassy meadows, and sunlit dells. There can be thousands of people within its borders, but Golden Gate Park is so large that one can easily find solitary tranquility in a misty forest grove or by a peaceful pond. More than a century ago, the park was painstakingly reclaimed from sand dunes through the Herculean efforts of a Scottish landscape architect named John McLaren. The park superintendent for 55 years, McLaren so disliked statuary that he shrouded all human likeness in dense vegetation. Most statues remain "lost" today.

Along John F. Kennedy Drive, about seven blocks into the park, is the

hard-to-miss **Conservatory of Flowers**. The incredible glass structure was built in 1878, modeled after the Palm House at London's Kew Gardens. Housing wonderful collections of rare palms and other tropical flora the atmosphere inside is one of color unleashed. A seasonal flowerbed in front is a natural announcement to its entrance, and the grounds around the conservatory have fine collections o fuchsias and azaleas.

The park has feasts for the mind as well as the eyes. Further along JFK Drive, a road branches off to the left for the **Music Concourse**, an esplanade built in 1894 offering Sunday concerts On one side of the Music Concourse is the **California Academy of Sciences** ❺ (tel: 415-379-8000; www.calacademy org; daily 9.30am–5pm, from 11am Sun). With a ground-breaking design produced by Pritzker Prize-winning architect Renzo Piano, it is among the world's greenest museums, with a 2.5-acre (1-hectare) "living" roof o native grasses, porthole skylights, and solar panels that supply the museum's power. The complex also includes the **Steinhart Aquarium**, the **Morrison Planetarium**, coral reef exhibits, and a live rainforest with orchids, macaws butterflies, bats, scorpions, turtles and an enormous anaconda.

The fabulous **de Young Museum** ❼ (50 Hagiwara Tea Garden Drive; tel 415-750-3600; https://deyoung.famsf.org Apr–Nov Tue–Sun 9.30am–5.15pm stands perilously close to the San Andreas fault, and the gallery was severely damaged in the 1989 earth quake. To withstand future seismic incidents, the new building – a bold monolithic structure with a copper skin that will slowly turn green – is able to move up to 3ft (90cm). It has one of the best collections of American painting in the US as well as art from Oceania Latin America, Africa, and Meso America. The tower at the northeast corner is 144ft (44 meters) high and has views all the way to Downtown and the Pacific Ocean.

Next door, the beautiful **Japanese Tea Garden** (http://japaneseteagardensf.com) is a harmonious blend of architecture, landscaping, and pools, and is one of the most visited and loved sites in the park. Built in 1894, it was created by George Turner Marsh, a successful dealer in Asian art. Marsh hired a renowned Japanese gardener, Makota Hagiwara, who planted traditional dwarf bonsai conifers, elms, and cherry trees. Hagiwara (whose family is said to have invented the fortune cookie) also designed the winding brooks with their moss-covered rocks, rises, and carp pond. A wooden gateway, a wishing bridge, and a five-story pagoda complete the landscape.

Across from the tea garden, the **San Francisco Botanical Garden** (tel: 415-661-1316; www.sfbotanicalgarden.org; open daily from 7.30am, for closing times check website), is an urban oasis of extraordinary beauty that delights the senses with some 7,500 plant species on 70 acres (28 hectares). Specialty gardens include a Succulent Garden in which limestone walls warm giant aloe plants and cactus while woodpeckers nest, and the Moon Viewing Garden where magnolias, Japanese maples, and camellias surround a reflecting pond with a platform used to view the autumn moon.

Further north along Martin Luther King Jr. Drive is the lovely, sweet-smelling Garden of Shakespeare's Flowers, with "lady-smocks," rosemary, and 150 other species mentioned in Shakespeare's writings.

THE BEACHES AND NORTHERN COAST

At the far western end of Golden Gate Park is Ocean Beach. Although the beach has dramatic ocean views, only the hardiest souls and little kids dip their toes into the ice-cold water.

Farther north along the coast is **Cliff House** , (https://cliffhouse.com), a restaurant that overlooks the Pacific Ocean, where you can peer down upon barking seals clinging wetly to the rocks below. The present Cliff House is the fifth to have been built here since 1863; each of its predecessors has burned down or suffered some other disaster.

North of the Cliff House is verdant **Lincoln Park**, whose 270 acres (109 hectares) include an 18-hole municipal golf course and the stunning neoclassical French-style **California Palace of the Legion of Honor** (100 34th Avenue; tel: 415-750-3600; www.legionofhonor.famsf.org; Tue–Sun 9.30am–5.15pm). Smack-dab in some of the hottest real estate in town, the fine art museum, renovated at a cost of $35 million in 1995, is spectacular; at the entrance is one of five existing bronze casts of Rodin's *The Thinker*.

The cliffs wind east along a protected area known as the **Golden Gate National Recreation Area** (the largest urban park in the world), under the Golden Gate Bridge.

Japanese Tea Garden in Golden Gate Park.

📷 SAN FRANCISCO'S CABLE CARS

Much more than just a means of transport, San Francisco's cable cars are an iconic feature of the city. They've been designated a National Landmark, starred in countless movies and TV shows, and featured on a postage stamp.

Even from their earliest days, San Francisco's famous cable cars impressed visitors. "They turn corners almost at right angles, cross over other lines and for aught I know run up the sides of houses," wrote Rudyard Kipling, who visited in 1889 on his way to India.

Operating on three routes – the Powell–Mason, Powell–Hyde and California lines – San Francisco's cable cars are among the last in the United States, at least 100 cities having abandoned them for buses. Underestimating the draw of this tourist attraction, San Francisco tried to get rid of the cars in 1947, but a vigorous local campaign saved them by a City Charter.

Today the cable cars transport over 9 million passengers a year, more than half of them local commuters. It is the visitors, of course, who buy the engraved knives, belt buckles, posters, and T-shirts emblazoned with pictures of the beloved cars, or dig into their wallets to pay for genuine cable car bells. The most enjoyable routes for visitors are the Powell–Mason and Powell–Hyde lines, which share a terminus at Powell and Market and then diverge in Nob Hill on different routes to Fisherman's Wharf (Powell–Hyde is more scenic, passing through Russian Hill and the top of Lombard Street).

Cable car winding machinery at the Cable Car Barn an Powerhouse Museum.

Cable car on Nob Hill. At the beginning of the 20th century, 600 cars rolled over 115 miles (185km) of trac but a fleet of electric trams powered by overhead wire hastened their demise.

Some of the tour buses are painted to resemble their more famous stablemates.

The cable car turntable at Powell and Market streets is the starting point for two lines, the Powell–Mason and the Powell–Hyde. The third cable car line is the California Street line that runs east–west.

Andrew Smith Hallidie

The cable-car system was created in 1873 by Andrew Hallidie, a British-born engineer with a reputation for building suspension bridges and a background in mining engineering. Seven years before, it's said, he saw a horse slip, breaking a chain on the overloaded streetcar it was pulling uphill. Hallidie set about devising a system that would eliminate such accidents.

Although Hallidie and his friends put up $20,000 to get the cable cars operating, it was Benjamin Brooks, the son of a local lawyer, who was awarded a franchise in 1870 to operate a similar system, but failed to raise the necessary financing.

When the Hallidie plan came to fruition, skepticism was the order of the day. "I'd like to see it happen," said realtor L.C. Carlson, "but I don't know who is going to want to ride the dang thing."

Critics of the system still abide today. Although the cars run at only 9.5 mph (15 kmh), they can't duck potential collisions and their braking system has been called "unimprovable" or "blacksmith shop crudity at its worst" by columnist Dick Nolan.

...bit at the Cable Car Museum on Mason Street.

...le cars on Market Street, c.1899.

Andrew Smith Hallidie.

GREATER SAN FRANCISCO BAY AREA

From the sequoias of Muir Woods to Jack London's Oakland, the people's Berkeley, and the high-tech communities of Silicon Valley, the Bay Area is as diverse as San Francisco itself.

Outside San Francisco are as many fascinating sights and delights as there are in the city. Mountains, redwood forests, and wonderful Pacific beaches beckon, as well as intriguing Silicon Valley, Oakland, and Berkeley. Travel is easy: several bridges span the bay; an underground train system (BART) links the East Bay, South Bay and the San Francisco International Airport (SFO) with the city; ferries crisscross the water; and trains run up and down the peninsula. Getting around by car, though, is the most attractive way to explore the coasts, hills, and valleys.

MARIN COUNTY

Encircling San Francisco Bay from the north, and lying at the tip of a metropolitan, Marin County is home to tens of thousands of acres of pristine coastline, unspoiled redwood groves and mountain meadows, and pretty beaches. This luxurious green belt offers seemingly limitless options for hikers and nature-lovers, while old-fashioned towns and charming bed and breakfasts lend themselves to relaxed weekend getaways.

SAUSALITO

The first – or last – stop for most Marin visitors is **Sausalito ❶**, tucked inside the bay to the east behind the Golden Gate. There is a ferry service to the

Sausalito dock from San Francisco. The waterside shops, the warrens of pricey but perfect boutiques, and the houses perched behind them on a steep slope draw inevitable comparisons to towns on the Mediterranean Riviera. The Spanish word *saucelito* (meaning "little willow") is said to have been the name's origin. There is, in fact, very little to do in Sausalito except stroll around, have lunch or dinner in one of the restaurants – where California Cuisine is a specialty – and admire all the boats and pretty people.

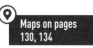

Main attractions

Sausalito
Mount Tamalpais
Muir Woods National
  Monument
Jack London Square,
  Oakland
Oakland Museum of
  California
University of California
Stanford University
Winchester Mystery House

Maps on pages
130, 134

View from Mount Tamalpais.

Bay Area

MOUNT TAMALPAIS

In recent years, **Mount Tamalpais ②** has become a weekend traffic jam of hikers, mountain bikers, and runners. Still, there seems to be enough beauty to go around. Over 30 miles (50km) of trails wind their way through 6,000 acres (2,400 hectares), as well as many more miles of hiking in the contiguous watershed lands owned by the water municipalities. On Mount Tam's lower elevations, often shrouded in fog, are stands of virgin redwood. Above, the mountain's chaparral-covered high slopes jut proudly into the sunshine, overlooking San Francisco Bay and the Pacific. It's a fantastic sight.

MUIR WOODS

At the very base of Mount Tamalpais is wonderful, woodsy **Muir Woods National Monument ③** (www.nps.gov/muwo). At the turn of the 20th century, the Marin Water District planned to condemn a property called Redwood Canyon, cut the timber on it, and with the profits build a dam and reservoir. The scheme so appalled one wealthy Marinite named William Kent that he bought the land outright, then cleverly deeded the redwood stand to the government, who turned it into a national monument. Kent modestly declined to have the monument named after him, out of deference to his old friend, naturalist John Muir.

Over 1 million tourists a year visit the giant sequoia trees here, which grow to 200ft (60 meters) in height, 16ft (5 meters) in diameter, live up to 1,000 years, and are spread out through Muir Woods' 300-plus acres (120 hectares). Energetic walkers might be advised to leave parked cars behind and head up the steep slope of Mount Tam on the **Ben Johnson Trail** through deeply shaded glens rife with ferns and mushrooms, past ever-changing groves of bay, tan oaks, madrona, and nutmeg.

THE MARIN HEADLANDS

Beyond Mount Tam, Marin County's green belt extends some 50 miles (80km) to the distant tip of Point Reyes National Seashore. The coastal country, known as the Marin Headlands (easily accessible off Highway 1 just north of

Muir Woods National Monument.

Sequoia trees in Muir Woods.

the Golden Gate Bridge; www.nps.gov), has miles of coastal and beach-bound trails. Stellar views can be had by driving up the Fort Baker Road.

Stinson Beach, at the foot of Mount Tamalpais, is San Francisco's favorite playground, popular among anglers hoping to hook surf perch and rockfish, and among bird-watchers who want to spy such out-of-the-way creatures as the sooty shearwater, brown pelican, Western grebe, killdeer, and millet. When the fog pulls back, the beach also attracts hordes of sunbathers. Stinson gets especially crowded on fine weekends, or when sweltering inland weather drives home-dwellers as near to the sea as it's possible to get.

POINT REYES

A triangular peninsula, **Point Reyes** ❹ is separated from the rest of the world by the main fissure line of the San Andreas fault, which is nudging Point Reyes northeast at an average rate of 2ins (5cm) a year. This 65,000-sq-mile (105-sq-km) seashore park, which draws over 2 million visitors a year,

Point Reyes lighthouse.

is one of the most frequented of the country's national parks.

Add quaint inns and diners in the little towns of **Inverness** and **Point Reyes Station**, and it seems as close to untouched paradise as you can get. The epicenter of the 1906 San Francisco earthquake was a half-mile from where the main park headquarters now stands on Bear Valley Road. On **Earthquake Trail**, visitors can see where the quake moved one old stone fence a distance of at least 15ft (5 meters).

To get to the park headquarters and most of the trailheads in the National Seashore, drivers must travel up Highway 1 past the town of **Olema** to Bear Valley Road. The park is open only to those who are willing to walk or ride a horse. The terrain is varied, much of it very steep. Gloomy forests suddenly open on lush, sweeping meadows, while the coast is rockbound with occasional pocket beaches. Hikers may see owls, foxes, raccoons, bobcats, deer, and almost every kind of bird imaginable, especially herons, egrets, and ducks.

A hike up wind-whipped, 1,400-ft (427-meter) **Mount Wittenberg** rewards out-of-breath hikers with a truly breathtaking view of the California coast: green-black forests and golden meadows that roll down to a coastline where the eye can track for miles without seeing a soul. Below is **Drakes Beach**, where the famous Elizabethan sea captain Sir Francis Drake is said to have set ashore in 1579 for ship repairs.

At the tip of the Point Reyes promontory perches a **lighthouse** that warns ships away from the treacherous coast. One of the foggiest places in Marin County, it usually has no view at all. When the fog lifts and at the right season, however, it is a good place from which to spot migrating whales.

On the northern edge of the seashore, Pierce Point Road meanders around to several beaches – **Abbotts**, **Kehoe**, and the most ruggedly dramatic, **McClures**. These beaches are not recommended for swimming because of the danger of sharks, undertow, and rip tides. It is better to head for Drakes Beach on the southern side, which is somewhat protected from winds.

THE EAST BAY

From the Black Panthers to Chez Panisse, the East Bay is as revolutionary as San Francisco. Built around the ports and the University of California, Oakland and Berkeley offer a slightly slower pace than their sister city, as well as craftsman-style homes and leafy, winding neighborhoods. But don't mistake this for suburbia: the lively political culture, widely diverse demographics, museums, and intellectual centers make these cities thriving metropolitan centers with a distinctly urban edge.

OAKLAND

Despite author Gertrude Stein's infamous quip that "there is no there there," **Oakland** ❺ long ago emerged from the shadow of its older sister to the west. In fact, things are looking pretty good in Oakland – especially for women: according to a recent US census, Oakland ranks third in the number of businesses owned by women. The tech boom that

Inside the lighthouse on the Point Reyes promontory.

Oakland and Berkeley

0 _____ 1 mile
0 _____ 1 km

N

ALBANY

Marin Ave
Gilman St
Hopkins St
Rose St
Cedar St
San Pablo Ave
North Berkeley
University Ave
Sacramento
7th St
4th Street
Cedar St
The Alameda
Spruce St
Shattuck Ave
Oxford St
Gourmet Ghetto
Berkeley Rose Garden
Grizzly Peak Blvd
Centennial Rd
CHARLES LEE TILDEN REGIONAL PARK
NORTH WATERFRONT PARK
580
Berkeley Marina
University Ave
Berkeley Marina
Hearst Ave
Lawrence Hall of Science
Sather Tower (Campanile)
Downtown Berkeley
Bancroft Way
Art Museum
University of California
University Botanical Gardens

BERKELEY
Dwight Way
Oregon St
People's Park
Way
Ave
College Ave
BERKELEY OPEN SPACE RESERVE
Claremont Ave
Claremont Resort Hotel and Spa

CITY CENTER / OLD OAKLAND inset

0 _____ 500 yds
0 _____ 500 m

14th St
12th St
10th St
8th St
7th St
Adeline St
Market St
Grand Ave
San Pablo Ave
Broadway
Telegraph Ave
Franklin St
Paramount Theatre
19th St Oakland
C Oakland City Hall
African American Museum and Library
H Preservation Park
Martin Luther King Jr. Way
Jefferson St
Clay St
CITY CENTER
G 12th St Oakland City Center
B Tribune Building
OLD OAKLAND
Broadway
Webster St
Harrison St
Alice St
14th St
12th St
11th St
CHINATOWN
Jack London Square
A
5th St
1st St
7th St
8th St
Oak Street
F Oakland Museum of California
Nimitz Freeway
Oakland Inner Harbor
Lake Merritt

13
Ashby
Ashby Ave
Alcatraz Ave
Telegraph Ave
Shattuck Ave
Market Street
M. L. Luther King Jr. Way
College Ave
Claremont Ave
Rockridge
24
Tunnel Road
REGIONAL PARK
CLAREMONT COUNTRY CLUB
Broadway Ter.
Claremood Dr.
Moraga Ave

Oakland Outer Harbor
Maritime St
West Grand Ave
Peralta St
30th St
West Grand Ave
Wood St
Peralta St
7th St
8th St
14th St
Market St
San Pablo Ave
Grove St
Telegraph Ave
Broadway
MacArthur
580
OAKLAND
Oakland West
M
Paramount Theatre
19th St Oakland
12th St Oakland City Center
African American Museum and Library
M
Tribune Building
7th St
5th St
Nimitz Freeway
Harrison St
14th St
980
Children's Fairyland
LAKESIDE PARK
E Lake Merritt
Valley Ave
Grand Ave
Broadway
Harrison St
MacArthur Blvd
PIEDMONT
M
Lake Merritt
Oakland Museum
Lakeshore Ave
Park Blvd
580
Park Blvd
MacArthur Freeway

Oakland Inner Harbor
Main St
Ave A
Ave F
Lagoon
Atlantic Ave
Main St
Atlantic Ave
ALAMEDA
880
E. 14th St
E. 12th St
E. 14th Ave
14th Ave
Foothill Blvd
E. 23rd St
21st St
Frutvale Ave
MacArthur Freeway
Oakland Zoo
D Mormon Temple
260
Brooklyn Basin
Oracle Arena & Oakland Alameda County Coliseum

dramatically escalated rental and home sales prices in San Francisco has also creeped into Oakland. Once still affordable for artists, teachers, and others not making big tech dollars, the rents and home prices have been steadily rising.

Oakland's version of Fisherman's Wharf is the restaurant and shopping pedestrian walk called **Jack London Square Ⓐ**. The author of *The Sea Wolf* and *The Call of the Wild*, who died in 1916, might not be impressed to see the overpriced restaurants and souvenir stores, but he'd be able to munch crab, listen to live music, and watch the sailboats pass by.

The **First and Last Chance Saloon**, which London frequented, is popular with tourists, and nearby is his sodroofed Yukon cabin, moved from Alaska to the waterfront in tribute to the city's most famous son.

Moored in the harbor is the USS Potomac, President Franklin D. Roosevelt's "floating White House," and now a National Historic Monument (www.usspotomac.org).

On Sundays a farmers' market is held in the part of the city called Old Oakland (around Washington Street at 8th Street) a neighborhood with stores, restaurants, and shops in its renovated buildings. Numerous cannabis clubs and marijuana dispensaries can be found in the cultural district nicknamed Oaksterdam, in the north end of downtown Oakland. Nearby, Oakland's Chinatown is more negotiable than its cousin across the bay.

Oakland's many landmarks include the handsome **Tribune Building Ⓑ**, with its distinctive tower, and the post-1989-earthquake renovated **Oakland City Hall Ⓒ**, with its wedding-cake cupola. The Art Deco palace, the Paramount Theatre, is the home of the Oakland Ballet and the Paramount Organ Pops, and shows old movies and newsreels. Other cultural attractions in Oakland are the Fox Theatre and monthly Art Murmurs (www.oaklandartmurmur.org), events

promoting local art and culture. In the hills above, the fivetowered, white granite **Mormon Temple Ⓓ** is the only Mormon temple in the state. From its lofty heights are wonderful views of the bay.

On the eastern edge of town is a natural landmark, **Lake Merritt Ⓔ**. This large saltwater lake and wildlife refuge, rimmed by Victorian houses and a necklace of lights, is the location of a 10-acre (4-hectare) theme park, **Children's Fairyland** (see margin).

Not far from the lake is the **Oakland Museum of California Ⓕ** (1000 Oak Street; tel: 510-318-8400; www.museumca.org; Wed–Thu 11am–5pm; Fri 11am–9pm , Sat–Sun 10am–6pm).

Landscaped with terraces and gardens and occupying three levels, it is considered the finest museum in the state for information on California's art, history, and natural science. The Cowell Hall of California History has a huge collection of artifacts, while the Gallery of California Art is known for its oil paintings.

Among Oakland's newer attractions are the **City Center Ⓖ**, a pedestrian mall with quaint restaurants, jazz concerts,

First and Last Chance Saloon.

City Hall, San Jose.

and art exhibits; **Preservation Park ⓗ**, a restored Victorian village complete with 19th-century street lamps and lush gardens; and the **African American Museum and Library** at 659 14th Street (www.oaklandlibrary.org). For many black Americans, Oakland has a special significance; it was here in the 1960s that the Black Panther Movement was founded. The politics espoused by the Panthers spread from here to the East Coast and then to college campuses around the country.

BERKELEY

Just north of Oakland is **Berkeley ⑥**, another East Bay rival of San Francisco. A city famous for social experimentation and the birth of the Free Speech movement, Berkeley has, in recent times, become slightly less flamboyant and slightly more commercial.

On the approach to Berkeley from Oakland, two buildings catch the eye. On a hillside toward the south is a fairytale white palace, otherwise known as the **Claremont Club & Spa** (tel: 510-843-3000; www.fairmont.com/claremont-berkeley), which, like San Francisco's

Palace of Fine Arts, was finished just before the Panama-Pacific Exposition of 1915. The other landmark is a tall, pointed structure, the university's bell tower. Its official name is **Sather Tower**, but it is known to everyone simply as "the campanile" because it's modeled after St Mark's campanile in Venice, Italy. Sather Tower belongs to the **University of California** (www.universityofcalifornia.edu), known simply as "Cal" and considered one of the country's finest public universities. Berkeley grew from a humble prep school operating out of a former fandango house in Oakland, to become part of the ninecampus University of California system.

To get the feel of Berkeley at its liveliest, visitors should take a walk down Telegraph Avenue from Dwight Way to the university. Students, townspeople, and "street people" pick their way between street vendors offering jewelry and pottery, and stores catering to modern students.

Berkeley's climate (it can be foggy in San Francisco but sunny across the bay) produces sweet scents in the **University Botanical Gardens** in Strawberry Canyon. Over 12,000 species thrive in the research facility here. Elsewhere in the Berkeley hills are other nature-based attractions: **Tilden Regional Park**, the **Berkeley Rose Garden**, and the **Lawrence Hall of Science**.

THE PENINSULA

The San Francisco **Peninsula**, a roughly 55-mile (89km) swath of high hills, tall trees, and beautiful estates, is wedged between the Pacific Ocean and San Francisco Bay. To its north is San Francisco. At its southern end lies the sprawl of **Silicon Valley** – or what used to be known as the Santa Clara Valley when apples and pears, not computers and silicon chips, were harvested here. In the valley, the peninsula's highlands segue into the affluent, high-tech communities of Palo Alto, Los Altos, Sunnyvale, Santa Clara, and San Jose. As the drive south on **El Camino Real** – the main thoroughfare that runs through all these cities down to San Jose – will prove, the only true borders between peninsula cities seem to be stoplights.

Where the commercial and spartan-finish industrial strips end, the wealthy suburban homes begin, spread like a heat rash across the ample flatlands.

The style of the peninsula is sophisticated, shamelessly commercial, and contemporary. Stanford University is the hub of academic and cultural activity. Mixed with the high-mindedness, however, is lots of new money (millionaires from scratch as common as tennis courts) and old money (San Mateo is one of the four wealthiest counties in California). Both types shop at the impressive **Stanford Shopping Center** (www.simon.com/mall/stanford-shopping-center).

STANFORD UNIVERSITY

A farm – a blue-blooded horse ranch – is exactly what the campus of renowned **Stanford University** ❼ (www.stanford.edu) was a little over a century ago when Leland Stanford and photographer Eadweard Muybridge began their experiments with moving images (which were to lead to the creation of motion pictures). Today, it is the academic lifeblood of the peninsula, located in the

University of California, Berkeley.

⊙ FREE SPEECH FOR ALL

The Free Speech movement of 1964 put Berkeley on the map. At issue was a UC Berkeley administration order limiting political activities on campus. This touched off massive student protests and, in turn, similar protests on campuses nationwide. Since then, the campus has been a center of political action.

In 1969, students took to the streets to stop the university's expansion in an area they wanted to preserve as **People's Park**. They prevailed, despite the intervention of 2,000 National Guard troops and violence that led to the death of an onlooker. Years on, People's Park drew more drug dealers and drifters from the city's homeless than it did students. But today, student unrest has turned more to rest and recreation, so the city has added basketball and volleyball courts to the park.

Colorful Californian.

northwestern corner of **Palo Alto**, a city known for its strict environmental policies and praised as one of the best "model little cities of the world." Architecturally, Stanford's handsome, rough-hewn sandstone buildings are Romanesque in style, though the red-tiled roofs, the burnt adobe color of the stone, and the wide arches give the university a Spanish mission look. The exception to the overall prosaic qualities is beautiful **Memorial Church**, which dominates the **Inner Quad** (also known as the central courtyard). The church is resplendent in stained glass and with a domed ceiling.

SAN JOSE

San Jose ⑧ was the first pueblo to be founded in Northern California by the Spanish, in 1777. Until 1956, the San Jose area was providing America with half its supply of prunes. But the orchards of five decades ago have now sprouted condominiums and industrial parks. Today, San Jose is the third-largest city in California, with a population that is booming due to the influx from

around the world of high-tech personnel and like-minded groupies.

It is a busy, fast-paced community (population of nearly one million), with several major hotels, nightclubs, and no fewer than 100 shopping centers that cater to all the techies with money to burn. Of these the most renowned is Santana Row. The **San Jose Museum of Art** (110 South Market Street; tel: 408-271-6840; www.sjmusart.org; Tue–Sun 11am–5pm) boasts nearly 1,500 works of art, new media, and installations including glass sculptures by Dale Chihuly and photographs by Ruth Bernard. For entertainment of a more eccentric bent there is the red-roofed, sprawling touristy but nonetheless fascinating **Winchester Mystery House** ⑨ (near Interstate 280 and State Highway 17; tel: 408-247-2101; www.winchestermysteryhouse.com; daily 9am–5pm) in downtown San Jose. It was built in convoluted stages by local eccentric Sarah L. Winchester, who inherited the fortune of her father-in-law, the famed gun manufacturer. Sarah was a spiritualist who believed that she would live as long as she kept adding to her house. Sixteen carpenters worked on the mansion for 36 years, adding stairways that lead to nowhere and doors without any rooms.

The spiritual realm is also the basis and reason for the **Rosicrucian Egyptian Museum and Planetarium** (tel: 408-947-3635; www.egyptianmuseum.org) in San Jose, on the way to **Santa Clara**. A recreated walk-in tomb of 2000 BC and the West Coast's largest collection of Egyptian, Babylonian, and Assyrian artifacts are contained within the building. The Ancient Mystical Order Rosae Crucis is an international philosophical order established nearly 3,500 years ago.

Anyone longing for fresh air and the sound of the sea should nip over to Highway 1 west of San Jose near the little town of **Pescadero,** where there is a particularly atmospheric site – **Pigeon Point Lighthouse**, the second-tallest lighthouse in the United States.

SILICON VALLEY

Endowed with the enterprising spirit of pioneers, Silicon Valley nurtured many of the technological advances that catapulted the world into the electronic age.

Silicon Valley stretches about 20 miles (32km) from the lower San Francisco peninsula to San Jose. Google, Adobe, Cisco, Yahoo, Apple, Facebook, and Intel are just a selection of the famous IT names based here. A large part of any history of modern computing will be a list of Silicon Valley milestones.

Formerly known as Santa Clara Valley and settled by farmers in the mid-1800s, it is bounded to the east by the San Francisco Bay and to the west by the Santa Cruz Mountains. It embraces 16 cities, including Palo Alto, home of Stanford University. In 1938, two Stanford students, David Packard and William Hewlett, living at 367 Addison Street in Palo Alto (now a State Historical Monument), founded what would one day become one of the world's corporate giants, Hewlett-Packard.

LOCAL HEROES

After receiving the Nobel Prize for the electronic transistor in 1956, Valley native William Shockley intended to build an empire, but the eight young engineers he hired all left to form Fairchild Semiconductor. It was here, in 1959, that Bob Noyce developed the miniature semiconductor set into silicon. Noyce, known to many as the father of Silicon Valley, co-founded Intel with Gordon Moore in 1968.

At 2066 Crist Drive in a Cupertino garage, Steve Jobs and Steve Wozniak turned out their first computer and later formed Apple Computer. Apple's headquarters are still located in Cupertino.

During the 1980s, personal computers replaced arcade games as the entertainment of choice. Then came email and the World Wide Web. At first these were mainly electronic noticeboards for tech geeks; now they are indispensable tools. When the internet started to catch on, with an estimated 18 million users in 1995, a frenzy began. Entrepreneurs were eager to dig from the emerging market, and people flocked to Silicon Valley, much as they had to the Sierras looking for gold in 1848. This time, instead of picks and pans, they brought business plans and laptops. Through the tumult and excitement of the dot-com boom, many got burned and the industry suffered a huge crash in 2002.

Life rose from the rubble. The world discovered Google as a search engine; on its stock flotation Google overtook Time-Warner as the world's most valuable media corporation; eBay gobbled up many of the old "bricks and mortar" auction houses; and Apple Computer took a market out from under Sony, replacing the once-ubiquitous Walkman with the now-ubiquitous iPod.

Social media mania quickly became the next Silicon Valley phenomenon with the rise of Facebook and Twitter. The communication, marketing, business, and political landscapes were forever altered by these seemingly innocuous but powerful media tools. A movie on the origins of Facebook, *The Social Network*, was nominated for a Best Picture Oscar at the 2011 Academy Awards.

Apple Park, headquarters of Apple Inc.

Enjoy an aerial view of Napa Valley from a hot air balloon.

WINE COUNTRY

Wine is grown all over the state, but the Napa and Sonoma valleys represent California Wine Country for most visitors. Apart from wineries, the region has plenty to entice the visitor, from trails to spa towns, and gorgeous scenery.

From the summit of Mount St Helena, a vast, rolling expanse of emerald vineyards stretches for miles below. Supported by a temperate climate and rich, drainable soil, the grape vines blanket the beautifully bucolic Napa, Sonoma, Mendocino, and Lake counties, together forming one of the most famous wine-growing regions in the world. Although wine is the main allure – for both San Francisco day-trippers and international visitors – the region also boasts a renowned farm-to-table restaurant scene, spas fed by hot springs, ballooning excursions, plenty of opportunities for biking, hiking, and camping, and even a wild animal park.

NAPA VALLEY

Rural Napa Valley, with its wealthy and genteel aura, was catapulted into wine industry fame after beating French wines in a 1976 tasting. Today it is the most famous of California's wine-producing regions. The 30-mile (50km) thrust of flat land nestles between the pine-forested Mayacamas Mountains and the buff-colored Howell Mountains, pinched off in the north by Mount St Helena. State Highway 29 and the Silverado Trail run parallel through the valley, passing long expanses of vineyards

Stained glass in Rhine House, Beringer Vineyards, Napa Valley.

broken up by farmhouses, stone wineries, and a series of small towns. If you are staying overnight, any of these towns makes a good launching point for exploring the valley. Otherwise, simply choose the wineries you want to visit and hit the road (with a designated driver, of course).

NAPA

The first Napa Valley town you enter when heading north from San Francisco is **Napa ❶** (www.visitnapavalley. com). The charming small town

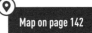 Map on page 142

Main attractions
Napa Wine Train
Oxbow Public Market, Napa
Yountville
Silverado Trail
Old Faithful Geyser
Downtown Sonoma

Wine Country

(whose name means "plenty" in the local Indian dialect) is a compact collection of shops, country inns, wineries, and eateries. Peruse boutiques on the main street through the quaint Downtown, grab a bite at an upscale restaurant, then get on the road to taste your way through wineries like Darioush, Paraduxx, Ceja, Frogs Leap, Vintners Collective, and Schramberg. If you don't feel like driving, consider a ride on the Napa Valley Wine Train.

The popular Oxbow Public Market is open daily (610 and 644 First Street; www.oxbowpublicmarket.com; 7.30am–9.30pm). Here you can choose from dozens of restaurants and specialty food purveyors, including Three Twins, serving scoops of organic ice cream; Hog Island, dishing out fresh oysters; and Ritual Coffee Roasters, pouring some the Bay Area's best coffee. On Tuesdays and Saturdays (8.30am–1pm), the Napa Farmers' Market is held at 105 Gasser Drive (https://napafarmersmarket. org).

YOUNTVILLE

In what must surely be one of history's most lucrative contracting deals, George Yount received his huge land grant for roofing General Vallejo's Petaluma adobe. Today, Yount's grave at the pioneer center is found across from Yountville's city-park picnic stop. The renovated brick and stone buildings in **Yountville** ❷ are home to exceptional restaurants, from Thomas Keller's world-renowned French Laundry (www.thomaskeller.com) to the more relaxed The Girl and the Fig (www.the girlandthefig.com).

Of course, the focus here is also on wine. **Domaine Chandon Winery** (tel: 888-242-6366; www.chandon.com) just west of town is owned by Chandon of Moët and Chandon fame, and produces sparkling wine in the *méthode champenoise*; that is, it is fermented in the same bottle from which it is poured. Just north of Oakville is the **Robert Mondavi Winery** (tel: 888-766-6328; www.robertmondaviwinery.com), a sleek operation, as befits such a famous local name.

⊙ Tip

Don't drive after wine tasting – in addition to the risks of getting in an accident, police frequently set up mandatory checkpoints along the main roads, where all cars are stopped to ensure drivers are sober. If you are not, penalties can be severe, so it's best to have a non-drinking designated driver.

On the Napa Valley Wine Train

⊙ THE WINE TRAIN

A one-of-a-kind fine-dining experience, with exceptional locally sourced Napa wines, awaits the passenger on this popular Wine Country attraction. The lavishly restored 1915 Pullman dining and lounge cars lend an air of opulence to this tasteful journey. The train whizzes past wineries along 36 miles (58km) of track in the heart of the Napa Valley during the three-hour tour. The Wine Train operates year-round and offers a variety of packages – from champagne brunch to a moonlight escape. Special trains operate on all holidays, and they offer winemakers' dinners and murder mystery rides. Optional excursions include tours of the Raymond Winery and Grgich Hills Estate. For more information: tel: 800-427-4124; www.winetrain.com.

Chefs at work in the kitchens of Sonoma's The Girl and the Fig restaurant, producing seasonal, French-inspired food.

The Girl and the Fig restaurant in Sonoma.

ST HELENA

The undisputed capital of the Napa Valley is **St Helena** ❸, noted for its dozens of wineries, historic stone buildings, picnic parks, chic shops, pricey hotels, and the CIA (see page 147). The **Robert Louis Stevenson Museum** (1490 Library Lane; tel: 707-963-3757; http://stevensonmuseum.org; Tue–Sat noon–4pm) is stuffed with Robert Louis Stevenson memorabilia and collectables like first editions of his work and souvenirs of his global jaunts.

South of town, the **Louis M. Martini Winery** (tel: 800-321-9463; www.louismartini.com), run by one of the valley's oldest winemaking clans, offers reasonably priced wines in an unpretentious setting. Two historic wineries lie just north of St Helena. Jacob and Frederick started the **Beringer Vineyards** (tel: 707-257-5771; www.beringer.com) in 1876, modeling the Rhine House (1883) after their ancestral estate in Mainz, Germany. They dug limestone caves for aging wine. Today's winery, owned by Foster's (yes, the Australian beer people) features Fumé Blanc and Cabernet Sauvignon in the mansion tasting room. Outside, spacious lawns and a regal row of elms fronts the winery.

The building of the other founding father, **Charles Krug Winery** (tel 707-967-2200; www.charleskrug.com) dates from 1874. The lavish Greystone building nearby was the world's largest stone winery when it was erected in 1889 by mining magnate William Bourn; today, the mansion is run by the California headquarters of the **Culinary Institute of America**, a brilliant cooking school with a restaurant that is open to visitors.

To take a break from wine tasting, visit the **Bale Grist Mill State Historic Park** ❹ (tel: 707-963-2236 open Fri–Mon 10am–4pm), 3 miles (5km) north of St Helena. The center of Napa social activity in the mid-19th century, the historic 1846 mill is where settlers once ground their corn and wheat into flour or meal. Milling demonstrations and historic tours are held on weekends.

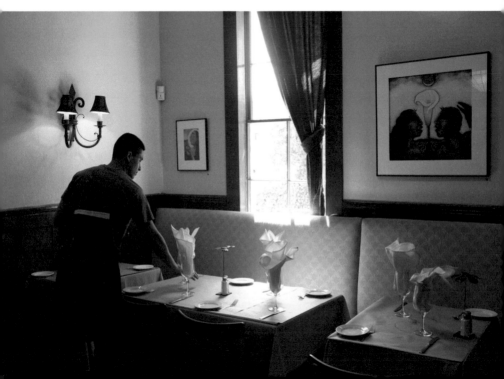

Between Bale Grist and the town of Calistoga are two excellent places to stop. **Sterling Vineyards** (tel: 800-726-6136; www.sterlingvineyards.com) – part Spanish mission, part fantasy – reigns over the upper valley atop a knoll. A sky tram whisks visitors 300ft (91 meters) up for a self-guided tour. The tram fee is offset against the purchase of Sauvignon Blanc and other wines. Close by is **Clos Pegase** (tel: 707-942-4981; www.clospegase.com), designed in 1986 by architect Michael Graves in sleek, modern style. Clos Pegase is known almost as much for its art collection as for its wines.

LAKE COUNTY

St Helena is also the turn-off to a warm-water paradise. The tragedy-ridden Berryessa family lost sons and soil in the Mexican War; today, their Napa land grant is better known as **Lake Berryessa ❺**, reached via State Highway 128 from St Helena or State Highway 121 from Napa. Fishermen pull in trout, bass, and catfish, while sailors, waterskiers, campers,

and swimmers have their choice of several resorts around this lake, which has more miles of shoreline than Lake Tahoe. Bring along some of your favorite vintage and enjoy your wine in a picnic setting.

Back on State Highway 29 and past **Robert Louis Stevenson State Park,** the road heads towards **Lake County** and its bold, friendly, visitor-seeking wineries scattered around **Clear Lake ❻**, California's largest natural lake (Lake Tahoe lies partly in Nevada). Besides producing Cabernet Sauvignon, Zinfandel, and Sauvignon Blanc grapes, Lake County is famous for Bartlett pears and walnuts. Resorts and campgrounds ring the lake, and there's good walking in **Clear Lake State Park** at the foot of conical **Mount Konocti**, an extinct volcano.

CALISTOGA

The one-street spa town of **Calistoga ❼** is a little gem. Wooden hangings shading the shopfronts give it a Wild West feel, while treatment centers

⊙ Tip

Hot-air ballooning is a popular adventure in the Napa Valley, offering gorgeous views from above. Some packages include a champagne breakfast upon landing. For operators try: Balloons Above the Valley (tel: 800-464-6824; www.balloonrides.com); Calistoga Balloons (tel: 707-942-5758; www.calistogaballoons.com); or Napa Valley Balloons Inc. (tel: 707-944-0228; www.napavalleyballoons.com).

Beringer Vineyards' historic Rhine House.

Bottle of white from the Beringer Vineyards, where Cabernet Sauvignon, Merlot, Pinot Noir, Chardonnay, and Sauvignon Blanc are produced.

Chateau Montelena produces Zinfandel, Riesling, Cabernet Sauvignon, and Chardonnay.

including Indian Springs, Calistoga Spa Hot Springs, and Solage make use of mineral springs and hot, therapeutic mud. After treatments, head to on-site pools heated by hot springs to completely relax.

Calistoga is surrounded by numerous wineries. Of note for its historic (1882) lakeside setting with a Chinese feel is **Chateau Montelena** (tel: 707-942-5105; www.montelena.com), which produces classic Chardonnay and Cabernet Sauvignon. A limited number of reservations are accepted for the picnic sites on Jade Lake in view of the pagoda.

Two miles (3km) north of town, Old Faithful Geyser (tel: 707-942-6463; www.oldfaithfulgeyser.com; daily, 8:30am–7pm, until 5pm in winter) spouts jets of boiling water 60–100ft (18–30 meters) into the sky every half-hour. Although the tickets are somewhat expensive for what takes place, there are tables inside the little waiting area, so you can have a pleasant picnic while waiting for the water to take off. Just to the west is the Petrified Forest (4100 Petrified Forest Road), where redwoods were turned to stone millions of years ago. Docent-led tours (included in the admission price) guide visitors through an ash fall, meadow, and view of Mount St Helena, and discuss the area's geology, flora, and fauna.

Seven miles (11km) north of Calistoga is Robert Louis Stevenson State Park, named for the famous author of Treasure Island, who honeymooned there in 1880. On a 5-mile (8km) hike to the top of Mount St Helena, a marker notes where his cabin once stood. On clear days, Mount Shasta can be seen 192 miles (309km) away from the peak.

SONOMA VALLEY

More slow-paced and rustic than Napa, Sonoma County is a patchwork of country roads, towns, orchards, ridges, and hills. West of Napa, Sonoma is only about one hour's (without traffic) drive from San Francisco. US 101, the Wine Country's only freeway, runs the length of **Sonoma County**

⊘ THE SILVERADO TRAIL

More quiet and scenic than State Highway 29, the **Silverado Trail** was built as the road from Mount St Helena's cinnabar mines to Napa's river docks. Today the elevated, two-lane road above the valley floor runs parallel to State Highway 29 between the towns of Napa and Calistoga, offering panoramic views, wineries, and hidden valleys deep in the Howell Mountains. **Stag's Leap**, a rocky promontory near Yountville where a 16-point Roosevelt elk once plunged to its death, overlooks the award-winning **Stag's Leap Wine Cellars** (www.cask23.com) and **Clos du Val** (www.closduval.com). Towards St Helena, popular stops include the **Rutherford Hill Winery** (www.rutherfordhill.com), an ark-like structure with picnic grounds, and **Auberge du Soleil** where you can dine on a terrace overlooking verdant vineyards.

north to south, entering it near **Petaluma ⑧**. The freeway continues on through Santa Rosa, Healdsburg (gateway to the Alexander, Dry Creek, and Russian River valleys), and Cloverdale, which is located on the Mendocino County border. State Highway 12 runs through Sonoma Valley to Santa Rosa, passing the towns of Sonoma and Kenwood.

The **Sonoma Valley** is steeped in wine and wineries, and literary and political history. Sonoma is a native Patwin word meaning "Land of Chief Nose," after an Indian leader with a prominent proboscis. Founding father Mariano Vallejo romanticized Sonoma Valley as the "Valley of the Moon" (author Jack London later borrowed the name for a book about frazzled urbanites rejuvenated by clean country living).

SONOMA

Father Altimira founded California's last mission, **San Francisco de Solano**, in 1823. General Vallejo set up the town in 1835, making **Sonoma ⑨** the northernmost outpost of a Catholic, Spanish-speaking realm that, at its peak, extended all the way to the tip of South America. It briefly became a republic after the Bear Flag Revolt in 1846, when Americans stormed Vallejo's home. Although Vallejo and the missionaries at Mission San Francisco de Solano dabbled in winemaking, the local residents really only recognized the region's vinicultural potential after Hungarian political refugee Count Agoston Haraszthy founded Buena Vista Winery in 1957 and began winemaking in earnest.

Today, downtown Sonoma is picturesque, relaxed, and well-heeled. Upscale restaurants and art galleries ring its tree-shaded **Sonoma Plaza**. Several restored adobes are also found around the plaza and on nearby streets, including the Mission

(tel: 707-938-9560); Vallejo's old house, **Lachryma Montis** (tel: 707-938-9559); and the **Sonoma Barracks** (tel: 707-939-9420), all part of the **Sonoma State Historic Park** (20 E Spain Street; daily 10am–5pm).

Two blocks from the plaza stand **Sebastiani Vineyards** (tel: 707-933-3200; www.sebastiani.com), on lands once cultivated by the people of the San Francisco de Solano Mission. This winery is still owned by the Sebastiani family.

East of Sonoma, the **Buena Vista Winery** Tasting Room (tel: 800-926-1266; www.buenavistawinery.com) retains connections with Count Haraszthy; his original cellars are still standing and his image adorns the label of the winery's Founder's red wine. South of town, the Gundlach and Bundschu families were involved in winemaking for more than 125 years, and Gundlach-Bundschu (tel: 707-938-5277; www.gunbun.com) wines are exported around the globe.

Nearby, the pricey, beautifully decorated **Fairmont Sonoma Mission**

Old Faithful Geyser, Calistoga.

☉ Tip

Not into wine? Enjoy a few rounds on the links, instead. Golfing options in Napa Valley include the Silverado Resort and Spa, which has hosted tour events since the 1960s (www.silveradoresort.com), Chardonnay Golf Club (www.chardonnaygolfclub.com), Eagle Vines Golf Club (www.eaglevinesgolfclub.com), or Napa Golf course (www.playnapa.com).

Inn and Spa (tel: 707-938-9000; www.fairmont.com/sonoma) offers health and fitness facilities (with its own source of thermal mineral water).

North on State Highway 121, the **Valley of the Moon Winery** (tel: 707-939-4500; www.valleyofthemoonwinery.com) occupies part of George Hearst's 19th-century vineyards (George was the father of tycoon William Hearst). North on State Highway 1 is the town of Kenwood. The **Kenwood Vineyards** (tel: 707-282-4281; www.kenwoodvineyards.com) features Zinfandel, Cabernet Sauvignon, and Chenin Blanc, while Chardonnay lovers head for **Château St Jean** (tel: 707-257-5784; www.chateaustjean.com), with its beautiful backdrop of the Sonoma Mountains and excellent whites.

SANTA ROSA

Famed botanist Luther Burbank picked the area around **Santa Rosa** ⑩, on State Highway 12, as "the chosen spot of all the earth" to conduct his plant experiments in hybridization. He developed more than 800 new plants, including many fruits, vegetables, and flowers, yet relished few of them except asparagus. Visitors can tour the **Luther Burbank Home and Gardens** (tel: 707-524-5445; www.lutherburbank.org; check for tour and visiting information). Children will want to head for Santa Rosa's **Snoopy's Gallery**, (www.snoopyshomeice.com) selling the widest range of Snoopy products in the world, thanks to the fame of Santa Rosaite and dog creator Charles Schultz.

The town's trinity of adjoining parks form a 5,000-acre (12,000-hectare) urban oasis with a children's amusement park and lake in **Howarth Park**; camping, picnicking, and boating in **Spring Lake Park**; and hiking and equestrian trails in **Annadel State Park**.

ALEXANDER, DRY CREEK, AND RUSSIAN RIVER VALLEYS

North of Santa Rosa, **Healdsburg** ⑪ is where the Alexander, Dry Creek, and Russian River valleys meet. A beach on the river encourages

Sonoma Valley vines.

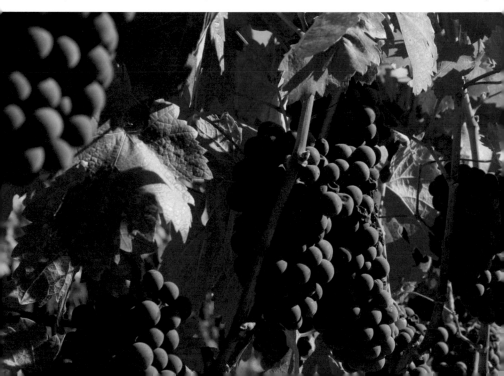

swimming, fishing, and canoeing. There's also a tree-shaded, Spanish-style plaza dating from the 1960s. The Healdsburg Museum (www.healdsburgmuseum.org) on Mattheson Street, housed in the old Carnegie Library building, displays Pomo tribal artifacts and 19th-century exhibits from the region.

There are more than 60 wineries within a half-hour's drive of Healdsburg, and the industry's growth and the concomitant rise in tourism have been bringing almost a million visitors a year to this pretty town. Opposite the 130-year-old Belle du Jour Inn on Healdsburg Avenue is the tasting room of the Simi Winery (tel: 800-746-4880; www.simiwinery.com). One entry in the 1942 guestbook is by Alfred Hitchcock, who drew a sketch of himself and noted, "The port here is far too good for most people." There are numerous other wineries in the area, especially in the picturesque Alexander Valley, east of US 101. State Highway 253 snakes westward from US 101 just south of Ukiah to join northbound State Highway 128 at Boonville. This narrow, often-wooded country road meanders through the valley past grazing sheep, vineyards, and orchards all the way to Navarro and beyond to the coast.

Winemaking first began here more than a century ago, when many frustrated gold-seekers settled and planted vineyards. **Boonville** ⑫ is a delightful little place. You can eat well and stay comfortably at the Boonville Hotel (tel: 707-895-2210; www.boonvillehotel.com), which calls itself a "roadhouse," defined in Funk and Wagnall's 19th-century dictionary as "an inn or restaurant in a rural locality which caters especially to transient pleasure-seekers."

Other worthwhile stops include the Anderson Valley Historical Society Museum (12340 Hwy 128; www.andersonvalleymuseum.org), in a red, one-room schoolhouse north of Mountain View Road; the Buckhorn Saloon; and the Anderson Valley Brewing Company (www.avbc.com; daily 11am–6pm).

Getting married at a Napa Valley vineyard.

ALONG THE NORTH COAST

California's huge stands of protected redwood trees and a tight legislative reign on development mean that urban civilization has been kept at bay on this wild coastline.

Few places in America are as beautifully wild as California's North Coast. North of Sonoma Valley, stunning coastline links together state parks and sleepy seaside towns such as Bodega Bay and Mendocino, which offer scenic bluff views and plenty of opportunities for beachcombing, hiking, and wildlife spotting. In the upper reaches of the rugged north, it is easy to contemplate miles of majestic coastline, inland hills, and towering redwood groves without spotting a living soul.

The absence of development is partly due to the California Coastal Commission, formed in the 1970s when the state seemed fated to become a 400-mile (600km) ribbon of private marinas and ocean-view condominiums. Visitors hardly complain – the quiet north coast is all the more lovely for the relative solitude you can find here.

BODEGA BAY TO FORT ROSS

North of Point Reyes National Seashore is **Bodega Bay ❶**, named for the Spanish explorer Juan Francisco de la Bodega y Quadra. Bodega Bay's bluffs offer sweeping views from Point Reyes to Fort Ross, and are a popular whale-watching spot from January through April. For more wildlife-spotting, the bird sanctuary

at Doran Beach is arguably the best bird-watching site in Sonoma County. Visit the Sonoma Coast Visitors Center (913 State Highway 1; tel: 707-377-4459; www.sonomacounty.com/chamberscvbs/sonoma-coast-visitors-center) for more information.

North of Bodega Bay, most of the Sonoma County coast is a state beach, with no camping but comfortable access, plenty of parking, thrilling views, and appropriate beach names like **Mussel Point, Salmon Creek, Hog Back, Shell Beach,** and

Map on page 152

Map on page 152

Main attractions
Bodega Bay
Fort Ross
Mendocino
Whale watching
Avenue of the Giants
Redwood National Park

Bodega Bay.

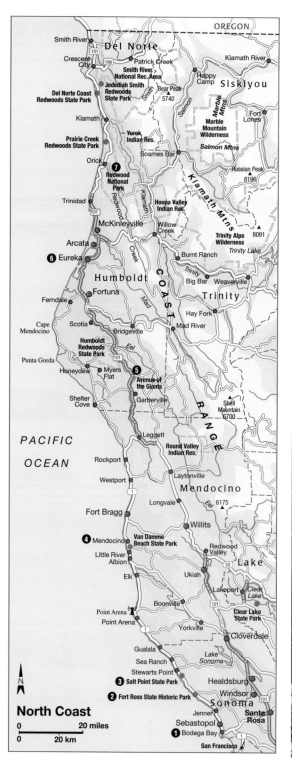

North Coast

0   20 miles

0   20 km

Goat Rock. As you travel north on Highway 1 from Bodega Bay, the prevailing scenery is cypress trees, pines, old barns, and grazing sheep and cows, often shrouded in fog. As real estate, this grazing land is so valuable that local ranchers are termed "boutique farmers," because they don't really have to farm: they could sell the land for easily more money than they'd make in a lifetime of farming.

North of **Jenner**, Highway 1 weaves through daily fog, rolling pastures, and sudden canyons that drop 1,000ft (over 300 meters) into the blue and foamy Pacific. The road passes historic **Fort Ross** ❷ (www.fortross.org; Fri–Mon 10am–4.30pm), a careful reconstruction of the original fort built by Russian traders in the early 19th century. There are tours, but the best way to see the fort is to stroll through and around on your own. The small Russian Orthodox chapel is worth a special stop.

One compelling way to pass an afternoon in north Sonoma County s to visit the coastal tide pools. At **Salt Point State Park** ❸, a popular place for abalone divers, visitors can explore the rocky tide pools at low tides to see marine life up close. Additional park activities include hiking, horseback riding, fishing, and diving.

MENDOCINO COUNTY

Travelers enter Mendocino County just north of Sea Ranch, at **Gualala**, which is notable for its fine old hotel in the center of town. Fifteen miles (24km) north, a coastal access path leads to **Point Arena**, a tiny bayside beach that comprises several dozen weathered mobile homes, two disintegrating and dangerous piers, and a few shops selling bait and fishing tackle. However, bed and breakfast inns are springing up all along the coast as city dwellers buy up Victorian homes, preserve them, fill them with antiques, and surrender with relief to a lifestyle change in the countryside.

The Coast Guard's **Point Arena Lighthouse** (http://pointarenalighthouse.

com) occupies the point of the US mainland closest to Hawaii. Many ships have crashed near Point Arena; lots of free literature is available to tell visitors which ships, and where, and what was lost as a result.

Set 156 miles (251km) north of San Francisco on a long bluff above a small bay, **Mendocino** ❹ is a cultured town with an arts center (with year-round events) and many galleries. A century-old former logging village, Mendocino was all but deserted in the early 20th century, but saw a cultural renaissance in the 1950s as artists and musicians moved in.

Today it's a lovely, low-key place, much of the pleasure coming from just strolling around. Gingerbread houses cling to windswept headlands, and there are white picket fences and ancient wooden water towers. Still, with more than 20 bed-and-breakfast inns, the small town becomes hectic on weekends. Two nearby state parks, **Van Damme** and **Russian Gulch**, offer camping, hiking, birdwatching, fishing, beachcombing,

Mendocino has attracted the more creative types since re-inventing itself in the 1950s.

and other quiet pleasures. To the north, the city of **Fort Bragg** is a down-to-earth, working-class town established in 1857 as a US military post. A mill built in 1885 served the town's lumber industry until 2002; its closure then was a huge blow to the local economy. Some of the best of its unpretentiousness can be found in **Noyo Harbor**, a sunny inlet lined by docks, characterful boats, and seafood restaurants.

HUMBOLDT COUNTY

Much of the North Coast's mystique is due to the majestically tall redwood trees, which have survived attempts to transform them into everything from lumber and ashtrays to mulch for suburban rose gardens. Most of California's remaining old-growth redwoods are now protected in parks.

North of Garberville, a breathtaking 33-mile (53km) scenic drive called the **Avenue of the Giants** ❺ follows the South Fork of the Eel River through 55,000-acre (22,000-hectare)

Humboldt Redwoods State Park. The giants – redwood trees, otherwise known as *Sequoia sempervirens* – are breathtakingly tall and sometimes surprisingly wide. Their size can, and has been, marketed: "Drive through a living tree" is the come-on from the **Drive Thru Tree** in the town of **Myers Flat**.

Those seeking to avoid this kind of commercialism can take the difficult road west from Garberville over the **King Mountains** to **Shelter Cove**. North of this isolated outpost is **Petrolia**, site of California's first oil well.

An honest glimpse into the spirit of the early settler life along the North Coast is aptly afforded by **Scotia**, a crisp little company town built entirely of redwood – the wooden visitor center is in the style of a classic Greek temple – and dominated by the former **Pacific Lumber Company mill** (now operated by Humboldt Redwood Company), the world's largest redwood mill. The Pacific Lumber Company owned the town until the company went bankrupt in 2008.

Gray whale breaching.

EUREKA

From the moment you arrive, it is obvious that **Eureka ⑥** is a good place to buy such commodities as sewer pipe, lumber, a slab of redwood burl, a life-sized statue of a lumberjack carved from a redwood log, or a fresh fish dinner. Often shrouded in fog, it is the largest Pacific Coast enclave in North America north of San Francisco. A sprawling, busy, industrial place, still with a large fishing industry, Eureka is also the location of the North Coast's only institution of higher learning, called, appropriately enough, **Humboldt State University**.

Eureka's ubiquitous and impressive Victorian architecture in the **Old Town** is highlighted by the **Carson House** at the end of 2nd Street. Visitors can't go inside this much-photographed house because it is now a private men's club, which makes it seem all the more Victorian. Anyone interested in this type of architecture will want to head to the little town of **Ferndale**, 10 miles (16km) southwest of Eureka, which has a very good sampling of well-maintained Victorian buildings.

The coast around Mendocino.

REDWOOD NATIONAL PARK

Orick is the gateway to **Redwood National Park ⑦**, established in 1968 to consolidate 40 miles (60km) of majestic forested coastline under

Victorian architecture in Eureka's Old Town.

Marijuana is now legal for recreational use in California.

federal jurisdiction. The 106,000-acre (42,900-hectare) national park encompasses three state parks: Prairie Creek Redwoods, **Del Norte Coast Redwoods State Park**, and **Jedediah Smith Redwoods State Park**.

There are five visitor centers throughout the park (most open daily 9am–5pm), and many campsites (tel: 707-465-7335; www.nps.gov for reservations). The Kuchel Visitor Center (tel: 707-465-7765) is located 1 mile (1.6km) south of Orick on US 101 and gives out trail maps, directions, and shuttle-bus information for excursions up **Redwood Creek**, to the southeast. There, three of the tallest trees ever identified are clustered in the **Tall Trees Grove**. The tallest, at 368ft (112 meters) in height, was the world's tallest known tree when it was discovered in 1963.

Other notable sites include the Lady Bird Johnson Grove, an old-growth forest named for the former First Lady. It is difficult to recommend much of the scenery north of the **Klamath River** bridge, however, because you probably won't see much of it; fog can come in thick and fast and without warning. Be sure to take a sweater, just in case.

CRESCENT CITY

Crescent City – a grim, gray gathering of plain houses and vacant lots around a semi-circular harbor – has never fully recovered from a 1964 tsunami which devastated the town. More recently, tsunami waves generated by the 2011 earthquake off Japan caused more damage and destruction.

Fifteen minutes east of Crescent City on US 199 heading toward Grants Pass, Oregon, the last undammed river in California flows gin-clear through the 90°F (32°C) summer twilight. Although the **Smith River** is wild, its accommodations are civilized. There's a lodge on **Patrick Creek** (www.patrickcreeklodge. com) with a restaurant and bar. There are clean campgrounds, public and private, under the peeling red madronas. The attractions here are simple: boulder-lined banks, clear pools, good fishing – and no redwood souvenirs.

Although there are no drive-through trees in Redwood National Park, there are three located along the Pacific Highway: the Klamath Tour Thru Tree, the Shrine Drive-Thru Tree, and the Chandelier Tree.

SHRINE
DRIVE-THRU TREE

AGE 3000   HEIGHT 275 FT.
DIA. 21 FT.   CIR. 64 FT.
MYERS FLAT, CALIFORNIA

The Sundial Bridge in Redding was designed by architect Santiago Calatrava, who designed a similar one in Buenos Aires, Argentina.

THE HIGH NORTH

The key to unlocking the secrets of the north is State Highway 299. This two-lane blacktop cuts across some of the state's least-populated wilderness.

Mountainous State Highway 299 should be savored like a fine wine and, if possible, should take at least five days to travel along. On its winding trek, it cuts across a remote domain of mountains, valleys, volcanoes, rivers, canyons, and basins. The best time to visit is mid-April to mid-November, but even under the best of weather conditions, rockslides and heart-stopping curves make driving this road no experience for the timid or the impatient.

THE KLAMATH MOUNTAINS

Coming from the Pacific Coast, State Highway 299 branches off US 101 at Arcata, north of Eureka, and crosses the low **Coast Range** to reach the wilderness realm of the **Klamath** and **Trinity** rivers. These two principal rivers drain the Coast Range and **Klamath Mountains**. The Klamaths comprise a series of smaller ranges: the **Siskiyou**, the **Trinity**, the **Trinity Alps**, the **Marble**, the **Scott Bar**, the **South Fork,** and the **Salmon** mountains. They cover about 12,000 sq miles (31,000 sq km) of Northern California and southern Oregon. **Mount Hilton** is the highest peak in the region.

There is something very wild about the Klamaths: with more than 70ins (1,800mm) of annual rainfall in some parts, they sustain a lush forest of ferns, hemlocks, pines, and spruce. Except for the highest of the Trinity Alps, glaciers are rare, so most peaks retain a raw, jagged quality and river canyons lack the graceful horseshoe shape of their glaciated Sierra Nevada counterparts.

Some native tribes still inhabit the area. The Hoopa and Klamath tribes own ancestral fishing rights and still set their traps and dip their nets at the foot of Ishi Pishi Falls. Guides with graceful rowboats, called

Main attractions
Trinity Alps Wilderness Area
Lassen Volcanic National Park
Mount Shasta
Lava Beds National Monument

Map on page 160

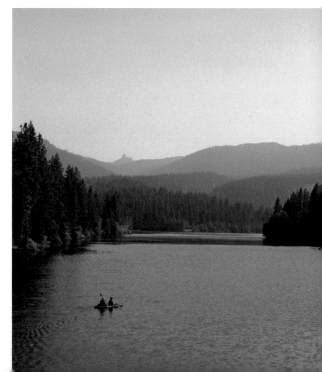

Lake Siskiyou, near Mount Shasta.

The Taoist temple in Joss House State Historic Park looks at the role Chinese immigrants played in the state's early history.

"MacKenzies," will lead you to the finest holding pools. Stealthy visitors are sometimes rewarded with sightings of eagle, river otter, great blue heron, duck, fox, bobcat, and the occasional great bear.

The rivers and streams bear names that join in a confluence of Native American mythology and the whims of 19th-century prospectors: Klamath, Ukunom, Trinity, Salmon, Smith. Fishing and floating on these rivers is by no means limited to

natives; the streams are big and cool in hot summers, and rafting and fishing guides take visitors down many of the most inviting canyons. Salmon and steelhead trout still spawn in these rivers and the fall run is unparalleled in the state.

Three national forests contain most of California's Klamaths – Klamath, Shasta, and Trinity. Within these forests are more strictly protected wilderness areas. The best-known and most popular is the vast **Trinity Alps Wilderness Area ❶**, a region of high, craggy peaks and sparkling lakes, laced with hundreds of miles of trails for hiking and camping. Ranger stations along State Highway 299 at **Burnt Ranch**, **Big Bar** and Weaverville, and on State Highway 3 at **Trinity Center**, will issue free permits, answer flora and fauna questions, and provide up-to-date information on weather and trail conditions.

Redwood trees can be found here, especially in the old-growth state parks of these northern coastal mountains. Some of these majestic giants

1,000 years old and reaching 300ft (90 meters) into the sky, are the largest living things on earth. Sun filtering through the redwood canopy as if through leaded glass, the cool enveloping shade, and the imposing sense of age often draw comparisons to the cathedrals of Europe.

About 10 miles (16km) east of the Trinity River bridge marking the Humboldt–Trinity county line, near the community of Burnt Ranch, State Highway 299 passes just south of **Ironside Mountain** (5,255ft/1,602 meters). Ironside's sheer, scenic face is the eroded, exposed tip of a much larger piece of granite – the Ironside Mountain Batholith. About 165 million years old, this batholith is typical of other such intrusions in the Sierra Nevada and Klamaths, which distinguish the Klamaths from the neighboring Coast Range.

WEAVERVILLE

For residents of Trinity County a "night on the town" usually means a trip to **Weaverville ❷**, the county seat, with a population of around 3,600. It saw its glory days during the mid-19th century, when it was a supply post for Klamath region gold prospectors. Gold hunters still haunt the creeks of Trinity County, but lumbering sustains the economy.

Weaverville is the site of the **Joss House State Historic Park** (www.parks. ca.gov; Thu–Sun 10am–4pm), a tribute to Chinese history in California, particularly of the Gold Rush days. Here, the oldest Chinese temple still in use in the state is open daily; guided tours are available. Nearby is the eclectic **JJ "Jake" Jackson Museum** (www.trinity museum.org), focusing on local history.

Weaverville is also the gateway to **Trinity** and **Lewiston lakes**, part of the expansive **Whiskeytown National Recreation Area** (www.nps.gov). A short drive north of town, these lakes were created in the 1960s with the damming of the upper Trinity River. They offer outdoor recreation opportunities in the form of fishing, hiking, boating, and camping.

Although lumber ranks first, marijuana ranks second in Trinity County's cash crops. This juxtaposition

Chinese temple in Joss House State Historic Park.

Whitewater rafting on the Trinity River.

VOLCANIC LEGACY

It is thanks to the collapse of an ancient volcano, leaving a giant crater in which Lassen Park lies, that visitors can enjoy geothermal features such as bubbling mudpots and steaming pools and vents.

Bumpass Hell.

of enterprises – one traditional, one contraband – is typical of Trinity. Trinity County's population breaks into two groups – true locals, and those who have come here since the end of the 1960s. Generally, old-timers tend to be conservative, the newcomers less so – but both groups share an individualism and a jealous regard for the natural environment. While Trinity often votes Republican, it also displays an abiding sensitivity to ecological issues. This is less ideology than simple self-interest.

Many residents hunt for their own food and draw water directly from springs, rivers, and creeks. (The bedrock of granite and serpentine is too impermeable for aquifers.) So when the county's residents tried to stop the federal government from spraying Trinity's woodlands with an herbicide many feared would end up in water supplies, no politicians – Democrat or Republican – openly opposed the grassroots effort. This closeness to one another and to the land breeds a native suspicion of outsiders.

THE CASCADES

The **Cascades** run almost due north from California to Canada's British Columbia. In California, the range stretches 40 to 50 miles (70 to 80km) across. Farther north, glaciers dominate the range. Here in California, only the highest peaks bear these relics from the Ice Age. The dominant snow-capped Cascade peaks are young volcanoes; some, like Washington's Mount St Helens, are still active. Unlike the Klamaths, the higher Cascade peaks present a sharply vertical profile of high conical peaks surrounded by lower mountains of the 4,500 to 5,000ft (1,400 to 1,500-meter) range.

There are few better places to study volcanology than **Lassen Volcanic National Park ❸**. The park is reached via State Highway 36 stretching east from **Red Bluff**, State Highway 44 east from Redding, or State Highway 89 south from State Highway 299 beyond Burney. Backpackers will find hot springs and geysers throughout the huge park. Lassen Peak (elevation 10,457ft/3,187 meters) marks the southern terminus f the Cascade Range, and is one of only wo Cascade volcanoes to have erupted n the 20th century: Mount Lassen blew ts lid in 1914.

Much of 108,000-acre (43,700-hec-are) Lassen Park lies within a cal-lera, the giant crater left by the collapse of an ancient volcano. Out of his caldera, Lassen Peak later rose o dominate this expanse of wilder-iess, but there are small volcanoes n the park as well; check out the iubbling mudpots of **Bumpass Hell**, a steaming valley of active geother-nal pools and vents. There are lakes, ivers, meadows, pine forests, and ine trails for hiking and camping.

Just east of Lassen Park lies **Eagle Lake**, an anomalous, highly alkaline iody of water straddling the Eastern Sierras on one side, sage desert on the ther, and home to a splendid species of iversize Eagle Lake rainbow trout found iowhere else in the state. As the name if the lake implies, osprey, golden eagle, ind bald eagle – the national bird – are iften seen skimming this lake for unsus-iecting fish. Nearby Lake Almanor,

a massive man-made reservoir, is a resort area with plentiful opportunities for waterskiing, sailing, lake trolling (slowly dragging a fishing line through deep water), and sunbathing.

All the mountains of this region are notorious for their massive deer herds, stealthy cougar (aptly called "mountain lions," but smaller and much more solitary than their handsome African cousins), black bear, and North Ameri-ca's only antelope, the pronghorn.

Northwest of Lassen, near the town of Weed, an ancient volcano named **Mount Shasta** ❹ (14,162 ft/4,317 meters) and the southern point of the volcanic Cascade Range that extends all the way to Alaska, stands soli-tary sentinel at the head of the Sac-ramento Valley. The glacier-capped peak is a moderately difficult all-day climb in the summer, with climbers offered a sweeping view of the Cen-tral Valley to the south, the Trinities to the southwest, and the Sierras to the southeast. In the winter, the moun-tain is buried in snow, but still open to enthusiastic skiers.

ⓘ **Fact**

The far northern corner of the state, still partly populated by Native American tribes, is home to the legendary Sasquatch, or, as more modern locals call him, Bigfoot. This huge, reclusive, ape-like creature, whose red fur camouflages him among the towering redwood trees and river canyons, has been sighted many times, but the scientific community says that it is either a hoax or wrongly identified animals.

Mount Lassen.

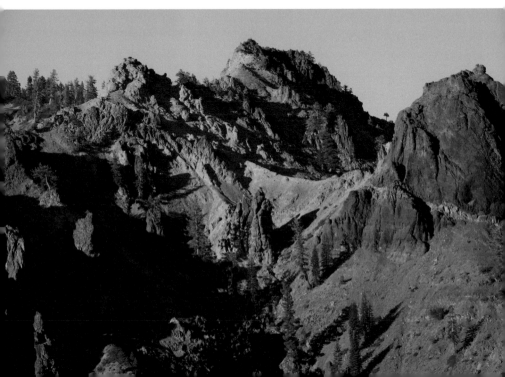

Most of the California Cascades fall within two national forests, **Lassen** and **Shasta**. At Shasta's southern boundary lies another prime wilderness, **Plumas National Forest** ❺. These upland woods cover the northern end of the Sierra Nevada and cradle the **Feather River**, one of the state's best-known wild streams.

Between Redding and Burney, a distance of 53 miles (85km), State Highway 299 climbs into a gently undulating country of ranches and volcanic debris. The red rocks that litter the landscape and pastures to the south of the road were deposited by hot mud flows from the eruption of Mount Maidu 7 million years ago. This posthumously named volcano collapsed to form the caldera within Lassen Park. Just beyond the lumber and livestock marketing center of **Burney** is the State Highway 89 intersection.

FALLS AND FORESTS

Lava tunnel at Lava Beds National Monument.

About 6 miles (10km) north of Burney is pretty, moss-covered 129ft (39-meter) **Burney Falls**. East of Burney

is **Fall River Mills**, and from here to the Nevada border, State Highway 299 runs across the basins and fault-block mountains of the **Modoc Plateau**, a lava plain similar to the Columbia Plateau to the north. For a large section of its route, the highway follows the deep canyon of the Pit River, the plateau's main drainage. The plateau extends over some 13,000 sq miles (34,000 sq km), taking in the whole of Modoc County and parts of Lassen, Shasta, and Siskiyou counties. Vestiges of volcanism make up much of the **Modoc National Forest**, a wonderful green expanse covering 1.97 million acres (800,000 hectares). A pristine example of this volcanic past is **Glass Mountain**, a huge flow of obsidian lava on the forest's western edge.

But the main focus of any geological tour of this region has to be **Lava Beds National Monument** ❻ (www.nps.gov). A more impressive example of basalt flows cannot be found than this moon-like landscape of lava flows, columns, and deep, dark caves.

⊙ OPEN RANGE

Visiting motorists should know that Trinity County, like most of California's north, has "open range." Cattle have never been a major part of the economy here, and open range is mostly a symbolic vestige of the region's frontier heritage. Open range means that cattle wander beyond their owner's unfenced rangelands. It also means that any driver whose vehicle strikes a cow has just purchased damaged livestock. Hikers must be careful to stay away from creek bottoms on which gold prospectors have staked claims. Likewise, those who come across a patch of marijuana should leave quickly before they are either shot at by its owner or arrested on suspicion of being its growers.

Mount Shasta, southern point of the Cascade Range.

California State Capitol.

CENTRAL VALLEY

Gold-seekers flocked here in the late 1800s, followed by thousands of Dust Bowl families during the Great Depression. Today, this important agricultural region is home to the state's capital, and many recreation areas and historic Gold Rush-era communities.

A large, flat basin in the heart of California, the 450-mile (720km) -long Central Valley encompasses California's capital city of Sacramento, a vast agricultural region, and the historic Gold Country.

The region first really became known to the world in 1848, when James Marshall discovered gold in the Sierra foothills, sparking a mass migration to the Mother Lode, California's richest mineral vein. Tucked just below the fork of the Sacramento and American rivers, Sacramento flourished as an arrival point for miners heading to the Sierra Nevada foothills to pan for gold. The Gold Rush is still a major part of the region's identity, especially in Sacramento's Old Town and towns along the Mother Lode that have been expensively restored to their former pioneer glory.

Today, the Central Valley's main source of wealth is agriculture. The San Joaquin valley is the lifeline of California's farming industry, producing more than half of the state's annual $40 billion plus in farm goods. Fresno County alone accounts for a significant portion of that, making it the number-one farming county in America.

SACRAMENTO

Located about two hours northeast of San Francisco and nestled in the middle of the Central Valley, the area surrounding **Sacramento ❶** is home to spacious tree-lined roads, expansive shopping malls, countless industrial parks, suburban tracts, and a tangle of multi-lane highways that joins it all together. The city itself boasts the state capitol and fascinating historic museums, and continues to develop rapidly as more residents from San Francisco and Los Angeles come to Sacramento in search of affordable housing.

In contrast to its glamorous coastal neighbor, San Francisco, Sacramento is a blazing furnace in midsummer,

Main attractions
Old Sacramento
California State Capitol
Sutter's Fort
Mark Twain's Cabin
Mercer Caverns
Auburn State Recreation Area
Gold panning

Maps on pages
168, 170

Governor's Mansion, downtown Sacramento.

with temperatures often passing 100°F (38°C) for days at a time. But the weather can still be pleasant, as humidity is low, it seldom rains for long, and the prevailing wind is a marine breeze from San Francisco Bay that cools the nights. In the winter, the city, which lays low in the 150-mile (240km) -long Sacramento Valley, is a resting bed for thick tule fog (a type of ground fog peculiar to the Central Valley), which, like the summer sun, can last for many weeks.

OLD SACRAMENTO

Beneath the imposing facade of Sacramento's mirrored-glass office buildings and slightly away from all the traffic lies the nostalgic neighborhood of **Old Sacramento** Ⓐ, a 28-acre (11-hectare) historic district along the Sacramento waterfront. Established in 1849, it was here that steamers from San Francisco once let off passengers headed for the gold fields. Today, wooden buildings, horse-drawn carriages, and cobblestone streets convey a distinct image of the Old West. The *Delta King* is a 1920s paddle steamboat that once regularly shuttled passengers between Sacramento and San Francisco on the Sacramento River. Today, it's permanently moored in Sacramento and operated as a hotel and restaurant.

Once the western terminus of the Pony Express overland mail service, Sacramento was also the western terminus of the Transcontinental Railroad. The station is now part of the **California State Railroad Museum** (125 I Street; tel: 916-323-9280; www.californiarailroad.museum; daily 10am–5pm), which delights kids and adults alike with its 50-plus restored engines.

The **Sacramento History Museum** is housed in a reproduction of the 1854 City Hall and Water Works building. Exhibits focused on the Sacramento region reflect on everyday life in the Native American period, celebrate the Pony Express, and commemorate the role Chinese immigrants played in the Gold Rush.

Another important collection is at the **Crocker Art Museum** Ⓑ (216 O Street; tel: 916-808-7000; www.crockerartmuseum.org; Tue–Sun 10am–5pm, until 9pm Thu). The oldest art museum west of the Mississippi River, it boasts one of the state's premier collections of Californian art, including works from the Gold Rush era to the present. Stop off at the **Visitor Center** (1608 I Street; tel: 916-226-5783) for a complete list of historic sites in Old Sacramento.

DOWNTOWN

Downtown Sacramento is dominated by the nicely restored **California State Capitol** Ⓒ (between 10th and 16th and L and N streets). Daily tours of the capitol building are offered on the hour (tel: 916-324-0333; daily 9am–5pm).

The capitol is surrounded by the 40-acre (16-hectare) **Capitol Park**, a manicured arboretum that has a vast collection of California flora

and examples of plants from different climates and continents. Not far from Capitol Park, the **California Museum** Ⓓ (1020 O Street; tel: 916-653-7524; www.californiamuseum.org; Tue–Sat 10am–5pm, Sun noon–5pm) is a fascinating mix of treasures from the California State Archives and cutting-edge multimedia exhibits, all designed to educate adults and children about California's history and influence on the world.

A 400-seat IMAX **theater**, next to the **Convention Center**, is another popular attraction. Also, while downtown, don't miss the handsome **Governor's Mansion** (corner of 6th and H streets), an 1877 Victorian building, complete with Italian marble fireplaces and gold-framed French mirrors, where 13 California governors lived between 1903 and 1967. Governor Jerry Brown moved into the newly refurbished mansion in 2015 making him the first governor to live there in five decades. The last governor to inhabit the mansion was Ronald Reagan, who stayed there for three months.

Sacramento's Old Town; migrants from San Francisco passed through here en route to the gold fields in the 19th century.

Actors in period dress in Old Sacramento.

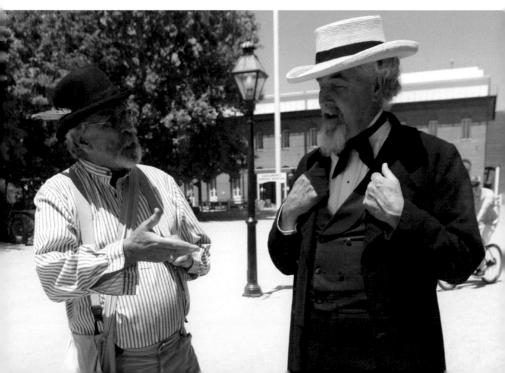

SUTTER'S FORT

Now almost overtaken by suburbs, **Sutter's Fort Ⓔ** (2701 L Street; tel: 916-445-4422; www.suttersfort.org; daily 10am–5pm) was once one of the most important in the West. It was an employee of John Sutter's who discovered gold in 1848, but 11 years earlier Sutter had already established the fort as a rest stop and refueling station for immigrants crossing the frontier from the east. The present site, which includes a prison and a bakery, has been reconstructed to give one of the most authentic pictures of pioneer life in the state.

SACRAMENTO RIVER DELTA

When the temperature gets too hot to handle, take the cue of thousands of recreational houseboaters, water-skiers, anglers, and sailors, and head south on State Highway 5 or 99 toward the **Sacramento River Delta**, where hundreds of miles of interconnected river channels percolate slowly toward San Francisco Bay and the Pacific Ocean.

This river country contains hundreds of islands; much of the area is accessible only by water. Still, even landlocked car passengers can choose from a variety of charming olde-worlde towns such as **Walnut Grove** and Locke.

Locke, created by Chinese laborers brought in to build the railroads, has a porticoed street with wooden sidewalks that is right out of the Old West. The deepwater port of **Stockton**, the "Gateway to the Delta," has 1860s homes, the **Haggin Museum** (www.hagginmuseum.org; Sat–Sun noon–5pm, Wed–Fri 1.30–5pm) which is full of local history, and several wineries.

SAN JOAQUIN VALLEY

Though its name is often mistakenly applied to California's entire Central Valley, the San Joaquin comprises just the southern two-thirds of this region. It follows the course of the **San Joaquin River**, flowing south to north to the Sacramento–San Joaquin Delta where both rivers empty into San Francisco Bay.

Tour guide at the reconstructed Sutter's Fort State Historic Park.

It doesn't take long to see that the valley is the lifeline of California. Interstate 5, running the length of it, is the main link between Los Angeles and the Bay Area, and the east–west routes to Lake Tahoe and the Sierras all cross the valley. The freeways are full of trucks piled high with tomatoes and ripe golden melons, or crates of canned peaches.

Recently, with substantial growth in population, the area's cities have experienced a boom as commercial and manufacturing centers, but employment in the valley is most closely tied to farming and rainfall. The San Joaquin Valley's soil, covering more than a million irrigated acres (405,000 hectares), supports some of the most productive farming in the world.

It is the abundance of that most precious of the state's resources – water – that makes the San Joaquin Valley a recreational as well as an agricultural heartland. Aside from the Sacramento River Delta and the mammoth irrigation projects it supports, several great rivers flow through the area – the San Joaquin, the **Stanislaus**, the **Tuolumne**, the **Merced**, the **Kings,** and, farther south, the **Kern**. Most are renowned for outstanding – and occasionally terrifying – stretches of whitewater rafting. This sport is for serious enthusiasts only, but there are gentler stretches of water where the faint-hearted will also feel at home.

LODI TO MERCED

In the northern part of the Central Valley and just 37 miles (60km) south of Sacramento, Lodi is recognized as a major center of wine production, especially Zinfandel. Robert Mondavi grew up here, and his well-known Woodbridge winery is located nearby in Woodbridge.

Another 45 minutes south is **Modesto ❷.** Like much of California, Modesto is a creation of Leland Stanford's Central Pacific Railroad. The Tuolumne River runs almost unnoticed through the southern fringes of town, but an early-20th-century steel arch along the main thoroughfare

Sutter's Fort, Sacramento.

Farmland in the San Joaquin Valley is used to grow grapes, citrus fruits, vegetables, and nuts.

promotes the town's virtues: "Water, Wealth, Contentment, Health." As in most of the valley, food production is king – here you can find an almond exchange, a mushroom farm, a cheese processor, and more local wineries.

Halfway between Modesto and Fresno, **Merced** is a major access point to Yosemite. The biggest attraction Merced County can call its own may be **Castle Air Force Base**, where lumbering B-52s provide a somewhat chilling background to the **Castle Air Museum's** (www.castleairmuseum.org; daily 9am–4pm) collection of vintage fighters.

FRESNO

The sleeping giant of central California, **Fresno ❸** is the only community in the United States within little more than an hour's drive of three national parks. From a simple train station by the edge of a wheat field, Fresno has become a city with 11 freeway exits and rows of high-rises. The financial and cultural as well as service and commercial center of the San Joaquin Valley, it is also as ethnically diverse, with large Mexican, Asian, Armenian, and Basque communities. Cultural institutions include the **Community Theater** and the **Fresno Philharmonic Orchestra**.

For people with children, **Roeding Park**, right off State Highway 99 in west Fresno, features a number of family amusements – a zoo, a Playland with rides, and Storyland, a quaint walk-through village where plaster fairytale figures tell their stories. **Woodward Park** in central Fresno has a Japanese Garden and a bird sanctuary.

Perhaps the most bizarre attraction is **Forestiere Underground Gardens** (tel: 559-271-0734; www.underground gardens.com, visit website for tour times). The gardens were once the beloved domicile of sculptor-horticulturist Baldasare Forestiere, a Sicilian immigrant, who single-handedly carved out the maze of 100 rooms, passageways, and courtyards over a period of 40 years.

GOLD COUNTRY

The Gold Rush may have ended, but it wasn't because they ran out of gold. They just ran out of the gold lying near the top of the ground. As the holes got deeper and more dangerous, the work got harder, slower, and more expensive, until finally it was no longer cost-efficient to dig.

Geologists say there is at least as much gold in the Mother Lode today as was taken out in the past 100-odd years. Latter-day gold miners say the seven million lbs (3.2 million kg) extracted by the old-timers was only 10 percent of the wealth that nature had deposited there. Either way, there is a good deal left – and quite a few people are looking for it. Modern mining operations dig deeper and deeper into the Sierra with automated machinery, but there are still the rough-hewn old-timers who crouch by mountain streams, squinting for the glimmer of gold flakes in shallow tin pans.

Potential prospectors seeking their fortunes in gold can check out one of the Gold Country panning exploration outfitters like Gold Country Adventures, (18170 Main Street, Jamestown; tel: 209-984-4653; www.goldprospecting.com) to learn how to pan for gold. They claim to find gold on every trip of two or more hours – the best part is finders' keepers – you keep all the gold you find. They also have a fascinating museum on the premises.

There's another rush going on in the Gold Country foothills from Mariposa to Nevada City, but it's real estate, not valuable minerals, that is at stake. Travelers on State Highway 49, the Gold Country's main highway, are likely to see more real-estate signs than ghost towns. The modern miner now competes with housing developers – not claim jumpers – for land. Still, for the most part, it is tourism, not treasure, that plays a key role in the area's resources.

SONORA

Sonora ❹, named for the Mexican state from which many of its first '49ers came, is a city and one that

San Joaquin Valley has some of the world's most productive farmland.

⊙ CALIFORNIA'S MIDWEST

Stuck between the magnificent California coast and the awe-inspiring Sierras, the San Joaquin Valley suffers the kind of image problem more associated with the Midwest than the Golden State. That's because, in many ways, it is the Midwest. Perhaps as many as 500,000 so-called "Okies" – the Dust Bowl victims of the Great Depression that gave life to John Steinbeck's The Grapes of Wrath – migrated here from Oklahoma and other places in the Midwest. Like ants on a honey trail, they piled into overloaded flivvers and streamed west on old US Route 66, through the chalk-dry Mojave Desert, past "bum barricades" and the abuse heaped on them by native Californians.

What became of them? One-eighth of the current California population – or nearly 3.75 million residents – claim Okie ancestry, and the core of that gritty, family-based community is still here in the heart of the San Joaquin. Stop by any town in San Joaquin Valley and, as one Dust Bowl survivor said himself, "You might as well be in Tulsa or Little Rock or Amarillo... Same music, same values, same churches, same politics." The music influence is felt in Sacramento too: The Dixieland Jazz Jubilee, held each May in Old Sacramento, is the world's largest celebration of Dixieland jazz, featuring more than 100 performers from around the world.

may be losing a struggle with the real-estate hustlers. But the houses and shopping centers have sprung up because Sonora is as beautiful as it was during the Gold Rush – and its quaint Downtown has remained true to the miners' spirit.

In the 1870s, there was a pocket mine at the north end of Sonora where the operators found a vein of nearly pure gold and recovered, they say, $160,000 worth of gold in one day. It was part of *La Veta Madre*, otherwise known as "**The Mother Lode**," from which the legends sprang. It is the kind of story that still keeps miners at work today, toiling in the dark tunnels.

COLUMBIA

A real gem of Tuolumne County these days is the town of **Columbia**. Just a few minutes north of Sonora and just off State Highway 49, this old town has been restored as the **Columbia State Historic Park ❺** (tel: 209-588-9128; www.parks.ca.gov). Columbia once had a population of 15,000, 50 saloons, competing daily

newspapers, and at least one church. Nearly $90 million in gold was mined there over a 20-year period. Much of restored Columbia is closed to cars, but the easy layout of the town makes it well worthwhile parking and walking around. The best sites are the Wells Fargo Express Office, the old schoolhouse (used until 1937), and the old city hotel.

Around Columbia, as in many of the Gold Country towns, there are several rock or gold shops whose proprietors may be willing to show visitors where to look for gold and perhaps even teach them how to mine. There are even tour companies that will set up trips to local mines.

CALAVERAS COUNTY

Back on State Highway 49, still headed north, a sign indicates the way to the summit of **Jackass Hill**. It is named for the animals so central to gold prospecting, and it is the place where Mark Twain lived in 1864. Twain's **cabin** has been reconstructed around the original hearth. During

Vintage airplane at Castle Air Museum.

he time Twain lived in the cabin, he wrote one of his most famous yarns, *The Celebrated Jumping Frog of Calaveras County*. The actual jumping frogs were supposed to have been a bit to the north in **Angels Camp ⑥**, where they can still be found.

From the Angels Camp area, a detour leads up into the mountains to the town of **Murphys**, a Gold Rush period settlement far enough off the track to be a natural museum. The impressive **Mercer Caverns ⑦** (www. mercercaverns.com), which are well worth a visit, are in this area. You descend 208 steps to see giant stalactites, stalagmites, and other cave formations formed by the dripping of limestone over centuries. Discovered in 1885, the cave is especially known for its rare frost-like aragonite floserri, which won a Grand prize at the 1900 Paris World Exposition. Farther up State Highway 4 is **Calaveras Big Trees State Park**, with magnificent sequoia trees.

San Andreas is another town whose present is a triumph of development interests, but whose past is alive with romantic echoes. Black Bart, a real stagecoach bandit, was tried here in 1883 for some of the 28 robberies he allegedly committed. Bart, a San Franciscan with expensive tastes and little income, embarked on a series of polite, bloodless robberies of the gold-laden stages. His shotgun was always unloaded and no one was ever hurt, but he served six years in San Quentin's rough prison. Then he disappeared.

In good weather, the drive from San Andreas to **West Point ⑧** on the Mountain Ranch and Railroad Flat roads is beautiful. A few of the 500 local mine shafts are now used as a site for ore-crushing, and even welcome visitors. If you stand in the mouth of a mine shaft, even in midsummer, you can see your breath condensing in the cold air seeping up from thousands of feet beneath the ground. Modern techniques of deep-rock mining differ little from those used by the '49ers. The gold pan and

⊘ Tip

In December and January, dense tule fog – a thick ground fog – blankets the area around the Sacramento and San Joaquin valleys for days at a time, making driving hazardous.

Playland in Roeding Park.

sluice boxes used by weekend miners are essentially the same tools that were used 100 years ago.

From West Point, it is possible to loop back west to **Mokelumne Hill**, a town once so rich in gold that its claims were limited to 16 sq ft (1.5 sq meters) in size. According to legend, the lust for wealth ran so high that there was a murder a week here for more than four months. On a more benign note, Mokelumne Hill is the site of the founding of the **E. Clampus Vitus Society**, a group devoted to good deeds and good times. The society is still around and active, and generally has an entry in any local parade or fair.

From **Sutter Creek** to Grass Valley, about 75 miles (120km), the countryside surrounding State Highway 49 is mostly a commuter suburb of Sacramento. For a more authentic look at the Old West, drive east to **Chaw'se Indian Grinding Rock State Historic Park** ❾ near the town of Jackson, one of the largest Native American sites in the United States. The park and its museum are a celebration of

the contributions made by the Miwok tribe.

PLACERVILLE, COLOMA, AND GRASS VALLEY

At the junction of State Highways 49 and 50 is **Placerville** ❿ once called Hangtown because of its chosen method of execution. Placerville was the nexus of wagon, mail, Pony Express, and telegraph routes, and consequently a busy and exciting place. Now it may be the only town in America with its own gold mine. The **Gold Bug Mine** (www.goldbugpark.org), north of town, is located in a public park where there are several other mines, and is open to visitors for inspection.

North of Placerville on State Highway 49 is **Coloma**, the birthplace of the Gold Rush. The **Marshall Gold Discovery State Historic Park** ⓫ is now at the spot where, in 1848, James Marshall was building a waterway for John Sutter's lumber mill and was distracted by something glittering in the water. The state has reconstructed the mill, though not exactly

Panning for gold at Columbia State Historic Park.

at the same place, since the **American River** has changed its course in the past century. Daily interpretive programs are held at the replica sawmill, and visitors can try their own hand at panning for gold.

At the junction of State Highway 49 and busy Interstate 80 is **Auburn** ⑫, home to the Auburn State Recreation Area. Located south of Interstate 80 on two forks of the American River, it stretches from Auburn to Colfax. Here you can hike, fish, camp, pan for gold, and ride whitewater rapids – some 30 private outfitters are licensed to offer whitewater trips in the area. When you tire of river recreation, visit the **Placer County Museum** (daily 10am–4pm) in Auburn; with its collections of Native American artifacts as well as gold-mining paraphernalia, it is counted as one of the best cultural attractions in the mountains. Nearby is the quirky Old Town Auburn **Firehouse**.

Auburn is a good place to jump off for a visit to Lake Tahoe (up Interstate 80) with a return via State Highway 20 near **Emigrant Gap**. Highway 20, the old Tahoe–Pacific Highway, is one of California's great drives. It rejoins State Highway 49 in the Nevada City–Grass Valley area.

Grass Valley ⑬ was once the center of the deep mines, and there are several splendid places to get a sense of what they were like. Some of them, including the **North Star**, have shafts that go hundreds of feet below sea level, though these shafts are now closed and flooded. The **Grass Valley Museum** (tel: 530-272-4725; www.saint-josephsculturalcenter.org/museum; Wed–Sat 12.30–3.30pm) in the town of Grass Valley is good for local history. **Empire Mine State Park**, east of town, is the site of the oldest and richest mine in California, which once produced no less than $100 million worth of gold before it was closed down in the mid-20th century.

Grass Valley is now very much in the 21st century and a center of high-technology industry, most notably the manufacture of equipment for television broadcasting.

Columbia State Historic Park.

Statue of a Pony Express rider in Sacramento, once the western terminus of the Pony Express overland mail service.

⊘ PANNING FOR GOLD

The Marshall Gold Discovery State Historic Park (310 Back Street, Coloma; tel: 530-622-3470; www.parks.ca.gov) is a great place to try your hand at gold panning. Sign up for a 45-minute gold-panning lesson to learn panning basics in park troughs, and then purchase your own pan and head to the South Fork of the American River. You can keep any gold you find.

There are also a number of other historic parks, ghost towns, and private camps in California where gold mining is possible, including the **Auburn State Recreation Area**, Amador County Park's Volcano Memorial Park, Bodie State Historic Park, San Joaquin River Gorge, and Jimtown Mining Camp. Depending on the site, you can borrow a pan or buy one.

⊙ Tip

For those who don't want to spend all their time meditating on history, Coloma is a pleasant place for a raft trip. A number of companies offer one-day and longer trips rafting down the American River, or check www.coloma.com.

NEVADA CITY

Nevada City is as old-fashioned as Grass Valley is up-to-date. It is the kind of place that attracted city people early. They busily converted the old factories and miners' stores into restaurants, museums, antiques stores, cool boutiques, and theaters, many of which have now been restored. There are a couple of pleasant bars, and the **National Hotel** (www.thenationalhotel.com), which is steeped in history, puts up overnight visitors in rooms furnished with antiques; there is a nice streetscape view from the second floor balcony. The town retains the feel of the old West.

Ten miles (16km) north of Nevada City is a large state historic park at the old **Malakoff Diggins** ⓮, a place that generated one of the very earliest pieces of environmental legislation. Visitors to the Malakoff mine can see the effects of hydraulic mining, a method of gold extraction in which high-powered streams of water were directed from cannons at the side of the mountain.

This method was highly effective but it devastated the mountain, and waterways were clogged with mud as far away as San Francisco Bay. The technique was banned as early as 1884 but the scars, which have been only slightly healed by time, are still grimly awesome.

It's an hour's drive from Nevada City to **Downieville**, which marks the end of this tour of the Gold Country. The country here is higher, cooler, and much less crowded than further south. From **Camptonville**, midway along the route from Nevada City, the pretty **Henness Pass Road** veers off into the mountains. In good weather it is a lovely side trip and there are a number of campgrounds a few miles toward the pass. Downieville itself is picture-perfect. It is a remote place hemmed in by steep hillsides, with a population of under a thousand people. Despite its size and seclusion, however, there are a few places for visitors to have a meal or relax for the night, taking in the sweet mountain air.

Pleasantly old-fashioned Nevada City.

Whitewater rafting on the Truckee River.

LAKE TAHOE & THE SIERRA NEVADA

There's a reason why both Californians and out-of-state visitors gush about Tahoe ski slopes and jaw-dropping views in Yosemite – they're just about as good as it gets. You'll never get bored, either – from skiing and hiking to camping and boating, the Sierras offer endless opportunities for outdoor adventure.

Lake Tahoe straddles both California and Nevada, and is a major tourist attraction for both states. Surrounded by the Sierra Nevada mountain range, the lake is a haven for nature lovers and sports enthusiasts in winter and summer.

LAKE TAHOE

"The lake burst upon us," wrote Mark Twain in *Roughing It*, "a noble sheet of blue water lifted 6,300 feet above the level of the sea, and walled in by a rim of snowclad mountain peaks... I thought it must surely be the fairest picture the whole earth affords."

Many would agree with this picture of **Lake Tahoe ❶**, located high in the Sierra Nevada about 50 miles (80km) southwest of Reno, Nevada. The crystal-blue lake, its 71-mile (114km) shoreline, and the surrounding region attract outdoor enthusiasts year-round, who come for skiing, snowboarding, hiking, biking, watersports, and lakeshore fun. The outdoor attractions do have competition for visitors' attention, however: roulette wheels and craps tables sing their sirens' call out from South Lake Tahoe casinos.

GETTING THERE

Getting to Lake Tahoe is easy and relatively inexpensive from San Francisco. The drive takes four to five hours in good weather and light traffic. On Friday

nights the weekend exodus from the San Francisco Bay area begins streaming up Interstate 80 or US 50 toward the lake, and traffic can be slow. In the winter, carry chains in case of ice and snow. Package tours are easy to find in the large cities, and can include transportation, ski lift tickets, accommodation, and food vouchers.

One delicious place that many locals make a point of stopping at on the way to Tahoe is Ikeda's California Country Market (13500 Lincoln Way, Auburn; tel: 530 885-4243; www.ikedas.com). Ikeda's

⊙ Main attractions
Lake Tahoe
Yosemite National Park
Sequoia and Kings Canyon
  national parks
Bodie State Historic Park
Devils Postpile National
  Monument

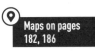

Maps on pages
182, 186

Lake Tahoe.

Lake Tahoe and the Sierra Nevada

0   20 miles
0   20 km

is famous for their freshly-baked pies that range from the traditional pecan, apple, and cherry to seasonal ones like wild blackberry, pumpkin, and apricot. They also carry a wide selection of groceries and fresh fruit and veggies, making it ideal for stocking up before heading to the mountains. Their restaurant serves breakfast, sandwiches, burgers and milkshakes.

TAHOE IN WINTER

Outdoor recreation is the lake area's lifeblood. In winter, that means downhill and cross-country skiing, and lots of snowboarding. If you don't care for skiing, the outdoors can still be the central focus. To get off the beaten track, **Lake Tahoe Adventures** (tel: 800-865-4679; www.laketahoeadventures.com) leads snowmobile tours through meadows, lakes, and mountain forest. Wilderness dinners, weddings, and overnights in igloos can be arranged. To take the wintry chill off, try a hot soak at **David Walley's Hot Springs Resort** (tel: 775-782-8155; www. davidwalleys-resort.com), located 12 miles (19km) east of South Lake Tahoe on Foothill Road in Genoa.

TAHOE IN SUMMER

When the snow has gone, rent in-line skates or a bicycle to explore the local roads, or a mountain bike to blaze down the bare ski runs at Squaw Valley. Several parks and reserves have well-marked hiking trails. The lake offers great fishing, as well as jet-skiing, waterskiing, and kayaking. There is usually good river rafting on the **Truckee River**. Check the local tourist office for information on operators and rental shops.

A great way to see Lake Tahoe is to take a ride on one of the large vessels that cruise around the lake all year round, which offer lunch, dinner, and dancing cruises, as well as sightseeing trips along the shoreline and through spectacular **Emerald Bay ❷**, an isolated, tree-lined wilderness tucked into the southwest corner of the lake.

Hikers and backpackers usually head for **Desolation Wilderness ❸**, a lake-studded area located west of Tahoe's Emerald Bay. A wilderness permit must be obtained for backpacking in Desolation Wilderness – it's a popular place that often fills to capacity in summer. The 165-mile (265km) **Tahoe Rim Trail** offers magnificent views and can be accessed from several points around the lake. The **Granite Peak** area is also good for backpacking, and the extremely pretty **Emerald Bay State Park**, as well as **DL Bliss** and **Sugar Pine Point** state parks, are excellent for short walks and picnics.

On any summer weekend, joggers and bicyclists take to the roads ringing the lake. The 75-mile (120km) circle makes a strenuous one-day bike ride or a leisurely two-day trip.

SOUTH LAKE TAHOE

The busiest part of the lake and just a stone's throw from Nevada, the town of South Lake Tahoe has both ski resorts and casinos. The latter can come in handy for skiers in the evening – most offer inexpensive all-you-can-eat buffet dinners to lure customers. Gambling is, of course, the area's biggest and most lucrative business.

YOSEMITE

Absolutely magnificent, **Yosemite National Park ❹** is one of America's most visited national parks, drawing over 5 million visitors each year to see its striking granite rock formations, pouring waterfalls, and lovely groves and meadows.

To its original inhabitants, the indigenous Ahwahneechee, Yosemite ("yo-seh-mih-tee") Valley was a holy place. Because of its isolation, the tribe managed to keep its mountain paradise a secret from outsiders until 1851, a full year after California attained statehood, when the US Cavalry arrived and herded the tribe members across the Sierras to a barren reservation near Mono Lake. As with much of the American West, subjugation of the Indians paved the way for settlement. During the decade following its "discovery," Yosemite Valley was fenced,

Snowboarding at one of Lake Tahoe's seven ski resorts.

Hiking the Mist Trail, which takes in two waterfalls and the combined view of Nevada Falls, Liberty Cap, and the back of Half Dome.

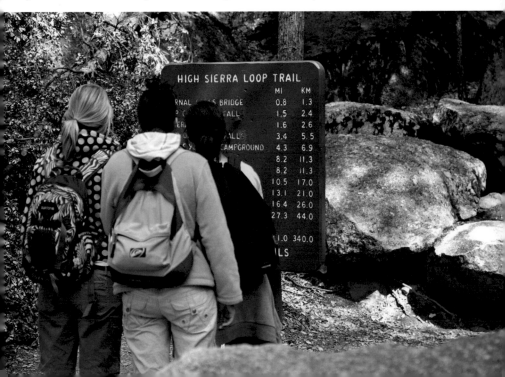

Tip

Another way to see the area is from above. Reno Tahoe Helicopters (tel: 530-544-2211; www.reno tahoehelicopters.com) take off from the Lake Tahoe airport in South Lake Tahoe. The Heavenly Gondola goes 2.5 miles (4km) up the mountain for views and trails departing from an observation deck. The Squaw Valley Cable Car also offers great panoramas year-round.

Hiking in the Lake Tahoe area.

farmed, and logged by homesteaders. Today, 94 percent of the park's 747,956 acres (302,687 hectares) is designated wilderness.

YOSEMITE VALLEY

Although the valley comprises only 8 sq miles (21 sq km) of the park's 1,169-sq-mile (3,027-sq-km) area, it plays host to more than 90 percent of all Yosemite's overnight visitors.

But there's a reason why the crowds come in such numbers. From the Yosemite Valley, many well-known sites can be seen, including Half Dome and Rainbow Falls. If you visit during a busy period, book your lodgings six months to one year in advance and be prepared for the Yosemite Valley to be very full.

Nowhere else in the world are there so many big waterfalls in such a small area, including 2,425ft (739-meter) **Yosemite Falls Ⓐ**, the highest in North America. When Ice Age glaciers scoured out an 8-mile (13km) -long, 1-mile (1.5km) -wide Yosemite Valley, they left behind several smaller hanging valleys on either side high but not dry conduits for free-leaping torrents whose very names suggest their infinite variety: **Ribbon, Bridalveil, Silver Strand, Staircase, Sentinel, Lehamite, Vernal, Nevada, Illilouette**. Visitors should note, however, that falls are often dry out of season, from late July through fall.

As the prehistoric ice melted and retreated, it exposed the colossal building blocks of the Sierra Nevada, shaped and polished into scenery on a grand scale – **El Capitan Ⓑ, Cathedral Rock, Three Brothers, Royal Arches, Clouds Rest**. In the daredevil world of technical rock climbing, El Capitan is a major challenge.

Roads in the east end of the valley near **Mirror Lake** have been restricted to shuttle buses, bicycles, and pedestrians. You can arrange to take a guided horseback trip at the valley stables near **Yosemite Village Ⓒ** (the first large developed area on the Yosemite loop road). Bicycles may be rented at the village and at **Yosemite Valley Lodge** (tel: 855-600-8964), and several bikeway trails make two-wheeled

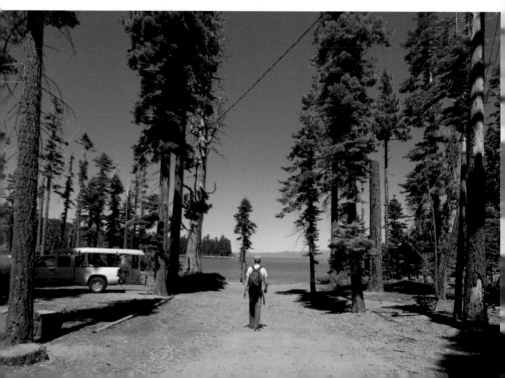

travel the most efficient choice of loco-motion. Lodgings runs the gamut from inexpensive cabins at the village to the palatial suite atop the Majestic Yosemite Hotel, with Yosemite Valley Lodge somewhere in the middle.

GLACIER POINT

To the south, State Highway 41 climbs 9 miles (15km) to **Chinquapin** junction, where a 15-mile (25km) paved road departs for **Glacier Point Ⓓ**. From this famed viewpoint, 3,200ft (980 meters) above the floor of Yosemite Valley, the entire park comes into unforgettable, stomach-clutching focus. No less compelling is the 80-mile (130km) vista to the east and south, a panorama of lakes, canyons, waterfalls, and the rugged peaks of Yosemite's High Sierra. Close at hand are the granite steps of the **Giant's Staircase Ⓔ**, where the Vernal and Nevada falls drop the raging waters of the **Merced River** 320 and 594ft (98 and 181 meters), respectively.

From Glacier Point, **Half Dome Ⓕ** is the most prominent landmark, a great solitary stone thumb thrusting skyward. What became of Half Dome's other half? In fact, the dome never had another half of solid rock, only slabs of granite on the sheer north face that were peeled away like onion skin by advancing Ice Age glaciers.

At the height of glaciation, 250,000 years ago, Glacier Point itself lay under 700ft (200 meters) of ice, and interpretive markers explain how the 2,000ft (600-meter)-thick Merced and Tenaya glaciers ground down from the high country to merge near Half Dome and hollow out vast Yosemite Valley. The mighty glacier filled the valley to its brim, and extended all the way down the Merced canyon to **El Portal**, 15 miles (24km) to the west.

MARIPOSA GROVE

Five miles (8km) south of **Wawona**, just inside the park's southern boundary, a short side road leads to the **Mariposa Grove Ⓖ** of giant sequoias, a preserve containing more than 500 mammoth redwood trees. It was here that naturalist John Muir and President Theodore Roosevelt slept under the stars.

View of Half Dome from Cook's Meadow, Yosemite.

Tunnel View in Yosemite.

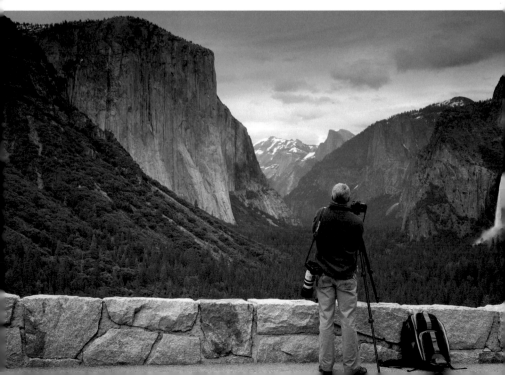

Roosevelt was persuaded by Muir that the forest should be added to the infant Yosemite National Park. The grove's largest tree, the **Grizzly Giant**, 200ft (60 meters) high and with a girth of 94ft (29 meters), is at least 3,800 years old. The best way to experience the trees is on foot, wandering among living things that were already giants when Christ walked the Holy Land.

TUOLUMNE MEADOWS

If Wawona and the Mariposa Grove are Yosemite's Black Forest, **Tuolumne Meadows** is its Switzerland. Reached by an hour's drive north from Yosemite Valley on the scenic road to the **Tioga Pass** ❶, and situated at 8,600ft (2,600 meters) above sea level, Tuolumne is the gateway to an alpine wilderness. The only way to see the more remote areas of the backcountry is to pick up your feet and hike, with the minimum of creature comforts carried in a backpack that may tip the scales at 50 lbs (23kg) or more. A less arduous alternative on some of the smoother trails is to arrange a horse-packing trip, details of which can be discovered locally or by calling Yosemite Park information services (tel: 209-372-0200).

Tuolumne is also the site of **Tuolumne Meadows Lodge** (tel: 209-372-1240), central star in the summer constellation of high Sierra camps. Arranged roughly in a circle, about 9 miles (14km) apart, these six permanent tented camps provide lodging, meals, and hot showers to hikers and horse-packers on the popular High Sierra Loop trail. Elevations of the camps vary from 7,150ft (2,180 meters) to 10,300ft (3,140 meters), and a night of acclimatization in Tuolumne is recommended before departure. In a typical year, camps are open from June 14 through September 1, with advance booking essential (www.recreation.gov).

SEQUOIA AND KINGS CANYON NATIONAL PARKS

Sequoia National Park ❺ and **Kings Canyon National Park** ❻ are less visited than Yosemite, but still attract over 1.2 million visitors each year. In

Yosemite National Park

some ways, these parks can out-boast Yosemite: the 7,000ft (2,000-meter) -deep Kings Canyon exceeds Yosemite Valley in sheer vertical relief, and the sequoia forests of the southern park are larger and more numerous than Yosemite's groves.

Sequoia/Kings Canyon is a wilderness park, with only two developed areas near its western boundaries. The back-country extends across the west slopes of the Sierras as far as the crest of the range, encompassing the headwaters of the Kern and San Joaquin rivers and the highest Sierra summits, including Mount Whitney.

A majority of the park's mountain trails are most easily reached from trailheads out of Lone Pine, Big Pine, and Bishop on the Sierra's east side, a 250-mile (400km) drive from park headquarters near **Three Rivers**. Permits are required for overnight back-country camping. The most scenic approach to the Kings Canyon section of the park, State Highway 180, begins in the sprawling agricultural city of Fresno (see page 172). A 52-mile (84km) drive from there through the Sierra foothills leads to the **General Grant Grove**, a stand of massive 3,000-year-old sequoia trees notable for the wide-open parkland that surrounds their bases.

Thirty-eight miles (61km) past the Grant Grove (where campground sites are available by advance reservation), State Highway 180 drops into Kings Canyon at **Cedar Grove**. In contrast to Yosemite Valley, this gaping chasm is V- rather than U-shaped; the smaller flow of the **Kings River** has yet to deposit enough alluvium to level out the canyon's floor. Two trailheads lead north and east toward the High Sierra, but the 6,500ft (1,980-meter) climbs on south-facing (and sun-broiled) slopes are only for the fit and experienced.

After backtracking to Grant Grove, visitors can proceed into the Sequoia section by following State Highway 198 south for 28 miles (45km) to **Giant Forest**. A short nature trail leads to the **General Sherman Tree**, a redwood much loved by photographers, who like to pose very small persons next to the very tall tree for contrast.

National Park Service ranger at Roaring River Falls, Kings Canyon.

Upper and Lower Yosemite Falls.

☉ BEAR COUNTRY

Grizzly bears no longer live in Yosemite, but the park is home to up to 500 wild black bears, which, despite their name, have mostly brown, cinnamon, and blonde fur.

With a great memory and a sense of smell seven times that of a bloodhound, bears are extremely good at finding your food; they'll even tear up your car for a piece of fruit or toothpaste hidden in the trunk. In fact, bears break into an average of 100 cars a year while looking for food.

As a result, it is very important to use food storage lockers in the park.

Attacks on humans are extremely rare, but they can be aggressive about food or their cubs.

Abandoned buildings at Bodie State Historic Park.

The tree is believed to be the earth's largest living thing. In recent years the park has removed many facilities in an attempt to restore the forest floor to its original ecosystem. With its **Giant Forest Museum**, built to showcase the huge sequoias and the diverse flora and fauna, Giant Forest is the closest thing to an urban center in the area. State Highway 198 continues southward past good camping and boating at **Lake Kaweah**, and drops back into the San Joaquin Valley at **Visalia**, 50 miles (80km) from the park boundary.

THE EASTERN SIERRA

Approached from the west, through the foothills of the Gold Country and on into Yosemite or Sequoia and Kings Canyon, the Sierra Nevada begins gently. Low, rolling hills studded with oak trees give way to pine-blanketed higher hills, which in turn give way to an accelerating crescendo of granite domes, spires and ridges. These culminate in the 13,000 to 14,000ft (4,000 to 4,300-meter) peaks of the crest. But there is nothing gradual about the Sierra when approached from

Climbing El Capitan.

the east, up US 395 from Southern California. On the east side, the mountains of the crest drop precipitously nearly 10,000 vertical feet (3,000 meters) in the space of a few miles, a single great front nearly 200 miles (300km) long. From **Walker Pass** at the southern end of the range to Tioga Pass on the eastern Yosemite boundary, not a single highway cleaves the scarp, the longest contiguous roadless area in the United States outside Alaska.

MONO LAKE TO MAMMOTH LAKE

At **Deadman Summit**, north of June Mountain, US 395 begins a long descent into Mono Basin, once the site of an inland sea. **Mono Lake ❼**, the last remnant of that sea, is the oldest continuously existing body of water in North America, and islands near the lake's northern shore are breeding grounds for 90 percent of the world's California seagulls. Eerie calcified rock formations on the shoreline are called tufa, and some of the best examples are strikingly preserved at **Mono Lake State Tufa Reserve**.

⊘ VISITING YOSEMITE

In spring, wildflowers carpet the meadows, and the roar of wild water resounds throughout the valley. In summer, Yosemite Valley's singular concentration of natural beauty has its far less felicitous human analogue, complete with crowded campgrounds and traffic jams.

Autumn brings a rich gold to the leaves of the oak trees, and the sun's lowering angle etches the granite domes and spires into sharper relief. Autumn also brings herds of wild deer, migrating to winter forage in the Sierra foothills.

Yosemite Valley is emptiest in winter, when the action shifts to the ski resort of Badger Pass, 21 miles (34km) away and 3,000ft (900 meters) higher. Badger's gentle slopes are ideal for families and novice-to-intermediate skiers who don't mind the 45-minute commute from the valley.

From May through November, or until the first winter snow falls, the town of **Lee Vining** on Mono Lake's western shore is the east entry to Yosemite National Park, via 9,990ft (3,045-meter) Tioga Pass. From Lee Vining, Tuolumne Meadows is a 45-minute drive away; it takes at least two hours to reach Yosemite Valley. Campgrounds are spaced every 15 miles (24km) or so, and, unlike the rest of the park's sites, can*not* be reserved in advance; just show up and see if space is available.

North of Mono Lake, the Sierra crest begins to lower, although "lower" in this case still means snowy summits 11,000ft (3,400 meters) high. Just under 12 miles (18km) north of Lee Vining, a graded side road leads 13 miles (21km) to **Bodie State Historic Park ❽**, which offers both an excellent panorama of the northern Sierras and a reasonably authentic glimpse into the life of a '49ers boomtown. Once the wildest camp in the West, Bodie was home to a ragtag collection of miners and confidence men who made silver fortunes by day and squandered them by night in opium dens, saloons, and bawdy-houses. Both professional and amateur photographers love Bodie Park, whose eerie, abandoned buildings perfectly evoke an era long past.

South past Tioga Pass is **Devils Postpile National Monument ❾**, just west of Mammoth Lakes. Its abrupt geometric pickets (80ft/24 meters high, 350yds/meters long) testify to the power of the twin forces that shaped the Sierras – fire and ice. There's some camping in summer at **Agnew Meadows** (just before the monument boundary on State Highway 203) and **Red's Meadows** (just after the boundary).

Winter sun fanatics head for **Mammoth Lakes**, one of the largest downhill ski resorts in America. In the snowy season, Mammoth is where Los Angeles goes skiing, and it is not uncommon to share lift lines with 20,000 other powder hounds. On the plus side, Mammoth offers gourmet dining at several eating establishments, plus good wine and cheese shops and, in summer, lots of outdoor activities, including hiking, canoeing and

Zumwalt Meadow in Kings Canyon National Park.

GENERAL SHERMAN

Posing by the General Sherman Tree in Giant Forest.

Sunset over Mount Whitney from Alabama Hills.

kayaking, fishing, golf, hot-air ballooning, and bird-watching.

OWENS VALLEY

Heading south further still, there is more dramatic scenery to be found at the shores of **Owens Lake**, near the hamlet of **Olancha**. To the west, the tawny, unforested peaks of the southern Sierras rise abruptly, cresting in granite pinnacles 12,000ft (3,600 meters) high. To the east, across the wide, shimmering lakebed, the softer, more rounded contours of the somewhat lower **Inyo Range** dissolve into black and purple foothills. These are the portals of **Owens Valley**, the deepest in America, and "The Land of Little Rain". The vegetation here is hardy desert flora, consisting as it does of scrub oak, mesquite, and sagebrush, but Owens Valley and the Inyos receive less than 10ins (25cm) of rain every year.

Just past the northern end of the lakebed, 21 miles (34km) north of Olancha, State Highway 136 departs east for Death Valley. Located at this junction is the **Visitor Center**, which dispenses maps, information, and wilderness permits for the extensive public lands under federal jurisdiction. In wintertime, the Visitor Center is a mandatory stop for the latest word on campground closures and road and weather conditions. In the busy summer season, rangers will direct travelers to campgrounds with vacant spaces.

On a patio outside the Visitor Center, telescopes are trained on the summit of **Mount Whitney** ⑩, at 14,494ft (4,418 meters) the highest mountain in the United States outside Alaska. A trail leads to the very top of Whitney, where portable latrines have been set up to cope with the tide of visitors. It's a strenuous three-day hike (two up, one down), but no technical skills are required, and thousands make the trip every summer. The hardest part can prove to be acquiring a reservation: many Mount Whitney trail permits are reserved up to a year in advance. For details or more information, call tel: 760-876-6200.

SKI RESORTS

Ski resorts in the Lake Tahoe area all offer equipment rentals and private and group lessons for both skiing and snowboarding, for kids and adults.

The ski season is usually November through May, and season, weekend, or day passes are available. Serious skiers tend to prefer the northern half of the lakeshore on the California side, particularly the area around **Tahoe City**. It's quieter and cleaner, and there's a bigger selection of ski areas. In addition to Squaw Valley, skiers can choose **Alpine Meadows**, **Sugar Bowl**, and **Northstar**. For cross-country skiing, the 90-trail Royal Gorge Cross-Country Ski Resort and the smaller Tahoe Cross Country Ski Area are both options in addition to the resorts below.

WHERE TO GO

Squaw Valley Alpine Meadows (2600 Alpine Meadow Road, Tahoe City; tel: 1-800-403-0206; http://squawalpine.com) The 14-lift Alpine Meadows is preferred by experienced skiers, as of its more than 100 runs, those rated "expert" make up 40 percent of the terrain, but kids' programs and ski and snowboard lessons are also available.

Squaw Valley (Olympic Valley, CA; tel: 1-800-403-0206; http://squawalpine.com) The majority of Squaw Valley's 4,000 acres (1,600 hectares) are better for beginning and intermediate skiers. But experts ski here too – Squaw Valley hosted the Olympic Winter Games in 1960. Squaw Valley and Alpine Meadows merged in 2007.

Heavenly Mountain Resort (South Lake Tahoe; tel: 775-586-7000; www.skiheavenly.com) On the south side, the very popular Heavenly straddles California and Nevada. It has a total of 29 lifts including five high-speed detachable quads plus a snowboard park, and a half-pipe. There are also tubing lanes for racing, and childcare for infants and kids up to 6 years old. The Heavenly Gondola takes passengers up to an observation deck at 9,200ft (2,800 meters). Located in South Lake Tahoe, Heavenly is the favorite ski area for those who like to duck into the casinos at night.

Kirkwood (State Highway 88, Kirkwood; tel: 209-258-6000; www.kirkwood.com) Although it's a bit further away from the action, Kirkwood is one of the best ski resorts in the area, with 12 lifts and 65 trails. You can also get outfitted for cross-country skiing and snowshoeing here.

Northstar (100 North Star Drive, Truckee, NV; tel: 530-562-1010; www.northstarcalifornia.com) One of the top options on the West Coast, this 2,420-acre (980-hectare) resort has 70 runs spread over two mountains. Here you can also cross-country ski, snowshoe, and ice-skate.

Sierra-at-Tahoe (1111 Sierra, Twin Bridges; tel: 530-659-7453; www.sierraattahoe.com) Another local favorite, the family-run resort west of South Lake Tahoe has bunny slopes and wide runs for beginners, and 200 acres (80 hectares) of back-country for experts to explore.

Sugar Bowl Ski Resort (Norden, CA; tel: 530-426-9000; www.sugarbowl.com). Opened in 1939, Sugar Bowl is a medium-sized resort that is particularly popular with skiers from the San Francisco Bay Area who want a shorter drive.

Lake Tahoe caters to downhill and cross-country skiers and snowboarders.

Vintage clothes shop in Santa Cruz.

MONTEREY PENINSULA AND THE BIG SUR COAST

The stretch of State Highway 1 from Santa Cruz to Big Sur is arguably California's most scenic route, passing beautiful state parks, rustic country inns, and great spots to surf.

Highway 1 south from San Francisco, also known as the Pacific Coast Highway (PCH) is perhaps one of the most spectacular routes in America. A series of razor-sharp switchbacks hug hills, plunge into valleys, and skirt the coast the entire way. Steep, rugged mountains loom on the left of the road, while on the right is nothing but a sheer drop to the wild, crashing waves below. The climate changes every few miles, from fog to rain to blinding sunshine. This is the *real* California.

On the way south to Santa Cruz is the delightful town of Pescadero, not far from the **Año Nuevo State Reserve ❶**. Off Highway 1, 20 miles (32km) north of Santa Cruz near the San Mateo–Santa Cruz county line, is where you will find whiskered, roly-poly elephant seal pups. These pups are born in January, when entire seal families are visible from lookout points along the beachfront. The seals can be viewed throughout the year in different phases of their lifecycle.

SANTA CRUZ

At the northern end of Monterey Bay is **Santa Cruz ❷**, a cool, green, redwood-shingled beach 77 miles (120km) southeast of San Francisco. The **University of California** opened its Santa Cruz campus in 1965 and

within a few years this influx of academic activity transformed what had previously been a quiet backwater town into an activist community. Santa Cruz was rejuvenated with excellent restaurants, cafés, pastry shops, and bookstores. Old buildings were refurbished, with cement block and aluminum replaced by natural redwood and hanging ferns.

Sunny Santa Cruz has sparkling clean air and is usually unaffected by the fog and chilly winds that hover off the coast, north and south. Popular

Main attractions

Santa Cruz Beach
  Boardwalk
Monterey Bay Aquarium
Carmel
Big Sur
Bixby Bridge
Hearst Castle
Pinnacles National
  Monument
Año Nuevo State Reserve

Map on page 194

Decorative tiles at Carmel Mission.

beaches include Natural Bridges State Beach, Bonny Doon, Pleasure Point Beach, and Twin Lakes State Beach. Surfing is very popular in Santa Cruz; to learn more, visit the Santa Cruz Surfing Museum (701 West Cliff Drive; tel: 831-420-6289; www.santacruzsurfingmuseum.org; Thu–Tue 10am–4pm, until 5pm in summer). Santa Cruz Pier is the place for all things fishy – fish restaurants, fish markets, and fishing facilities. One of the most popular attractions in Santa Cruz is the **Santa Cruz Beach Boardwalk** (www.beachboardwalk.com), with its 1911 carousel with hand-carved horses, the thrillingly rickety Giant Dipper rollercoaster built in 1924, an old-fashioned arcade containing shooting galleries, and a giant Ferris wheel. On Friday nights in the summer, the Beach Bandstand hosts free live concerts featuring music from the 1960s, 1970s, 1980s, and early 1990s at 6.30 and 8.30pm as well as free beach cinema screenings on Wednesday nights throughout the summer (end of June–mid-Aug).

⊘ AÑO NUEVO RESERVE

On the wild and undeveloped shores of the Año Nuevo State Reserve, northern elephant seals come ashore every winter to give birth to pups and breed. Starting in mid-December, the 2.5-ton bulls fight for breeding access to females. Already pregnant females come on shore to have pups in late December and January, and then nurse for about a month before weaning, mating, and departing to sea. In March, pups learn to swim in the tide pools before heading out to sea.

For a chance to watch the action, reserve tickets for the 2.5-hour naturalist-led tours (tel: 1-800-444-4445). To see them up close in a more subdued state, visit between April and August when they spend time on land molting. Weather can be extreme here, so come prepared for rain and muddy trails.

Leaving Santa Cruz, Highway 1 follows the coast in a beautiful arc around Monterey Bay. During the springtime, marigolds carpet the high sand dunes. The road passes near the beach town of **Capitola**, then stretches dramatically toward Big Sur. Break at produce and peanut stands for snacks, or at wineries in the mountains behind Santa Cruz for tastings (www.scmwa.com).

MONTEREY

The city of **Monterey** ❸ is located at the northern end of Monterey Peninsula. During World War II, Monterey was the sardine capital of the western hemisphere, processing some 200,000 tons a year. After the war, for reasons variously blamed on overfishing, changing tidal currents, and divine retribution, the sardines suddenly disappeared from Monterey Bay and all the canneries went broke.

Cannery Row, located along the waterfront on the northwest side of town just beyond the Presidio, has become a tourist attraction, its old buildings filled with bars, seafood restaurants, a wax museum, dozens of shops, and food vendors. Cannery Row is also home to one of the world's premier aquariums: the **Monterey Bay Aquarium** ❹ (886 Cannery Row; tel: 831-648-4800; www.montereybayaquarium.org; daily 10am–5pm). The enormous building, with its outdoor pools overlooking the sea, stands on the site of what was Cannery Row's largest cannery, the Hovden Cannery. Showcasing the incredible diversity of marine life from near and far, more than 100 galleries and exhibits include over 350,000 specimens, from sea otters, leopard sharks, bat rays, and giant octopuses, to towering underwater kelp forests. Although always crowded – it's the biggest aquarium in the US and attracts nearly two million visitors each year – this

spectacular sanctuary is worth any amount of waiting time.

In downtown Monterey, the main visitor attraction is **Fisherman's Wharf**, lined with restaurants and shops, with fish markets, an organ grinder with a monkey, and noisy sea lions which swim among the pilings, among the attractions. The real working wharf is found two blocks east.

To see the rest of Monterey, a 3-mile (5km) walking tour, called **The Path of History**, leads past key historical buildings and sites. These include the Customs House, the oldest public building in California, now a museum (www.mshpa.org); Pacific House, a two-story adobe with a Monterey balcony around the second floor; and impressive historical exhibits from the Spanish, Mexican, and early American periods.

Other attractions include **Colton Hall**, a two-story building with a classical portico which was the site of the state's first (1849) constitutional convention; Stevenson House, a smaller former hotel where the romantic (and sickly) Robert Louis Stevenson

⊙ Tip

It is possible to park for three hours for free in Santa Cruz at parking garages on both Front and Cedar streets.

One of the entrances to Santa Cruz's beach boardwalk.

⊘ Tip

To rent boats in the Santa Cruz area, check out Capitola and Santa Cruz Boat Rentals (tel: 831-462-2208 and 831-423-1739; http://capitolaboatand bait.com). They have the only motorized ocean skiffs for rent on Monterey Bay and are located on the Santa Cruz and Capitola wharves, the perfect spots to start and end a day of adventure on the water. Both offer boat rentals, fishing gear and other rental equipment. The Capitola shop also offers kayak rentals.

Feeding time in the kelp forest tank at Monterey Bay Aquarium.

lived for a few months while courting his wife; and the **Royal Presidio Chapel**, in constant use since 1794 and where US President Herbert Hoover was married.

The **Presidio**, founded in 1770 by Gaspar de Portolá, was one of a series of "royal forts" built on the west coast by Spain and now serves as the **Defense Language Institute Foreign Language Center** for the US government. Other points of interest in Monterey are the **Monterey Museum** of Art (www.montereyart.org), which focuses on Californian art and photography from the 19th century onwards, and the **Museum of Monterey** (5 Custom House Plaza; tel: 831-372-2608; www.museumofmonterey.org; Tue–Sun 10am–5pm), which includes models of sailing ships and boats, photography, and historic and decorative objects. In mid-September each year, the hugely popular **Monterey Jazz Festival** (tel: 831-373-3366; www.montereyjazzfestival.org) attracts many of the biggest names in music to the Monterey Fairgrounds; this is where Jimi Hendrix was brought to the attention of the world.

Diving is popular in Monterey, as is kayaking, which offers a delightful opportunity to get out among the otters and sea lions. The Monterey County Convention and Visitors Bureau (787 Munras Avenue, suite 110; tel: 888-221-1010; www.seemonterey.com; daily, check website for opening times) provides information on local companies that operate tours out to see the gray whales on their migration between Alaska and Baja California.

17-MILE DRIVE AND PEBBLE BEACH

Leaving Monterey, head south on Route 1 (PCH) toward Carmel-by-the-Sea. Pay to access the famous **17-Mile Drive** ❺ through one of five guarded gates. The route hugs the coast, meandering around the Peninsula, passing the **Del Monte Forest**, mansions, and the world-famous golf course, on the way to Pacific Grove. The scenic attraction known as Cypress Point is where you can see

⊘ A FISHY PAST

In the heady early years of Monterey's canning industry, the beaches were so deeply covered with fish guts, scales, and flies that a sickening stench covered the whole town. When the fishing boats came in heavy with their catch, canneries blew whistles and residents streamed down the hill to work amid the rumbling, rattling, squealing machinery of the canning plants. When the last sardine was cleaned, cut, cooked, and canned, the whistle blew again and the wet, smelly workers trudged back up the hill.

John Steinbeck famously described former Ocean View Avenue, now Cannery Row, as "a poem, a stink, a grating noise, a quality of light, a tone, a habit, a nostalgia, a dream." Today, thankfully, the beaches are bright and clean, and the air is sparkling fresh.

the eerie **Ghost Tree** and the **Lone Cypress**, a single gnarled and wind-sculpted Monterey Cypress near the top of a huge wave-battered rock — the official symbol of Pebble Beach.

The drive's other renowned attraction is the **Pebble Beach Golf Links**, host of five U.S. Opens, and considered by many to be America's greatest public golf course.

The 17-Mile Drive is undeniably beautiful but the attitude of the Pebble Beach Company toward tourists is somewhat condescending, and the landscape is littered with "no trespassing" signs threatening fines and imprisonment.

CARMEL-BY-THE-SEA

The southern gateway to the Monterey Peninsula is the town of **Carmel-by-the-Sea** ❻. A few chance factors made Carmel what it is today: starving writers and unemployed painters in flight from the devastation of the 1906 San Francisco earthquake; and canny property developers who, to reduce their taxes, covered the treeless acres with a thick, lush carpet of Monterey pines.

The result is one of the most charming seaside towns on the West Coast, one that has attracted artists and celebrities such as Sinclair Lewis, Ansel Adams, Robert Louis Stevenson, and Clint Eastwood. When the evening fog rolls in from the bay, the lights inside the cozy houses, combined with the faint whiff of wood smoke from roaring fires, give Carmel the peaceful feeling of a 19th-century European village. The town has grown from the affordable artist haven it once was, and now an air of preciousness graces Carmel.

Carmel's best-known attraction is **Carmel Mission** (https://carmelmission. org). Dating from 1771, it is the burial place of Father Junípero Serra and one of California's largest missions. Masses are still conducted daily, and self-guided or docent-led tours of the church and grounds are available.

Although some three or four million people visit each year – its popularity was boosted when actor Clint Eastwood

☉ Where

The town of Gilroy, to the east of Santa Cruz, is best known for its annual Garlic Festival (www.gilroy garlicfestival.com), held every July. Garlic bread, fries, popcorn, seafood, ice cream – everything is seasoned with garlic here. Its other claim to fame is the Gilroy Yamato Hot Springs. This center of healing had its heyday from the 1880s to the 1920s; it has since fallen into disrepair but it is slowly being refurbished by volunteers. For information, visit www.gilroy yamatohotsprings.org.

Cadillac on Cannery Row.

⊘ Fact

California-born John Steinbeck (1902–68) is possibly best known for his 1939 novel *The Grapes of Wrath*. His novel Cannery Row (1945) was set in Monterey and revolves around the lives of people living there during the Depression. He won the Nobel Prize in 1962.

Carmel Mission.

became mayor for a couple of terms – Carmel has resisted the glare of neon signs, fast-food franchises, and even street numbers. The plazas and little shopping malls attract pedestrians to wine shops and antiques stores, art galleries, and over 500 boutiques, especially on Ocean Avenue between San Antonio and Junipero avenues.

In the residential parts of town, the streets meander through the forest, sometimes even splitting in two to accommodate an especially praiseworthy specimen of pine. Sandy Carmel beach, at the bottom of the hill and within easy distance of the town, is undeniably stunning. For tours, contact Carmel Walks (tel: 831 223-4399; www.carmelwalks.com).

South of Carmel is **Point Lobos State Reserve**, a rocky park overlooking the sea. Nature trails crisscross the reserve, and big natural rock pools are home to lolling sea lions. Be sure to take water and a picnic: there are no food facilities.

Highway 1 south of Point Lobos begins to swoop and curve in dramatic fashion. The Santa Lucia Mountains rise steeply to the left, the foamy, raging sea to the right changes shape and color constantly. Only the two-lane road separates the two, which means the curling ribbon of road has its own distinct weather pattern. Although the sun may be shining brightly on the other side of the mountains, and can often be seen through the trees, Highway 1 can be distinctly chilly, and the fog comes on very quickly.

BIG SUR

Arguably California's most beautiful stretch of coastline, **Big Sur ❼** is a 90-mile (140km) stretch from Carmel to San Simeon, between the Santa Lucia range and the Pacific Ocean.

The stunning **Bixby Bridge**, north of Big Sur village, spans the steep walls of Rainbow Canyon and is one of the highest single-span concrete bridges in the world.

Until 1945, Big Sur was mainly populated by ranchers, loggers, and miners. But soon literary people

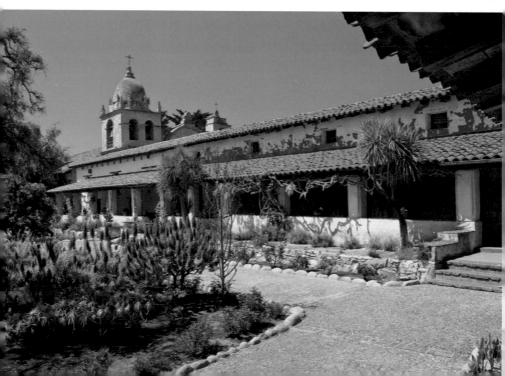

began arriving, attracted by the idea of living cheaply, growing marijuana in remote canyons, and communing with what long-time resident Henry Miller called "the face of the earth as the creator intended it to look." The **Henry Miller Memorial Library** (https://henrymiller.org), near **Nepenthe** restaurant (where everyone goes to enjoy a sunset over dinner; www.nepenthe.com), has works by and about this local hero.

Big Sur village is really little more than a huddle of shops and a post office. Places to stay in Big Sur are scarce, and, if you're planning a weekend visit, book early for any of them. In addition to a couple of campsites, a couple of motels and inns, there are a few very luxurious rustic resorts, notably the **Ventana Inn** (tel: 800-628-6500; www.ventanabigsur.com) and the **Post Ranch Inn** (tel: 831-667-2200; www.postranchinn.com), designed by local architect Mickey Muennig.

There are numerous local parks and wilderness areas to explore along this stretch of coast. Of special note is the stunning **Julia Pfeiffer Burns State Park**, with its twisting nature trails and silvery waterfall.

After winding past several state parks south of Big Sur village, Highway 1 passes the entrance to 1960s alternative haven the **Esalen Institute** (www.esalen.org), which has famous hot spring baths on a ledge over the ocean, before ending 16 miles (25km) north of **Hearst Castle** ❽ (see page 200).

Beyond Hearst Castle, Highway 1 branches off to hug the coast, passing close to **Morro Bay**, dominated by a 576ft (176-meter) rock just offshore. To take the fast track back to San Francisco, turn at Morro Bay onto State Highway 41, which eventually joins US 101.

Heading north, US 101 passes through the town of **King City** to **Pinnacles National Monument** ❾, a 24,000-acre (9,700-hectare; www.nps.gov) destination for hikers, climbers, campers, and bird-watchers. It is named for the unusual rock formations – massive monoliths and spires – formed by water and wind eroding volcanic rock.

Trail through Pinnacles National Monument.

📷 HEARST CASTLE AT SAN SIMEON

Tycoon William Randolph Hearst, the newspaper magnate, was larger than life and so is his mansion. Indeed, it is so lavish that it is often referred to as Hearst Castle, but he just used to call it "the ranch".

The massive, Baroque Hearst Castle was built by media tycoon William Randolph Hearst, who was the model for Orson Welles' 1941 movie *Citizen Kane*.

It was Hearst's father George, a multimillionaire from his gold, silver, and copper mines, who first acquired the 275,000-acre (111,300-hectare) ranch. On his parents' death, the younger Hearst hired his favorite architect, Julia Morgan, to design the highly ornate twin-towered main house, which ended up with 38 bedrooms, a Gothic dining room, two swimming pools, and three sumptuous guest houses.

Next, he stocked the grounds with exotic animals and filled the buildings with carvings, furnishings, and works of art from European castles and cathedrals. To hide from view a water tank on the adjoining hill, Hearst planted 6,000 pine trees. All in all, craftsmen had labored for 28 years to create La Cuesta Encantada, "the Enchanted Hill," with its acres of gardens, terraces, pools, and walkways, and four grand buildings with a total of 46 rooms and almost as many fireplaces.

Hearst, who at his death in 1951 was at the helm of a media empire including the country's largest newspaper chain, 14 US magazines, and 11 radio stations, lived in his 130-room hilltop mansion at San Simeon for 20 years until ill health caused him to move to Beverly Hills in 1947. The property is now a State Historical Monument.

Hearst Castle, 750 Hearst Castle Road, San Simeon; tel: 800-444-4445; www.hearstcastle.org; daily from 9am; many tours most days, reservations required.

The indoor Roman swimming pool took over three years to build. Replete with decorative tiles in Venetian glass and hammered gold, the pool room is big enough to hold twin tennis courts on its roof.

William Randolph Hearst.

Neptune Pool, an enormous outdoor swimming pool, was the favorite among the castle's guests. Marble colonnades and white marble statues front an impressive Greco-Roman temple facade.

Marion Davies.

Hollywood highlife

Hearst Castle frequently welcomed moviedom's elite. A special train with a jazz band and open bar brought party guests 210 miles (340km) from Hollywood to San Luis Obispo; limousines then transported them through the estate's grounds filled with lions, bears, ostriches, elephants, and leopards. Guest were free to wander, except during the mandatory late-night dinner. There were also special occasions: among the hundred guests at a covered-wagon party were the Warner Brothers, the Gary Coopers, and William Powell.

"The society people always wanted to meet the movie stars so I mixed them together," wrote actress Marion Davies, Hearst's longtime mistress. "Jean Harlow came up quite frequently. She was very nice and I liked her. She didn't have an awful lot to say… all the men used to flock around her. She was very attractive in an evening dress because she never wore anything under it." Clark Gable was another regular guest. "Women were always running after him but he'd just give them a look as if to say 'how crazy these people are' and he stayed pretty much to himself."

t nights the publisher would preside over dinner at the -century monastery table in the dining room. Liquor was tly banned (so guests drank in their rooms). After dinner, rst often showed an as-yet-unreleased movie. Gone With Wind, for example, was screened six months before its niere in December 1939.

of the bedrooms.

One of the three guest houses.

A rainbow arches over the sprawling city of Los Angeles.

Riding dune buggies at Pismo Beach.

SOUTHERN CALIFORNIA

A detailed guide to Southern California, with principal sights clearly cross-referenced by number to the maps.

Classic VW bus parked in the Ocean Beach neighborhood of San Diego.

Southern California is one of the few places on the planet where a few hours' drive can transport you from gorgeous sun-drenched beaches to majestic snow-capped mountains and from fertile green farmland to parched desert landscapes. The diversity of the geography is mirrored by the varied cities and attractions packed into the region. Modern Los Angeles, a sprawling, thriving, and often smoggy metropolis, is home to the cinema mecca of Hollywood and the thousands of stars and fame-seekers it attracts, as well as the blockbuster attractions of Disneyland and Universal Studios, and constantly evolving restaurant, nightlife, and cultural scenes. The state's second-largest city, sunny San Diego, boasts surfer-packed coastlines, easy access to Mexico, and one of the best zoos in the world. And the smaller cities have their own claims to fame, too: Palm Springs is globally renowned for its hot-spring-fed spas and is a mecca for gay men, Anza-Borrego for its spring flood of wildflowers, Pismo Beach for its massive sand dunes, and Ojai Valley for its exceptional wine and gorgeous sunset pink skies.

Beyond this, the desolate and scorching hot Mojave Desert and Death Valley seem like

Rodeo Drive in Los Angeles.

another planet. But elsewhere in the Southern California region, balmy weather is the norm; it seldom rains between April and November. The sunny climate not only feeds a thriving agricultural sector that has made California the country's agricultural powerhouse, but it has also helped create the healthy, upbeat attitude that Southern California is known for.

THE CENTRAL COAST

From beautiful beaches to an increasingly popular Wine Country, California's central coast and its small, relaxed towns make lovely escapes for serenity-seeking city folk.

California's central coast south from San Luis Obispo to Los Angeles is a lovely collection of small towns and scenic attractions. There's the sleepy college town of San Luis Obispo and nearby Pismo Beach, famous for its sand dunes and monarch butterflies. Nearby, the Santa Ynez and Santa Maria valleys are home to over 100 wineries, along with quaint towns like Scandinavian-influenced Solvang and flower-filled Lompoc. Then comes Santa Barbara, a beautiful coastal city with Spanish-style architecture and a relaxed, wealthy vibe – it's fittingly nicknamed the "American Riviera." For a detour, head inland to artsy Ojai or set off from seaside Ventura to explore the uninhabited Channel Islands. All of these towns can be explored easily by car – a drive directly from San Luis Obispo to Los Angeles takes about 3.5 hours. There are also small regional airports in Santa Barbara and San Luis Obispo.

SAN LUIS OBISPO

Roughly halfway between San Francisco and Los Angeles, **San Luis Obispo ❶** owes its beginnings to the 1772 mission, and its development to the 1894 arrival of the Southern Pacific Railroad. Today, the pleasant town is a frequent stopover for

visitors to the nearby Wine Country, as well as home to the students at Cal Poly (California Polytechnic State University).

The pedestrian-friendly downtown hosts a popular Thursday night farmers' market on Higuera Street that turns into a proper street festival, with entertainment and barbecues plus stalls selling produce such as flowers, herbs, nuts, honey, and marmalades.

The Victorian homes in the **Old Town** neighborhood around Buchon and Broad streets are worth exploring;

Main attractions
Guadalupe-Nipomo Dunes Preserve
Solvang
Stearns Wharf, Santa Barbara
Mission Santa Barbara
Channel Islands National Park

Maps on pages 209, 211

Gold Rush Steak House at the Madonna Inn Resort & Spa.

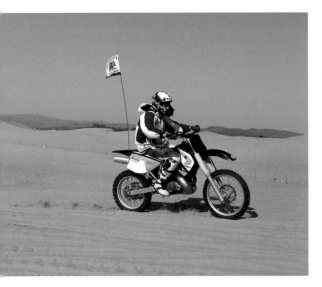

Riding a dirt bike on the sand dunes at Pismo Beach. Beach buggies and quad bikes can also be hired.

1880 Union Hotel, Los Alamos.

and explore the grounds. The San Luis Obispo Children's Museum (1010 Nipoma Street; tel: 805-545-5874; www.slocm.org) caters to visitors with shorter attention spans.

PISMO BEACH

If you're craving beach time, **Pismo Beach** delivers. It's the only real shore community on US 101 between San Francisco and Santa Barbara, and is ideal for sunning and surfing, Here also is the stunning **Guadalupe-Nipomo Dunes Preserve ❷** (tel: 805-343-2455; www.dunescenter.org), including the Mussel Rock Dunes, the world's highest coastal dunes.

From late November through February, hordes of colorful Monarch butterflies come to winter in groves of eucalyptus and Monterey pines. The groves are accessible from State Highway 1 at the southern city limits of Pismo Beach (daily guided walks 11am and 2pm).

If time permits, leave US 101 at the **Los Alamos ❸** turnoff to view the virtually one-block town with its

download self-guided historic walking tours to smartphones in advance at www.historycenterslo.org.

At the 1772 Mission San Luis Obispo de Toloso (751 Palm Street; tel: 805-781-8220; daily 9am–4pm, until 5pm in summer; www.missionsanluisobispo.org), visitors can view Chumas Indian artifacts in the museum antiques stores and frontier-style buildings. The **1880 Union Hotel** has a wonderful saloon and pool room as well as bedrooms and a restaurant furnished completely in 19th-century style. Even more unusual rooms are offered by the famously pink and kitschy **Madonna Inn** (tel: 805-543-3000; www.madonnainn.com).

SANTA YNEZ AND SANTA MARIA VALLEYS

Napa and Sonoma may be the best-known wine-producing regions in California, but the emerging and increasingly regarded **Santa Ynez** and **Santa Maria valley** wineries are well worth a visit. Spotlighted in the movie Sideways, the rural region is home to 100-plus wineries, including the high-profile **Firestone Vineyard** (tel: 805-688-3940; www.firestonewine. com) and the **Fess Parker Winery** (tel: 805-688-1545; www.fessparker. com). For a current list of local wineries and information on their tours and tastings, contact the Santa Barbara County Vintners' Association

(tel: 805-688-0881; www.sbcountywines. com).

One of this Wine Country's most notable towns is **Solvang** ④, an amusing and slightly camp replica of a Scandinavian town with horse-drawn streetcars, windmills, and Danish bakeries. The Hans Christian Andersen Museum (The Book Loft Building, 1680 Mission Drive; tel: 805-688-2052; www. solvangca.com/museum; daily 9am–6pm) has first, early, and illustrated editions of Andersen's works and original photographs and letters. To learn more about the history of Solvang and heritage of Denmark, visit the Elverhoj Museum (1624 Elverhoy Way; tel: 805-686-1211; www.elverhoj.org; Wed–Sun 11am–4pm).

Continuing south on US 101, the highway skirts past gorgeous beaches before passing through **Goleta**, home of a University of California branch, and then arriving in Santa Barbara.

SANTA BARBARA

Beautiful **Santa Barbara** ⑤ first found admiration as a health resort

Windmill in Solvang, the town founded by a group of Danes and built to resemble a Danish settlement.

Spanish-Moorish style of Santa Barbara's Court House

Stearns Wharf, Santa Barbara.

in the 1870s after New York journalist Charles Nordhoff glowingly touted its mineral springs. The sunny "American Riveria" is still an alluring getaway destination, boasting a Mediterranean climate, picturesque white stucco buildings topped with red-tiled roofs, and five miles (8km) of palm-tree-lined beaches, perfect for leisurely jogging, biking, rollerblading, and sunbathing.

One of the shore's main landmarks is the century-old **Stearns Wharf Ⓐ**, the oldest pier on the West Coast. Here visitors choose among seafood stands, restaurants, wine tasting, fishing, and the Santa Barbara Museum of Natural History's Sea Center (211 Stearns Wharf; tel: 805-962-2526; www.sbnature.org; daily 10am–5pm), where local jellyfish mesmerize visitors with their graceful undulations, and small sharks patrol a touch pool. Looking for larger marine life? Whale-watching boat trips depart from Stearns Wharf most days from February through September in search of

the heavyweight mammals heading north from the Baja coast with their offspring.

Take a short diversion to Chapala and Montecito streets to admire the massive **Moreton Bay fig tree Ⓑ** native to Australia and said to be the largest of its kind in America. Planted here in 1914, its branches have since grown to cover, at their widest spread, a length of 160ft (49 meters) and often shade the city's down-and-out homeless community. A bit further along the harbor is the Santa Barbara Maritime Museum (www.sbmm.org; Mon, Tue, Thu, Fri and Sun 10am–5pm, Sat 9am–3pm), with its ship models and floating exhibits.

For some beach life, Stearns Wharf is lined on either side with volleyball-court-filled beaches; East Beach is the long stretch of sand alongside Chase Palm Park, with showers, picnic facilities, and a playground.

Further down the eastern end of the shore, expensive hotels and the multicolored 21ft (6-meter) high **Chromatic Gate** stand on the

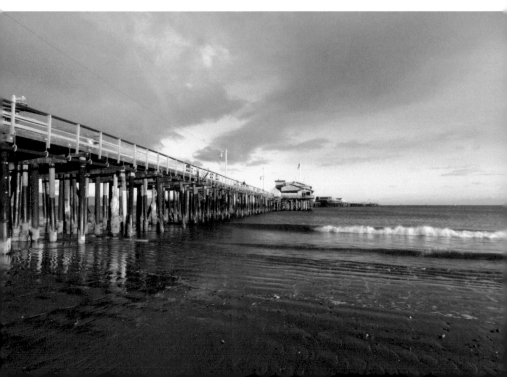

waterfront. The latter was the work of Herbert Bayer, last survivor of the seminal Bauhaus school, who spent the years before his death in the town. Nearby, the petite Santa Barbara Zoo (500 Ninos Drive; tel: 805-962-5339; www.sbzoo.org; daily 10am–5pm) houses 146 species – including gorillas, snow leopards, tropical birds, and giant anteaters – along with a small train and a petting zoo.

To explore downtown Santa Barbara, head up State Street, the main thoroughfare running northwest from the coast through Downtown. Turn right at E. De La Guerra Street to admire the **Casa de la Guerra** C (1827; www.sbthp.org/casa-de-la-guerra), the original home of the Presidio's commander and his family. Here the city council first met in 1850, an event still celebrated every August with a fiesta. The enticing cobbled area, **El Paseo** ("the walk" in Spanish), is an attractive place to shop and sip coffee at outdoor cafés around the fountain.

The next block of E. De La Guerra, bordered by the **Canedo Adobe**

(1782), is where the city began, centered around the **Presidio** D with its chapel, restored adobes, and the **Historical Society Museum** (www.sbhistorical.org). Continue up Anacapa Street and turn left on Carrillo to visit the **Hill-Carrillo Adobe**. The city's first home with a wooden floor,

Danish-style Solvang.

> Tip

The Downtown–Waterfront Shuttle provides frequent service along State Street and the Waterfront area. Shuttle buses and bus stops are marked with blue and black sailboat symbols and the shuttles travel on State Street from Sola Street to Stearns Wharf and along Cabrillo Boulevard. The shuttle fare is $1.75 cents one-way. State Street service stops every block and runs daily every 10 minutes (10am–6pm).

it was built by Daniel Hill in 1826 for his Spanish bride.

Further up Anacapa is the handsome 1929 Spanish-Moorish **Court House** ❸ (1100 Anacapa Street; tel: 805-962-6464; Mon–Fri 8am–5pm, Sat–Sun 10am–5pm). Admire the lobby's mosaics and murals, then take the elevator up to the tower for a lovely 360-degree view of gently sloping roofs and the multilevel lawn below. The Santa Barbara Public Library is around the corner on Anapamu Street and the **Museum of Art** (www.sbma.net; Tue–Sun 11am–5pm Thu 5–8pm) is close by on State Street.

A short drive up State Street and right on E. Los Olivos Street brings you to **Mission Santa Barbara** ❻ (Laguna and Los Olivos streets; tel: 805-682-4713; www.santabarbaramission.org; daily 9am–5pm), one of the most beautiful of the remaining missions. Founded in 1786, it was damaged in both of the area's major earthquakes (1812 and 1925) but lovingly restored, and is still in use as a parish church. The museum displays relics from the days when

Chumash Indians lived and worked at the mission.

Just two blocks north, the **Museum of Natural History** ❼ (2559 Puesta del Sol; tel: 805-682-4711; www.sbnature.org; daily 10am–5pm), shares more about Native American and in particular Chumash life, and also has collections focusing on animals, birds, reptiles, and fish. Among the highlights are a life size blue whale skeleton, the Nature Trail along Mission Creek, the Space Lab and Gladwin Planetarium.

A mile to the west up Mission Canyon Road, trails at the **Botanic Garden** ❽ (tel: 805-682-4726; www.sbbg.org/explore-garden) meander through 78 acres (32 hectares) of native flowers, shrubs, and cacti.

OJAI

Hidden away on the edge of the Los Padres National Forest, **Ojai** ❾ (pronounced *Oh*-hi) is a sleepy but happy town full of artists and writers. From the Pacific Coast Highway, take state Highway 33 for 15 miles (24km), or

Mission Santa Barbara.

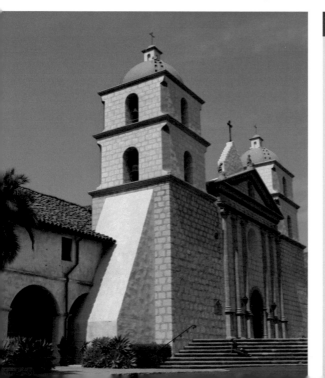

> MONTECITO

Just on the eastern outskirts of Santa Barbara, Montecito has long been a good place to spot celebs. The charming Montecito Inn (tel: 800-843-2017; www.montecitoinn.com) was popular with refugees from Hollywood in the 1920s when one of its original owners was Charlie Chaplin. Montecito's other legendary hotel is San Ysidro Ranch (tel: 805-565-1700; www.sanysidroranch.com), one of the places John F. Kennedy honeymooned with his wife, Jackie; where Lauren Bacall says she fell in love with Humphrey Bogart; and the site of a midnight wedding in 1940 between Laurence Olivier and Vivien Leigh. Today Butterfly Beach (at Olive Mill Road) is often frequented by celebrities; it lies across the street from the posh Biltmore Hotel.

head inland 35 miles (56km) from Santa Barbara on US highway 101 then state highway 150.

On the main street, a graceful tower offsets a row of shops behind a covered arcade. The predominantly Spanish-style architecture owes its origins to glass tycoon Edward Drummond Libby, who in 1917 built the elegant **Oaks Hotel** opposite the library.

To see exhibits on the environmental, cultural, and historical factors that shaped the Ojai valley, visit the **Ojai Valley Museum** (130 W. Ojai Avenue; tel: 805-640-1390; www.ojaivalleymuseum.org; Tue–Sat 10am–4pm, Sun noon–4pm). It is located in the St Thomas Aquinas Chapel (c.1918) and doubles as the **Ojai Visitor Center.**

Large annual events in Ojai include a spring tennis tournament, an arts festival in May, a classical music festival in June, and a film festival in October.

West of Ojai, you can take State Highway 150 to wind along some 60 miles (100km) of the shoreline of **Lake Casitas**, but the scenery is even better along the coast.

VENTURA AND THE CHANNEL ISLANDS

Just north of Los Angeles, **Ventura** is dominated by an ostentatious city hall perched on the hillside. The grand civic giant is outshone in style and grace, however, by the 230-year-old **Mission San Buenaventura** (211 E. Main Street; tel: 805-648-4496; www.sanbuenaventuramission.org) with its pretty garden. Founded in 1782 by Father Junípero Serra, it sits on the edge of a restored "Olde Towne" area filled with antiques shops.

Ventura also serves as a main departure point for the **Channel Islands National Park** ❼. The only national park in Southern California, it encompasses the Anacapa, Santa Cruz, San Miguel, Santa Rosa, and Santa Barbara islands. The beautiful and desolate Santa Barbara Island is especially popular, with its 640 acres (260 hectares) offering a haven for birds, sea lions, and seals. For trip-planning help, visit the National Park Service Visitors Center (1901 Spinaker Drive; tel: 805-658-5730; www.nps.gov).

Museum exhibit at Mission Santa Barbara. The Mission is still home to a group of Franciscan friars, and has a retreat center as well as the church and museum.

Webster Point area of Santa Barbara Island.

⊘ CHANNEL ISLANDS

One of the least visited of America's national parks (with fewer than 250,000 annual visitors), the isolated Channel Islands are often called the "North American Galapagos." Over 150 endemic or unique species are found here, including the island fox, island spotted skunk, and island night lizard. The pygmy mammoth once lived here too, standing just 4–8ft (1–2 meters) high at the shoulders, compared to the 12–14ft (3.5–4-meter)-tall mainland mammoths. Why so much smaller? Separated from their mainland counterparts, these mammoths evolved due to food scarcity.

Today, 99 percent of Southern California sea birds nest and feed here, including bald eagles and peregrine falcons, while sea lions, whales, dolphins, and giant black sea bass swim in the surrounding waters.

Universal Studios

Autry National Museum of the American West, LA Zoo, and Botanical Gardens

Los Angeles

0   2 miles
0   2 km

GRIFFITH PARK ⑮

FOREST LAWN MEMORIAL PARK ⑯

Hollywood Reservoir

Griffith Park Observatory

Hollywood Bowl
Hollywood Heritage Museum
RUNYON CANYON PARK
Grauman's Chinese Theatre
Hollywood Blvd
HOLLYWOOD
DE LONGPRE PARK
Sunset Gower Studios
KTLA-TV
HOLLYWOOD FOREVER CEMETERY
⑫ Paramount Pictures
WILSHIRE COUNTRY CLUB (PRIVATE)
LA Museum of the Holocaust
The Grove
K PARK
La Brea Tar Pits
Peterson Automotive Museum
Miracle Mile
Wiltern Theater

Los Feliz Blvd
Franklin Ave
Hollywood/Western
Hollywood/Highland
Hollywood/Vine
Gower Gulch Sunset
Vermont/Sunset
Silver Lake Reservoir
Santa Monica Blvd
Vermont/Santa Monica
Beverly Blvd
Vermont/Beverley
ECHO PARK
3rd St
Vermont/Beverly
MACARTHUR PARK ⑰
Wilshire/Western
Wilshire/Normandie
Wilshire/Vermont
Westlake/MacArthur Park
KOREATOWN

ELYSIAN PARK
Dodger Stadium
Chinatown
DOWNTOWN
Civic Center/Grand Park
Union Station
MOCA
City Hall
Pershing Sq.
Fine Arts Bldg
Little Tokyo / Arts District

Olympic Blvd
7th Street/Metro Center
Convention Center
LA Live
Staples Center
Pico

Santa Monica Freeway
Washington Blvd
LATTC/Ortho Institute
Grand/LATTC
San Pedro St
Jefferson/USC
University of Southern California (USC)
Expo/Vermont
Expo Park/USC
Natural History Museum
California Science Center & IMAX
EXPOSITION PARK
Memorial Coliseum
Martin Luther King Jr Blvd
Expo/Crenshaw
Expo/Western
Watts Towers

Downtown

0   500 yds
0   500 m

Cathedral of Our Lady of the Angels
Ahmanson Theatre
Music Center
Hall of Administration
Dorothy Chandler Pavilion
CIVIC CENTER
County Courthouse
Hall of Records
Former Hall of Justice
US Courthouse
El Pueblo de Los Angeles ①
LA Plaza ②
El Pueblo de Los Angeles Historic Park ③
Pico Hse
Chinese American Museum
Union Station

Promenade Towers & Bunker Towers
BUNKER HILL
④ Walt Disney Concert Hall
Los Angeles World Trade Center
Museum of Contemporary Art (MOCA)
⑤ Wells Fargo History Museum
California Plaza
Civic Center/Grand Park
Law Library
State Offices
LA Times Building
Criminal Courts Building
City Hall ①
Los Angeles Mall
Federal Building

EDWARD VINCENT JR. PARK
Angels Flight
Grand Central Market
Million Dollar Theater
⑦ Bradbury Building
Civic Plaza
Parker Center
LITTLE TOKYO
MOCA at the Geffen Contemporary
Little Tokyo/Arts District

US Bank Tower
⑥ Millennium Biltmore
New Otani Hotel
Japanese American National Museum

INGLEWOOD PARK CEMETERY

LOS ANGELES

Sun-drenched beaches, Hollywood celebrities, fabulous food, blockbuster theme parks... La La land is a vast metropolis with many identities and many cities within one.

A huge, sprawling city with more than 18 million residents, Greater Los Angeles is California's biggest city and a metropolis with multiple (and often opposing) personalities. There's the MOCA's modern art and the cliff-side Getty Center, innovative fine dining from celebrity chefs and street-side food carts, slick clubs and hipster dives, and designer Rodeo Drive and tiny vintage shops. Movie buffs can soak up Hollywood and television show tapings, while beach lovers have plenty to keep them busy: from the exclusive Malibu colony to the roller-blading boardwalk of Venice, Los Angeles wouldn't be Los Angeles without its photogenic beaches. A forward-looking city from the start, Los Angeles has been a mecca for the young and hopeful since the 1950s, and it is still a magnet for the adventurous, for those seeking to begin a new life, and especially those looking to become a star or at least see one.

DOWNTOWN

It isn't the bustling central hub of the city you might expect given its name, but the Downtown district of Los Angeles still represents both new and old faces of the city. Millions of dollars have been spent to spruce up the neighborhood with modern architecture,

Hand- and footprints outside TCL's Chinese Theatre.

cultural institutions, and high-end lofts, now interspersed among the ornate movie palaces and other unforgettable fixtures of the city's past.

One such historic landmark is the restored **City Hall** ❶. In keeping with its public-spirit function, the mortar with which City Hall was built contained sand from every California county and water from every mission. You can take a fascinating walking tour of this landmark and its magnificent rotunda through the Los Angeles Conservancy (tel: 213-623-2489; www.

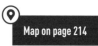
Main attractions
El Pueblo de Los Angeles
Museum of Contemporary Art
Hollywood Walk of Fame
West Hollywood
Griffith Park and Observatory
LA County Museum of Art
La Brea Tar Pits
Getty Center
Getty Villa
Venice Beach Boardwalk

Map on page 214

○ Tip

Parking Downtown is difficult unless you choose to leave your car on the edge of the area, in a lot opposite The Original Pantry (it never closes), for example, at 9th and Figueroa streets. For those on foot, the bus along 7th operates every few minutes in the downtown area from 6.30am on weekdays and from 10am on weekends. Between Grand, Hill, 3rd and 4th streets, the old-fashioned Angels Flight funicular (www.angelsflight.com) takes just 70 seconds to ride up steep Bunker Hill.

Dancers celebrate at a Hispanic festival in El Pueblo de Los Angeles.

laconservancy.org). A quirky claim to fame of City Hall is that it featured as part of the Daily Planet building in TV's Superman series.

From City Hall, you can drive or take a bus to **El Pueblo de Los Angeles** ❷, the oldest section of the city. It was here in 1780 that the city's El Pueblo de Nuestra Señora a la Reina de Los Angeles came into being on what was then Wine Street. Busy **Olvera Street**, a lively pedestrian marketplace, teems with working craftspeople, Mexican stalls, and strolling mariachi who serenade diners sipping frozen margaritas under the sidewalk awning of La Golondrina, the city's first brick building (c.1855). This was home to the Pelanconi family whose piano, a neighborly gift, sits across the street in the older Avila Adobe. The Avila Adobe, the home of a prosperous rancher who died in 1832, was deserted for years and condemned by the city as unsafe. It was saved from demolition by a civic-minded group and acquired by the state in 1953. Since then, it has been restored pretty much as it was left by

his widow when she died, using some of the original furnishings.

Other preserved buildings include Pico House, the city's first three-story building and once its finest hotel with 82 bedrooms, 21 parlors, two interior courtyards, and a French restaurant; the Garnier Building (1890); and the Hellman Quon building, which was originally a Chinese store but is now managed by the Parks Department who offer morning tours of the neighborhood. In the firehouse is a picture of Blackie, the city's last fire horse.

Adjacent to the marketplace is **LA Plaza de Cultura y Artes (LA Plaza)**, the nation's premier center of Mexican-American culture and arts, which opened in 2011 (www.lapca.org). Here you'll find interactive exhibits, a re-creation of 1920s-era Main Street, a short film series, and a large public garden.

Nearby is majestic **Union Station** ❸. Opened in 1939, it is one of the country's last grand railway stations. Its leather seats, marble floors, and stratospheric ceiling have been seen in scores of old newsreels. Just behind the station is the glass-roofed Gateway Transit Center, the mural- and fountain-filled transportation hub of the region today.

Not far from Union Station, the austere **Cathedral of Our Lady of the Angels** (555 West Temple Street; tel: 213-680-5200; www.olacathedral. com; Mon–Fri 6.30am–6pm, Sat 9am–6pm, Sun 7am–6pm) is the home of LA's Catholic archdiocese. Designed by architect José Rafael Moneo, the exterior is all jutting angles, while inside, daylight seeps through thin alabaster panes into a cavernous, polished space. Visitors can park in the underground garage (entrance on Hill Street), and grab a simple lunch in the plaza's café.

The grand **Walt Disney Concert Hall** ❹ (111 South Grand Avenue; tel: 323-850-2000; www.laphil.com; tours most days), where the LA Philharmonic performs, is just a block and a half away from the cathedral. Opened in 2003, it was designed by renowned architect Frank Gehry to be one of the world's most acoustically sophisticated concert halls. The exterior's striking stainless steel curves make the main auditorium a bit of a surprise: it's warm and inviting with golden-hued Douglas fir panels and an enormous organ centrepiece. The Hall is part of the Music Center's campus, which includes the Dorothy Chandler Pavilion, the Ahmanson Theatre, and the Mark Taper Forum.

A block further along Grand Avenue is the **Museum of Contemporary Art (MOCA)** ❺ (tel: 213-626-6222; Mon, Wed and Fri 11am–6pm, Thu 11am–8pm, Sat–Sun 11am–5pm), which harbors American and European art from the 1940s to the present, including work from Mark Rothko, Diane Arbus, and Franz Kline. In addition to this postmodern architectural gem designed by Arata Isozaki, the permanent collection is also housed in the **Geffen Contemporary at MOCA** (152 North Central Avenue; tel: 213-625-4390; www.moca.org), a former police car warehouse, in Little Tokyo, and at West Hollywood's **MOCA** Pacific Design

Walt Disney Concert Hall.

Center (8687 Melrose Avenue; tel: 310-289-5223; www.moca.org). California Plaza (350 Grand Avenue) is a good spot for a quick lunch, with take-away food counters, numerous tables, and a spectacular waterfall.

A few blocks away up Bunker Hill are the LA Central Library at 5th and Grand streets, and Pershing Square, flanked by the awe-inspiring **Millennium Biltmore** , with its ornate lobby and photographs of attendees at the 1937 Academy Awards. It was here that MGM's art director is said to have used a napkin to sketch a design for a still-unnamed Oscar statue. Not far away, admire the gilded façade of the **Figueroa Tower**, built in 1989. A subtle fountain by Eric Orr stands outside the Figueroa at Wilshire building while inside one of the 80ft (24-meter) high Art Deco lobbies, among acres of brown marble, sit two of the largest plants ever seen in captivity. A remarkable late-1980s addition to LA's soaring skyline is the **US Bank Tower**, one of the tallest buildings in the west of the country.

At 7th and Fig, a stylish mall with a sunken plaza and open-air food court sits among three-story palm trees shading stores. Scattered around are several artworks, including a stooping bronze businessman on the north side of Ernst & Young Plaza.

At 811 West 7th, the Fine Arts Building has a medieval-style lobby with 15 chandeliers and a tiled fountain, and hosts exhibitions. The stepped, white form of the 777 Tower ("subtle profiles and strong silhouettes," says one critic) was created by Argentine-born Cesar Pelli, also responsible for the distinctive Pacific Design Center (known locally as "the Blue Whale") in West Hollywood. A few blocks away, adjacent to the **Staples Center,** is the **LA Live entertainment complex,** where you can catch a show at the Nokia Theatre, or peruse the four-floor Grammy Museum (www.grammymuseum.org), dedicated to the history of the Grammy Awards.

Back on Broadway is the ornate, 1893-built **Bradbury Building** , whose winding iron staircases, open

TCL's Chinese Theatre.

elevators, and rich woodwork have long endeared it to moviemakers. It featured in Ridley Scott's cult movie *Blade Runner* and also passed for private eye Philip Marlowe's down-at-the-heels office in the 1969 adaptation of Raymond Chandler's *The Little Sister*.

Opposite the Bradbury is the lively **Grand Central Market** (www.grandcentralmarket.com), which adjoins one of the city's earliest movie palaces, the Million Dollar Theater (www.milliondollar.la) at 307 South Broadway. Founded by showman Sid Grauman, it had a gala opening in 1918 with Charlie Chaplin, Mary Pickford, and Lillian Gish in attendance. The last of the grand movie palaces, S. Charles Lee's Los Angeles Theatre (www.los-angeles-theatre.com), which opened with the premiere of Charlie Chaplin's City Lights (in 1931), is still operating down the street. Three other notable buildings are the Mayan Theater (Hill and 11th streets), now a nightspot, where Norma Jean Baker is said to have appeared as a stripper long before she became Marilyn Monroe, and the 1928

Oviatt Building (South Olive and 6th streets), whose lobby has more than one ton of Lalique glass.

Head east to explore **Little Tokyo**, where you'll encounter interesting shops in Little Tokyo Square, lush Japanese gardens, Buddhist temples, and the **Japanese American National Museum** (100 N. Central Avenue; tel: 213-625-0414; www.janm.org; Tue–Wed, Fri–Sun 11am–5pm, Thu noon–8pm).

HOLLYWOOD

Home to TCL's Chinese Theatre (formally Grauman's Chinese Theatre), the Hollywood Walk of Stars, the Hollywood sign, and the Hollywood Bowl, Hollywood is one of Los Angeles' iconic neighborhoods.

Start off at **TCL Chinese Theatre ❽**, the famous landmark most notable for its forecourt of famous footprints. Nearby are the Hollywood First National Bank Building (a neo-Gothic structure created by the same architects, Meyer and Holler) at the corner of Highland Avenue, and, east of La Brea, the glamorous

Head to Little Tokyo to find an enclave of Japanese culture.

The Watts Towers sculpture in the Downtown suburb of Watts.

⦿ WATTS TOWERS

In the Downtown suburb of Watts, in Los Angeles' South Central area, is one of the city's most astonishing sculptures: the Watts Towers (1727 E. 107th Street; tel: 213-847 4646; www.wattstowers.org). Created between 1921 and 1954 by Simon Rodia, a penniless Italian tilesetter, the trio of lacy columns was intended as an affectionate tribute to his adopted land. Composed of broken bottles, pottery shards, tiles, pebbles, and steel rods all stuccoed together and covered with 70,000 seashells, the towers are a set of sculptures so far ahead of their time that they were unappreciated for years: vandals tried to destroy them and the city planned to pull them down.

The towers, the highest of which reaches 100ft (30 meters), were reprieved after attempts to dismantle them using steel cables pulled by a tractor – in full view of TV cameras – were unsuccessful. In time, the towers started to accumulate the adulation they had long deserved, but Rodia died in poverty in 1965 at the age of 86, having left town and deeded the site to a friend. The towers can be seen behind the fence even when the adjoining Watts Towers Arts Center, which displays works by African-Americans, is closed.

Star on the Hollywood Walk of Fame.

Hollywood Roosevelt Hotel (www.the hollywoodroosevelt.com), site of the first public Oscars ceremony in 1929.

The Dolby Theatre, where the Oscars ceremony is staged, is part of the shop- and restaurant-filled **Hollywood & Highland Center ⑨**. In 30-minute guided tours (tel: 323-308-6300; www.dolbytheatre.com), visitors get access to VIP areas and the low-down on the gossip and glitz of the event.

The old Max Factor building (a former speakeasy) on Highland just south of Hollywood is now the **Hollywood Museum** (tel: 323-464-7776; http://the-hollywoodmuseum.com; Wed–Sun 10am–5pm), which displays hundreds of costumes, film posters, and artifacts, including Cary Grant's Rolls-Royce.

Across the street is the approach to the **Hollywood Bowl**, an 18,000-seat amphitheater staging "Symphonies Under the Stars" concerts all summer, not to mention jazz, world music, and major rock performances.

The **Hollywood Walk of Fame ⑩** (www.walkoffame.com) is the area today that most visitors think of as the heart

Concert at the Hollywood Bowl.

of Hollywood: the celebrated brass and terrazzo stars run along Hollywood Boulevard westwards from Vine Street, with Marilyn Monroe's star positioned outside the McDonald's restaurant. The walk was part of a major restoration of the street back in 1958 when the first batch of stars to be cemented into the sidewalk included Burt Lancaster, Ronald Colman, and Joanne Woodward. Only one star, Barbra Streisand, in 1976, failed to make the obligatory appearance at a dedication ceremony, although it's presumed that she or her agent paid the usual fee of around $15,000 to be commemorated in this quintessential Hollywood way.

After years of neglect, Hollywood Boulevard is making a comeback: witness the **Egyptian Theatre ⑪** in the 6700 block. The theater is a 1,700-seat replica of a palace in Thebes; in its heyday, the theater had a man on the roof in white robes announcing the times of the movie screenings. Now the property of the American Cinematheque, this restored theater presents a movie about Hollywood history on weekends; classics and previews of independent films are also screened (tel: 323-461-2020; www.egyptiantheatre.com; monthly tours.) There is also the spectacular **Pantages**, which wows visitors with its grand lobby and Art Deco chandeliers.

Other nearby landmarks include the **Musso & Frank Grill** (http://mussoandfrank.com), a rendezvous built in 1919 and frequented by writers Nathanael West, William Faulkner, and Raymond Chandler; and Larry Edmunds Bookshop (http://larryedmunds.com), a peerless source of Hollywoodiana, the best place for movie souvenirs in town.

Not far is 6751 Hollywood Boulevard, the former site of **Frederick's of Hollywood**. Now their provocative lingerie is only available online. Steep Whitley Terrace heads up to **Whitley Heights**, a community of elegant mansions much favored by movie stars of the Gloria Swanson era, preceding the rise of Beverly Hills. Access is easier, however, off Highland Avenue, just before the big yellow barn (moved here long ago) that served as the original de Mille

and Lasky studio, now the **Hollywood Heritage Museum** (tel: 323-874-4005; www.hollywoodheritage.org; Sat–Sun noon–4pm).

THE STUDIOS

Most of the movie studios that earned Hollywood its reputation have gone, but the famous gate seen in the film Sunset Boulevard still guards the entrance to **Paramount Pictures** ⑫, (5555 Melrose at Van Ness Avenue; tel: 323-956-1777; www.paramount.com), where The Ten Commandments and all the Godfather movies were also made. Fans who were not even born when silent star Rudolph Valentino died in 1926 seek out his grave (and those of Douglas Fairbanks, Cecil B. de Mille, Eleanor Powell, and Marion Davies) in the adjoining Hollywood Forever Cemetery, formerly the Hollywood Memorial Park Cemetery.

Memories of all the low-budget Westerns churned out in moviedom's early days are evoked by the aptly named **Gower Gulch**, now the site of a shopping center resembling

The iconic Hollywood sign on Mt Lee in the Hollywood Hills.

⏺ Tip

Hollywood Boulevard peters out into hillside suburbia beyond La Brea, but, if you are driving, it is worth continuing for a few blocks along Franklin to take a look at the Yamashiro restaurant, a re-created Japanese palace, and its Victorian neighbor, the Magic Castle. Only in Los Angeles...!

a Western movie set, opposite Sunset Gower Studios on the corner at Sunset and Gower. Across the street, at Columbia Square, is where Hollywood's first film studio, the Nestor Film Company, paid just $40 to rent a defunct tavern in 1911.

Four blocks east, the KTLA TV station replaced the old **Warner Brothers studios**, where, in 1927, Al Jolson emoted in The Jazz Singer. Just north of Sunset on nearby Vine Street, Cecil B. de Mille and Jesse Lasky in 1913 filmed The Squaw Man, Hollywood's first full-length feature.

A bust of Rudolph Valentino stands in the minuscule **De Longpre Park** (below Sunset at Cherokee), named after the turn-of-the-20th-century flower painter whose gorgeous house and gardens near Wilcox Street and Hollywood Boulevard was Hollywood's first tourist attraction. Kansas-born Harvey Wilcox and his wife, Daeida, were the founders late in the 19th century of a temperance community they called "Hollywood" that encircled their orchards.

WEST HOLLYWOOD

Tourists often assume that the "Sunset Strip" refers to the entire length of Sunset Boulevard. In reality, it begins and ends at West Hollywood's city limits, one of LA's most hip and happening neighborhoods. Just a few decades old, "WeHo" has a large gay community and a stylish outlook. By day, a chic crowd meanders from elegant art gallery to bohemian clothing shop to intimate café; by night the same people glide between classy bistro, slick hotel lounge, and pulsating music club.

The castle-like **Chateau Marmont** ⓭, on Sunset near Laurel Canyon (tel: 323-656 1010) is almost an historic monument, in part because of guests such as Greta Garbo and Howard Hughes, and its notoriety as the place where John Belushi died; in part because of its current laid-back but starry ambience. The hotel is, loosely, the eastern edge of the Strip. From here, temples of cool march down the boulevard on ever-higher heels, its role-call including the Standard and Mondrian hotels,

⏺ LA COUNTY MUSEUM OF ART

Established in 1961, the LA County Museum of Art (LACMA) is the largest art museum in the western United States, and attracts over one and a half million visitors each year. Housed in a seven-building complex spanning 20 acres (80 hectares), the collection includes more than 135,000 objects from ancient times to the present.

Particular strengths include its significant Asian art – the LACMA boasts the most comprehensive Korean art holdings outside of Korea and Japan – and its Southeast Asian art galleries are particularly notable for their early Tibetan and Nepalese paintings, sculpture, furniture, and decorative arts.

It also has a significant 1,700-piece Islamic art collection, including glazed ceramics, enameled glass, carved wood and stone, inlaid metalwork, and calligraphy.

Strong Latin American holdings range from pre-Columbian masterpieces to modern and contemporary works by the likes of Diego Rivera, Frieda Kahlo, Rufino

Tamayo, and Jose Clemente Orozco.

In December 2007, the museum expanded its modern art holdings with the gift of the Janice and Henry Lazaroff collection, including works by Edgar Degas, Pablo Picasso, Camille Pissaro, and Alberto Giacometti.

Among its European masterpieces are Georges de la Tour's Magdalen with the Smoking Flame (c.1638–40), Rembrandt van Rijn's Raising of Lazarus (c.1630), Edgar Degas's The Bellelli Sisters (1862–64), and Paul Cézanne's Sous-Bois (1894).

In 2012, the museum inaugurated artist Michael Heizer's monumental sculpture titled Levitated Mass. Originally conceived in 1969, the sculpture consists of a 456ft (139-meter) -long concrete slot, over which sits a 340-ton granite boulder.

For younger art enthusiasts The Boone Children's Gallery, which is free to enter, invites people of all ages to come and create their own art, with staff providing information on brush painting and passing on helpful tips and techniques.

the House of Blues, the Comedy Store, the Whiskey a Go-Go, the Viper Room, and the Roxy.

Some delightful Spanish-style architecture can be found in the West Hollywood blocks lying between Sunset Boulevard and Fountain Avenue, west of Crescent Heights. The Villa Primavera (1300 North Harper), as well as the Patio del Moro (8229 Fountain) and the Villa Andalusia (1473 North Havenhurst), were the work of the husband-and-wife architectural team of Arthur and Nina Zwebell; others, including Villa D'Este (1355 North Laurel), were done by the Davis brothers, Pierpont and Walter. All date to the 1920s, as does the apartment house located at 1305 North Harper where Marlene Dietrich is said to have stayed when she first arrived in 1930.

Mi Casa (1406 North Havenhurst) is the genuine foreign article: an irresistible row of balconied apartments around twin patios brought over from Ronda, Spain, in 1926, and since designated as a national historic place.

The city's denizens have always had an ambivalent attitude about the local architecture and what survives seems to be largely a matter of chance.

Dominating the hill above Sunset is **Greystone Mansion** ⓮. The 18-acre (7-hectare) garden (www.greystonemansion.org) is a popular spot for visitors, although the house (905 Loma Vista Drive) itself usually remains closed. It is, however, often rented out to movie companies for location filming. Built at a cost of $6 million in 1926 by the city's first oil millionaire, Charles Doheny, the 50-room mansion is now owned by the city of Beverly Hills. Down La Cienega at Beverly Boulevard is the Beverly Center (www.beverlycenter.com). For 30 years, until 1974, an amusement park and oil wells stood on the site of what is now an eight-level mall with 140 shops and restaurants and 13 movie theaters.

GRIFFITH PARK

Griffith Park ⓯ (tel: 323-644-2050; www.laparks.org/griffithpark) is an immense preserve that begins at Los

Farmers' Market

Feliz Boulevard and extends all the way to the Ventura freeway. At 4,000 acres (1,620 hectares), the park is the nation's largest, and is home to a **zoo**, a wonderful **observatory**, an **open-air theater**, a **train museum**, numerous recreation areas, and the excellent **Autry Museum of the American West** (tel: 323-667-2000; www.theautry.org; Tue–Fri 10am–4pm, Sat–Sun 10am–5pm), which focuses on the diverse people and culture as well as history of the American West. Among exhibits are film memorabilia, firearms and paintings as well as over 500,000 pieces of art, including one of the largest collections of the Native American Art in the country.

Perched on the south-facing slope of Mount Hollywood in the park is the Griffith Park Observatory (2800 East Observatory Road; tel: 213-473-0800; www.griffithobservatory.org; Tue–Fri noon–10pm, Sat–Sun 10am–10pm). In addition to is grounds, massive telescopes, and exhibits, the observatory offers public star parties and planetarium shows, the latter in the impressive 285-seat Samuel Oschin Planetarium, arguably the best in the world.

Forest Lawn Memorial Park ⑯ (the park literature studiously avoids the word "cemetery") has two peaceful locations flanking Griffith Park: **Glendale** and the **Hollywood Hills** (tel: 800-204-3131). The Glendale location was the inspiration for Evelyn Waugh's *The Loved One*, and is a must-see. Ultimately a final resting place (for many Hollywood stars, including Clark Gable, Carole Lombard, Nat King Cole, and Jean Harlow), Forest Lawn also has reproductions of famous churches from around the world, a stained-glass interpretation of da Vinci's *The Last Supper,* and the world's largest religious painting, *The Crucifixion,* by Jan Stykam, measuring 195 by 45ft (59 by 14 meters). The Hollywood Hills site is dedicated to early American history, and features bronze and marble statuary, including a replica of the Liberty Bell in Philadelphia. Later residents include Buster Keaton, Stan Laurel, and Liberace.

Shopping in Beverly Hills.

WESTLAKE, MIRACLE MILE, AND LA BREA

West of Downtown, Wilshire is showing its age nowadays, although the Metro Line subway has brought life to otherwise seedy **MacArthur Park** and the Art Deco landmark of the former Bullock's department store has been refurbished and now houses a law library. The Ambassador Hotel once stood at 3400 Wilshire Boulevard, drawing showbiz types to its Coconut Grove and in the 1960s becoming infamous as the site of Robert Kennedy's assassination.

Miracle Mile's Museum Row, on Wilshire near Fairfax, has Old Masters and other fine paintings, which hang in the **LA County Museum of Art (LACMA)** ⑱ (tel: 323-857-6000; www.lacma.org; Mon, Tue, Thu 11am–5pm, Fri 11am–8pm, Sat–Sun 10am–7pm.)

Focusing on a much older collection, the **La Brea Tar Pits** ⑲ at the Page Museum (tel: 323-934-7243; www.tarpits.org; daily 9.30am–5pm) is a major tourist attraction. In the 1860s, Rancho La Brea had been bought for $2.50 per acre by Major Henry Hancock, who quarried asphalt and shipped tar to San Francisco to pave streets. The oil company geologists who, in 1989, started uncovering fossils here identified some of the bones as belonging to extinct sabre-toothed tigers, dire wolves, and giant sloths.

After a decade of oil drilling, Henry's son, George, allowed LA County to examine the site, deeding the 23-acre (9-hectare) ranch to the county in 1913. The skeleton of a woman from 9,000 years ago was found, but no other humans among what were literally millions of bones. The museum opened in 1972; excavations for the building uncovered skeletons of complete animals, which had been trapped in the tar as they came to drink.

There's alfresco eating just a few blocks north at the **Farmers' Market**, where, from 1934, farmers parked their trucks and sold produce from the back. Next door is a huge open-air shopping mall, **The Grove**, complete with several dozen stores (ranging from Coach and

Griffith Observatory.

La Brea Tar Pits.

☉ NATURAL CHALLENGES

Los Angeles is kept alive by water pumped in from hundreds of miles away. Windswept fires race across arid hillsides, devouring entire estates in a matter of hours. Spring rainfalls slip-slide celebrity-owned, million-dollar mansions down precarious slopes. Storm tides topple beach homes and century-old piers. Every year, there are earthquakes – on a minor scale in recent years, but everybody knows the Big One, a massive quake on the San Andreas fault, is overdue. Still, despite all the hazards, Angelenos remain fairly sunny and optimistic in their outlook. Perhaps local publisher Jeremy Tarcher summed it up best. "We are still the city of the future," he said, "even if nobody knows what the future is."

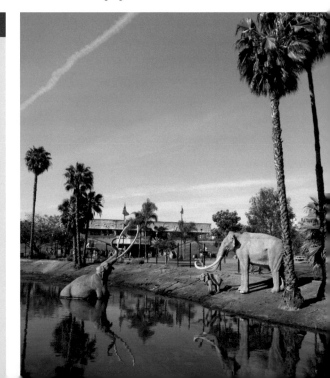

The Los Angeles Zoo and Botanical Gardens (5333 Zoo Drive; tel: 323-644-4200; www.lazoo.org; daily 10am–5pm) is home to more than 1,100 mammals, birds, amphibians and reptiles including Chinese giant salamanders, crocodiles, scorpions, rare tortoises, and blue frogs. Other highlights include Sumatran tigers, snow leopards and Reggie the alligator, who was dumped by his owners and spent two years evading captivity before being brought to the zoo.

The Getty Villa is a museum of ancient art in Malibu.

Sephora to Topshop and Anthropologie), a movie theater, and restaurants. The mall and market are connected by a free shuttle service.

In 2010, the Los Angeles Museum of the Holocaust (www.lamoth.org; Mon–Thu and Sat–Sun 10am–5pm, Fri 10am–2pm), opened its new permanent home next to the Holocaust Memorial in Pan Pacific Park. Here you'll find the West Coast's largest archive of documents, relics, and other primary source materials from the Holocaust period.

BEVERLY HILLS

Drilling for oil on what was once the Rancho Rodeo de las Aguas is what led to the birth of Beverly Hills; the unsuccessful oil prospectors subsequently decided to develop the land. One-acre lots were offered for under $1,000 along the length of Sunset Boulevard. In 1912, Burton Green built the **Beverly Hills Hotel** ⑳ to be the focal point of the new community.

One of Beverly Hills' earliest homes is the **Virginia Robinson House and Gardens** ㉑ (tel: 310 550-2087; www.

robinsongardens.org; Tue–Sat 10am–1pm, tours by appointment only), built in 1911 for the son and daughter-in-law of the owner of the Robinson department store chain. Lushly landscaped gardens include a mini-forest of palm trees and flower-filled terraces.

Filmdom's elite built ever-bigger homes in this elegant area, fanning out into the hills and canyons, and around **Mulholland Drive**, the spectacular highway that runs for 50 miles (80km) along the crest of the Santa Monica Mountains all the way down to the coast just north of Malibu.

Greta Garbo and John Gilbert shared idyllic poolside afternoons together in a mansion at Seabright and Tower Grove Drive; Rudolph Valentino luxuriated in Falcon's Lair at 1436 Bella Drive; not too far away, the home of Roman Polanski and Sharon Tate at 10050 Cicelo Drive was the scene of the 1969 murders by members of the infamous Charles Manson "family."

At the canyon's lower end, along immaculate **North Roxbury Drive**, lived Marlene Dietrich (No. 822),

Jimmy Stewart (No. 918), Lucille Ball (No. 1000), and Jack Benny (No. 1002). Greta Garbo's home was nearby at 1027 Chevy Chase Drive and William Randolph Hearst's mistress, Marion Davies, had a home at 1700 Lexington Road. At the time of his death in 1951, Hearst was living with Ms. Davies in a house on Beverly Drive, noted for the huge palms that line the street. With some 30,000 trees, Beverly Hills has almost one per resident.

Land was cheaper down around Santa Monica Boulevard when the community first began, but these days you'd hardly know it considering the prices along famous **Rodeo Drive** ㉒, especially between Santa Monica and Wilshire where designer stores such as Gucci, Hermès, Chanel, Fendi, and Cartier have branches – "the most staggering display of luxury in the western world," says novelist Judith Krantz. Two Rodeo Drive, with its cobbled street and bow windows, is a replica of what only Hollywood could believe to be an olde-worlde European backwater; across the street, the late entrepreneur Fred Hayman's red-and-yellow boutique-cum-bar has a working fireplace surrounded by photos of celebrity customers.

Even **City Hall**, with its handsome tiled dome, is a splendid sight, part of the Spanish Renaissance-style Beverly Hills Civic Center. More interesting architecturally, however, is the intriguingly bizarre **Witch's House**, at 516 Walden Drive, which began life as a 1921 movie set designed to look like the home of the fairy tale witch in Hansel and Gretel. It was later moved to this site. Conscious of its worldwide fame, Beverly Hills maintains an informed, active Visitors Bureau at 9400 South Santa Monica Blvd (tel: 310-248-1015; www.lovebeverlyhills.com; Mon–Fri 9am–5pm, Sat–Sun 10am-5pm).

If you happen to be in LA on a rare rainy day, head for the **Paley Center for Media** (465 North Beverly Drive; tel: 310-786-1000; https://media.paleycenter.org; Wed–Sun noon–5pm), where visitors can listen to news and watch old TV shows. About a mile (1.5km) south is the **Museum of Tolerance** (9786 West Pico Boulevard; tel: 310-772-2505; www.museumoftolerance.com; Sun–Fri 10am–5pm, check website for hours), a sobering look at the history of racism in the US and the Holocaust experience in Germany.

Santa Monica and Wilshire boulevards intersect at the far side of Beverly Hills, beside the **Electric Fountain** that caused sightseeing traffic jams when it was first built in the 1930s. Santa Monica Boulevard heads west past the skyscrapers (filled mostly with corporate law offices and the like) of Century City, centered around the luxurious Century Plaza Hotel and another upscale shopping center, before terminating at Santa Monica. Century City's 180-acre (73-hectare) site was once part of the studio back lot of 20th Century Fox.

⊘ BEVERLY HILLS HOTEL

The Beverly Hills Hotel, the famous pink palace, is a legend in Los Angeles. Here Elizabeth Taylor honeymooned in a bungalow and reclusive resident Howard Hughes ordered pineapple upside-down cake from room service almost every night. For a long time, Katharine Hepburn took lessons from the hotel's tennis pro and one day, after six sets, dove in the pool fully clothed. She was also known to curl up outside Spencer Tracy's locked door, waiting for him to let her in after a drinking bout. Greta Garbo chose the hotel as a hideaway in 1932 and Clark Gable checked in to dodge the press after separating from his wife, Rita. At the Fountain Café, Marilyn Monroe and Yves Montand romanced over afternoon tea in 1959.

When the world's then richest man, Hassanal Bolkiah, Sultan of Brunei, bought the hotel for $185 million in 1987, he ordered extensive renovations. The number of rooms was cut from 253 to 194 and gilded ceilings were added to the lobby. New additions included a kosher kitchen.

Some things, of course, stayed the same. The menu of the Polo Lounge, where Will Rogers and Darryl Zanuck dropped in after their matches, still features the Neil McCarthy salad, named for the polo-playing millionaire who died in 1972. In 2012, the hotel was named the first historic landmark in Beverly Hills.

⊙ Eat

Straddling the border with Venice on Rose Avenue at Main Street is the iconic Rose Café (http://rosecafevenice.com), where locally created artworks are sold in a small shop that's part of this lively boho spot. Sip espresso and nibble sinfully rich pastries while sitting on stools at high tables or on the outside patio.

Decorative tiles in Adamson House, Malibu.

WESTWOOD, BEL-AIR, AND BRENTWOOD

Wilshire Boulevard swerves slightly to the northwest heading out of Beverly Hills along the southern flank of the shopping complex **Westwood Village**, once the headquarters of William Fox's newsreel operations and now home to the interesting Hammer Museum (10899 Wilshire Boulevard; tel: 310-443 7000; www.hammer.ucla.edu; Tue–Fri 11am–8pm, Sat–Sun until 5pm), which exhibits a mix of European paintings, da Vinci drawings, and traveling art shows. The movie theaters at Westwood are often the places for sneak previews and low-key movie premieres; it's also one of the places where off-duty movie stars take their kids on Saturday afternoons.

Westwood also adjoins the tree-shaded **University of California** (UCLA) campus. UCLA's 130 buildings include Schoenberg Hall (named after the composer who taught here), Bunche Hall Library, and the New Wight Gallery, all open to the public. The college's main entrance is on Hilgard Avenue, south of Sunset. A first stop should include one of 11 information and parking booths around the campus.

The gated community of ultra-chic Bel Air is north of Sunset, the road up through Stone Canyon passing what some think of as LA's most beautiful hideaway hotel, the **Hotel Bel Air**. Grace Kelly lived here for much of her movie career.

Back on Sunset, the boulevard begins a series of dizzying loops and curves passing through Brentwood, site of the impressive **Getty Center** ㉓ (see page 236). One of Raymond Chandler's many homes was at 12216 Shetland Place and Marilyn Monroe died in a bungalow at 12305 Fifth Helena Drive; both located just off Sunset. Sunset continues through Pacific Palisades before sweeping down to the Pacific Coast Highway.

On the way to the coast, it's worth turning off to the right for the challenging, uphill drive to the Will Rogers State Historic Park (www.parks.ca.gov). The cowboy philosopher, who

⊙ GETTY VILLA

Where Sunset hits the Pacific Coast Highway (PCH) is 1 mile southeast of the Getty Villa (www.getty.edu; Wed–Mon 10am–5pm; timed ticket required). The villa, one of America's most beautiful museums, has reopened as an evocative and highly suitable permanent home to the Greek and Roman exhibits. These treasures were formerly displayed in highly cramped quarters or more often, packed away in storage. But when the Getty Center (see page 236) opened and many items moved to the clifftop museum, the Getty Villa came into its own. Up the highway from the villa is Topanga County beach with a full range of public facilities, but somewhat territorially minded surfers.

had been America's top box-office star, died in a plane crash in 1935. Ten years later, the ranch was turned over to the state, which has maintained it as a museum pretty much as it was when Rogers lived.

MALIBU

Head west on Pacific Coast Highway (PCH) to reach the wealthy seaside community of **Malibu** ㉔, with its free state beach and pier. Southwest of the pier is the historic **Adamson House** (tel: 310-456-8432; www.adamsonhouse. org; Thu–Sat 11am–3pm). The Adamson House was built in 1929 by Rhoda Adamson, daughter of Frederick Rindge, Malibu's founder and major landholder. (Frederick Rindge bought hundreds of acres of surrounding land for as little as $10 an acre back in 1892.) The house is as attractive outside as it is inside, and even when it is closed you can drive or walk up the lane (or even come in from off the beach) and admire the tiled terrace, the lovely fountains, bottle-glass windows, and well-kept gardens.

A display in the museum, which features old photographs, explains that the real Malibu Gold is real estate: Bing Crosby's house cost him $8,700 in 1931 and was bought for almost $2 million by Robert Redford half a century later. Harold Lloyd's 1928 house cost him $6,400, but singer Linda Ronstadt paid $1.3 million in 1985. Now they sell for tens of millions.

Just northeast of the lagoon (a preserved wetland in which you can sometimes spot ducks, herons, and pelicans) is **Malibu Pier**, built by Rindge just before he died in 1905. The pier is open to the public and is a fun place to while away an amusing hour or two.

Dozens of stars live hidden away here, some of them along the well-guarded beachfront Malibu Colony at the junction of PCH and Webb Way, but the only place they're likely to be seen in public is the Colony shopping center about a mile to the west of the pier.

Broad Beach, like so much of the Malibu coastline, is private but only down to the mean high-tide line – meaning that as long as you stay on

Venice Beach.

Malibu Beach.

wet sand, you have every right to be there. Easily missed access to the beach is in the 3100 and 3200 block of Broad Beach Road. Zuma Beach and Point Dume State Beach are public and often crowded. Up in Malibu's Santa Monica Mountains, the environmentally friendly **Ramirez Canyon Park** (tel: 310-589-2850; by appointment) occupies the 22.5-acre (9-hectare) site of what was formerly one of Barbra Streisand's estates, donated by the singer in 1993. Walking paths shaded by sycamore, walnut, and pine trees wind along Ramirez Creek.

SANTA MONICA

Once, it took a full day's stagecoach ride to get to **Santa Monica** from Downtown, but, when the freeway opened in 1966, the trip was cut to half an hour: Los Angelenos had discovered the beach. Whereas previously the city's seashores had been the preserve of fishermen and those wealthy enough to build bungalows by the sea, suddenly everyone was sporting a tan and hanging ten. Today Santa Monica

is the largest coastal town in the 100-mile (160-km) stretch between Oxnard and Long Beach.

This deceptively casual town embraces both a metropolitan sophistication and a beach-town atmosphere. Many people in the media, arts, and design choose to live here, and almost every visitor to Los Angeles under the age of 35 chooses to at least visit, or more often, stay here. It's a great place to walk around and, so unusual for LA, no car is necessary. The Visitor Information Kiosk at 1400 Ocean Avenue, open daily 9–5pm, is a great place to start. To the south is a Camera Obscura Art Lab, for which the admission is via the Senior Recreation Center.

At the northern end of Santa Monica, the enormous mansions along the beach were mostly built by moviedom's elite. The grandest, at 415 Pacific Coast Highway, was the 118-room compound designed by William Randolph Hearst's favorite architect, Julia Morgan, for the newspaper tycoon and his paramour, Marion

Ferris wheel on Santa Monica Pier.

Ø LA DETECTIVES

The "Bay City" setting of many of Raymond Chandler's detective novels is where Wilshire and Sunset boulevards meet the ocean. Discussing the locale, Chandler's biographer Frank MacShane said he felt the detective story was an entirely appropriate form for LA because such stories "could involve an extraordinary range of humanity from the very rich to the very poor and can encompass a great many different places."

Chandler, the revered documenter of Los Angeles of the 1940s, felt Los Angeles was a city "rich and vigorous and full of pride... a city lost and beaten and full of emptiness."

Davies. In 1945, the house was sold for $600,000 to Joseph Drown, owner of the Hotel Bel Air, who turned it into a beach hotel and club (today it is the public Annenberg Community Beach House, www.annenbergbeachhouse.com).

In those days, before the breakwater extended the beach, the sea came to within 50ft (15 meters) of most of these homes. It was another famous architect, Richard Neutra, who created Mae West's home at No. 514, while Wallace Neff, who designed Pickfair (Douglas Fairbanks' and Mary Pickford's estate), was responsible for the home of Louis B. Mayer's son-in-law, producer William Goetz, at No. 522.

The century-old **Santa Monica Pier** has numerous amusement arcades, a carousel you might recognize from *The Sting* and *Forest Gump*, and eating places and fishing stands from which visitors have gorgeous views of Pacific sunsets and beaches curving gently around the bay. Unfortunately, the ocean here is often too polluted for safe swimming mainly due to consecutive years of below-average rainfall.

Affluent "industry" people stop by Santa Monica from Malibu or their offices nearby to shop or use the excellent library, and people from all over the area frequent the spacious pedestrian mall, the **Third Street Promenade**. The promenade leads to attractive Santa Monica Place, an upscale mall designed by acclaimed local architect Frank Gehry, replete with major department stores, scores of eating places, and several cinemas nearby.

Eucalyptus-fringed **Palisades Park**, overlooking the pier, was given to the city in 1892 for use "forever" by Santa Monica's founders, Col. Robert Baker and his partner, silver tycoon John P. Jones. Jones's house at the corner of Wilshire was where the **Fairmont Miramar Hotel** now sits; the enormous fig tree outside the lobby was planted by a member of his family more than a century ago. Greta Garbo spent her first three years living at the Miramar when she first came to the US in 1924. The pool was seen in the "Bermuda" sequence

Santa Monica Pier is a great place to watch a Pacific sunset.

of *That Touch of Mink* with Cary Grant and Doris Day.

South of the pier, a walkway and bicycle path extends all the way down to Venice. Buses run up and down Ocean Avenue, close to Main Street with its terrific shops, cafés, and California Heritage Museum (tel: 310-392 8537; www.californiaheritagemuseum.org; Wed–Sun 11am–4pm). At 2427 Main Street is Santa Monica Travel & Tourism Visitor Center (tel: 310-393-7593; daily 9am–5pm).

VENICE

The closer you get to **Venice** , the odder the ambiance. An early favorite of such silent moviemakers as Charlie Chaplin and Carole Lombard, **Venice Boardwalk** is today jammed almost around the clock with characters who appear to be auditioning for some unannounced contemporary epic. Sights and sounds might include guitar-bearing rollerbladers in robes and turbans, bikini-clad beach bunnies, rainbow-haired punks, lunatic dreamers, outrageous con men, barely dressed cyclists, psychics, chain-saw jugglers, and the bicep-bound boasters of Muscle Beach.

But there is another, less-explored Venice a few blocks to the east. After noting the building on Windward Avenue whose colonnaded arches are meant to evoke visions of San Marco Square in Venice's Italian namesake, walk east to the post office, which was where once most of the canals met. Many are now paved over, but a walk of a few blocks to the southeast will bring you to what remains of the watery network, a charmingly tranquil area of shallowly filled canals lined with houses in myriad styles, mostly with gardens full of flowers that thrive in the hot sunshine, and where ducks and geese roam the walkways. If you are driving, the route is down Dell Avenue across the humpback bridges. The creator of this area was Abbott Kinney, whose name has been memorialized in Abbott Kinney Boulevard – connecting Main Street with Marina del Rey

Junk-food outlets mix with marijuana venders on Venice Beach's boardwalk.

– along which can be found interesting little cafés, restaurants, and lots of shops.

Some of the city's most interesting murals can be seen around Venice – Christina Schlesinger's Marc Chagall Comes to Venice Beach at 201 Ocean Front Walk and Emily Winters' Endangered Species six blocks down are notable – not far from the headquarters of SPARC (www.sparcinla.org), an organization which sponsors such public art such as the half-mile Great Wall of Los Angeles beside the Los Angeles River in Van Nuys.

MARINA DEL REY

This seaside place is close to the Los Angeles international airport (LAX), and is a good place for a stopover. The marina's tourist attraction is the charming but phony Fisherman's Village (the "lighthouse" is a fast-food stand) with a multitude of restaurants for lunch. These range from reasonably priced Mexican fare to more upscale Whiskey Red's (formerly Shanghai Red's, www.whiskeyreds.com),

which has the appealing ambiance of a century-old inn but has actually been there for only 40 years or so, since the marina began.

At the end of Basin D is a shallow-water family beach known as **Mother's Beach.** All the restaurants overlook the harbor – the world's largest artificial harbor for small craft – with its berths for 6,000 boats. From Beverly Hills, the bus runs down Robertson Boulevard all the way to Marina del Rey, which is also accessible by Santa Monica's Big Blue Bus.

Back on Ocean Avenue, take the Big Blue Bus up a few blocks to Ocean View Park and transfer to the bus that runs along the north side of Santa Monica Airport. At Clover Park, walk a couple of blocks down to the Museum of Flying (3100 Airport Avenue; www.museumofflying.com; Fri–Sun 10am–5pm), which focuses on the Douglas Aircraft Company (which built the DC-3 here in 1977) and houses about two dozen aircraft plus aviation art, artifacts, and the California Aviation Hall of Fame.

Venice's canals were created from marshland.

⊘ VENICE

When tobacco magnate Abbott Kinney invested millions in creating his Venice from worthless marshland in the early 1900s, he lined the canals with Japanese lanterns, imported gondolas, encircled the project with a miniature railroad, and sold scores of housing lots. Visitors who paid 25¢ to take the railroad from Downtown ended a busy day on the (now-abandoned) pier watching an armored trumpeter serenade the sunset from a replica of Juan Cabrillo's medieval flagship before retiring for the night in the St Mark's Hotel, modeled after the Doge's Palace in Venice, Italy.

Despite Kinney's ambitious plans, which included hiring Sarah Bernhardt and the Chicago Symphony Orchestra for his 3,500-seat auditorium before scaling down the attractions for more plebeian audiences, the project gradually deteriorated. Its collapse was speeded by the discovery of oil (there were 163 wells in the area by 1931) and by the shortage of fresh water. Like so many neighboring communities, Venice was obliged to come under the aegis of Los Angeles if it wanted a regular water supply. With incorporation came less tolerance for canals when paved roads could occupy the space. Moreover the envisaged water circulation system proved unworkable and the canals became stagnant. Since then extensive renovations have helped dredge the canals, refill them with water, repair the paths, and rebuild some of the bridges.

📷 J. PAUL GETTY MUSEUM AND THE GETTY CENTER

More than a dozen years in the making, the billion-dollar Getty Center, comprising art collections, gardens, a research center, and more, has been likened to a Tuscan hilltown by its award-winning architect, Richard Meier.

The white city on the hill high above the intersection of the Santa Monica and San Diego freeways has – like many examples of modern architecture – provoked both praise and criticism. Detractors have claimed it resembles an oversize refrigerator or a strip mall while one admirer claims it is "too good for Los Angeles." Richard Meier, winner of architecture's highest honor, the Pritzker Prize, was chosen for the commission after a worldwide search. He described the site as the most beautiful he had ever been invited to build upon, one whose light, landscape, and topography provided the cues for his design. The center, he says, "is both in the city and removed from it... evok[ing] a sense of both urbanity and contemplation."

The Museum at the Getty Center houses European artwork, ranging from sculpture to paintings, and European and American photographs.

Irises (1889) by the Dutch artist van Gogh is on show at the Getty Center's Museum.

The J. Paul Getty Museum's collections include European drawings, paintings, illuminated manuscripts, sculpture, French 17th- and 18th-century decorative arts, and photography, which are displayed in a series of five interconnecting buildings. However, the Getty Center site also includes six other buildings, including a research institute, a library, an auditorium, and a restaurant, most offering breathtaking views of the city, the sea, and the mountains. Between the museum and the research institute is a playful and imaginative central garden, designed by artist Robert Irwin.

There are two branches of the J. Paul Getty Museum: at the Getty Center in the Brentwood neighborhood of Los Angeles, and at the Getty Villa in Malibu.

J. Paul Getty, c.1935.

The reclusive billionaire

Minneapolis-born oil billionaire J. Paul Getty, who refused to fly and lived his last years as a virtual recluse in England, never saw the museum that bears his name. When his Malibu ranch house opened to the public to exhibit his art and antiquities, he was no longer in the country. From the oilfields of Kuwait in May 1954, he telegraphed regrets that he could not attend the opening: "I hope this museum, modest and unpretentious as it is, will give pleasure..."

Later, he remotely directed the construction of a new site, an elaborate reproduction of a Pompeian villa (now called the Getty Villa), which opened in 1974. When Getty died two years later, aged 83, Getty oil stock was left to the museum; this $700-million endowment has ballooned into billions. Planning for the ambitious Getty Center began almost immediately, but family lawsuits (eventually running up $26.4 million in legal fees) held up events until 1982.

With five marriages and innumerable mistresses, Getty had 26 children, but only one – his third son, Gordon – is connected with the museum today.

...wing British artist J.M.W. Turner's Modern Rome – ...mpo Vaccino (1839).

... Museum at the Getty Villa in Malibu is dedicated to ...ek, Roman, and Etruscan pieces.

Ancient sculpture at the Getty Villa.

DISNEYLAND AND AROUND LA

Pasadena, the San Fernando Valley, Anaheim… the fringes of the Los Angeles region offer historic houses, gardens galore, not to mention the magic of Disneyland and other family-friendly attractions.

Heading north of the Los Angeles Basin, in which the whole of downtown Los Angeles sits, you reach the San Fernando Valley. Better known locally as "the Valley," this valley encircled by the Traverse Ranges is home to beautiful gardens, historic missions, plenty of malls, and some 1.8million people.

East of Los Angeles, Pasadena boasts noteworthy gardens of its own at the Huntington Library, Art Collections and Botanical Gardens, not to mention an annual New Year's Day parade featuring elaborate floats made entirely of flowers. For year-round entertainment, head just south of Los Angeles. Despite the great popularity of newer theme parks, there's nothing quite like the original Disneyland, or the other family attractions around Anaheim.

PASADENA AND ENVIRONS

To the east of the San Fernando Valley and bordering almost on the San Gabriel Mountains, **Pasadena ❶** comes fully alive once a year during the Rose Bowl football game and the famous Tournament of Roses Parade, held on New Year's Day. Any other day of the year, the city's houses, museums, and gardens take center stage.

Near the freeway is the 18-room **Fenyes Mansion** (1905), home of the

Pasadena Museum of History (tel: 626-577-1660; https://pasadenahistory.org; Wed–Sun noon–5pm) where D.W. Griffith shot one of his first films. Half a block away is the impressive **Gamble House** (tel: 626-793-3334; http://gamble house.org; guided tours: Tue 11:30am–1:30, Thu–Fri 11.30am–4pm, Sat–Sun noon–4pm), built for David Gamble (of Procter & Gamble, America's biggest soap company) in 1908. Technically a California-style "bungalow," the terraced, wood-tiled house is a product of the turn of the 20th-century Arts and

◎ Main attractions
Norton Simon Museum
Huntington Library, Art Collections and Botanical Gardens
Universal Studios
Disneyland
Knott's Berry Farm

Map on page 240

Loop-the-loop at Knott's Berry Farm.

Crafts Movement of which the Greene brothers, Charles Sumner and Henry Mather, were noted members. Its interior is a knockout, but its impressive exterior makes it worth seeing even when the house is closed.

Just south of the freeway is the **Norton Simon Museum ❷** (411 W. Colorado at Orange Grove; tel: 626-449-6840; www.nortonsimon.org; Mon and Wed-Thu noon-5pm, Fri-Sat 11am-8pm, Sun 11am-5pm), where one the world's most impressive private art collections is held. Norton Simon (1907–93) was an industrialist who acquired a remarkable collection of both European and South and Southeast Asian art. Some of the most famous pieces in his collection are Madonna and Child with Book (c.1502–03) by Raphael, Portrait of a Boy (c.1655–60) by Rembrandt van Rijn, Mulberry Tree (1889) by Vincent van Gogh, Little Dancer Aged Fourteen (1878–81) by Edgar Degas, and Woman with a Book (1932) by Pablo Picasso. In addition to Simon's collection, the museum's 12,000-artwork collection includes pieces from the former Pasadena Art Museum. Each year, about 1,000 of the museum's 12,000 artworks are displayed.

The main local attraction, however, is the **Huntington Library, Art Collections, and Botanical Gardens ❸** (1151 Oxford Road, San Marino; tel: 626-405-2100; www.huntington.org; Wed-Mon 10am-5pm), the former gardens and library of multi-millionaire railroad magnate Henry Edwards Huntington. With his wife Arabella, Huntington assembled one of the most important collections of art and rare books in the country.

The main art gallery has several world-famous paintings: Thomas Gainsborough's *Blue Boy* (c.1770), Thomas Lawrence's *Pinkie* (1794), Sir Joshua Reynolds' *Sarah Siddons* (1784), and John Constable's *View on the Stour* (1822). The library has an astonishing five million items. Among those on display are a 1410 edition of Chaucer's *Canterbury Tales*, a Gutenberg Bible, Audubon prints, and an early Shakespeare folio.

The tranquil gardens occupy more than 100 acres (40 hectares). Beyond the lily pond are the colorful Subtropical Garden, the Australian Garden, and the Japanese and Zen gardens flanking a delightful 19th-century Japanese house. After crossing a little red bridge over the carp-filled lake and climbing some steps, you can take tea at the charming **Rose Garden Tea Room** (reservations required, book online or call 626-683-8131).

North of Pasadena, off the Angeles Crest Highway exit on Interstate 210, is fragrant **Descanso Gardens** ❹ (1418 Descanso Drive, La Cañada Flintridge; tel: 818-949-4200; www. descansogardens.org; daily 9am–5pm), which cover what remains of a 30,000-acre (12,000-hectare) ranch. The 165-acre (67-hectare) gardens can take several hours to explore. The oak and camellia woodlands constitute one of the largest camellia collections in the world, with more than 600 varieties. The woodlands began as carefully planned landscaping along the private drive leading to

a magnificent 22-room house built in 1938 by the energetic *Daily News* publisher E. Manchester Boddy.

The woodlands collection is augmented by winding trails, a lilac garden, the International Rosarium (a timeline of roses from Cleopatra's day to the present), and the Japanese Garden and Teahouse, which serves refreshments in summer. Something is always in bloom whenever you arrive: daffodils, tulips, and lilacs in the spring, chrysanthemums in the fall.

SAN FERNANDO VALLEY

Were it a city unto itself, the San Fernando Valley would be the fifth-largest in the country, topped only by New York, Chicago, Houston, and Los Angeles. Despite sporadic efforts to secede, the valley is not its own city, however – with the exception of holdouts Burbank and Glendale, which are separate cities. All the differently designated areas are merely neighborhoods in the City of Los Angeles, and compose nearly one-third of LA's population.

> **⊙ Tip**
>
> There are several ticket options available at Universal Studios including the 1-day General Admission (visit the website for details). Budget-conscious visitors can take the Metro Red Line from Downtown or Hollywood to the Universal City station.

In contrast to neighboring areas, the valley – about 24 miles (39km) wide and 12 miles (19km) north to south – is a staggeringly flat expanse of land bounded by the Ventura county line on the west, the San Gabriel mountains to the north, the Verdugo range on the east, and the Santa Monica Mountains and Hollywood Hills on the south. The west and south sides are the more affluent: cities like **Encino**, **Tarzana**, **Woodland Hills** and **West Hills** display few signs of opulence, but a quiet wealth predominates. Heavy industry is almost all concentrated in the northern area, around Pacoima, Sylmar, and San Fernando.

MOVIE AND TV STUDIOS

West of Griffith Park, in the Cahuenga Pass that joins Hollywood to the valley, is **Universal Studios ❺** (Hollywood 101; tel: 800-864 -8377; www.universalstudioshollywood.com; see website for hours), whose daily tours offer glimpses of the studio in what is in effect an amusement park. A 60-minute tram ride visits King Kong and the giant shark from *Jaws*, negotiates the perils of a flash flood, goes past the Bates Motel from Psycho and gets caught up in a thrilling car chase at 120 miles per hour on the Fast & Furious Supercharged set. Other attractions include *Jurassic Park: The* Ride, The Simpsons Ride, Harry Potter and the Forbidden Journey as well as Transformers: The Ride – 3D. Directly next door to the studios, **Universal CityWalk** (tel: 818-622-9841; www.citywalkhollywood.com) is a glittery mall with one-of-a-kind shops, a contemporary art gallery, and a 19-screen cinema.

To the west, in **Studio City**, is CBS **Studio Center** (tel: 818-655-5000) where sit-coms like Seinfeld have been made; there are no tours, but the public can apply for tickets to be members of the audience. InBurbank there are two studio tours, the NBC **Television Studios** (www.nbcuniversal.com) and **Warner Brothers Studios** (www.wbstudiotour.com). Also in Burbank is the unbelievably successful

San Fernando Valley.

Walt Disney Studios (www.waltdisney studios.com) but it is not open to the public.

GLENDALE

A few miles northeast, in the town of **Glendale ❻**, the **Brand Library and Art Center** (1601 W. Mountain Street at Grandview Avenue; Tue–Thu 11am–8pm, Fri–Sun 10am–5pm) houses the art and music section of the city's public library in a Moorish-style mansion. Inspired by the East Indian Pavilion at the 1893 Chicago World's Fair, it was built in 1904 by Leslie C. Brand, and the peaceful, landscaped grounds are perfect for picnicking.

The *Great Wall of Los Angeles* mural (west wall of the concrete flood control channel on Coldwater Canyon Avenue between Burbank Boulevard and Oxnard Street, North Hollywood; http://sparcinla.org) claims to be the world's longest mural. It recounts the history of California from dinosaurs to the present, and doesn't leave out the nasty bits.

One of the murals on *The Great Wall of Los Angeles*, Glendale.

FROM VAN NUYS TO ENCINO

Heading west along the Ventura Freeway, several great homes and gardens dot the valley neighborhoods. The **Japanese Garden** (6100 Woodley Avenue, Van Nuys; tel: 818-756-8166; www.suihoen.thejapanesegarden.com; Mon–Thu 11am–4pm and Sun 10am–4pm), a 6-acre (2-hectare) botanical delight, is littleknown

Arts and Crafts-designed Gamble House, Pasadena.

Shopping is a popular pastime in the Valley. There are mega-malls like the Sherman Oaks Galleria, which is halfway between Westfield Topanga to the west and Glendale Galleria nearer to LA; also at the western end are Westfield Promenade in Woodland Hills, and Town and Country Shopping Center and Plaza de Oro in the town of Encino. There's also 21-mile (34km) -long Ventura Boulevard, the Valley's upscale artery of restaurants and pricey shops.

Universal Studios.

despite having been created over two decades ago on the Donald C. Tillman Water Reclamation Plant. Tours visit three areas of the property designed in distinctly different styles: a dry karensansui, a wet garden, and an authentic tea ceremony garden with a tatami mat tea room. In summer, popular "sunset" tours are offered on weekdays.

Orcutt Ranch Horticultural Center (23600 Roscoe Boulevard, Canoga Park; tel: 818-346-7449; www.laparks. org) perfectly recalls a vanished moment in California history, with citrus groves bounded by ancient, majestic, and stately oaks. When the Orcutts purchased the 200-acre (80-hectare) estate in 1917, they named it Rancho Sombra del Roble, "ranch in the shadow of the oak," which is quite literally the case. There is one magnificent valley oak, 33ft (10 meters) in circumference that is estimated to be at least 700 years old. The orange groves are only open to the public on one weekend announced in July.

Shadow Ranch (22633 Vanowen Street, Canoga Park; tel: 818-883-3637; www.laparks.org; Mon–Fri 9am–6.30pm, Sat 10am– 4pm) is a restored 1870 ranch house built by LA pioneer Albert Workman and located on the remaining 9 acres (4 hectares) of a 60,000-acre (24,000-hectare) wheat ranch. It reopened in 2001, seven years after being damaged in the Northridge earthquake. The stands of eucalyptus are purported to be parents of the towering trees that now blanket the state, and the ranch is currently used as a community center.

At the valley's western end, near Mulholland Drive, is the **Leonis Adobe** (23537 Calabasas Road at Mulholland Drive; tel: 818-222-6511; www.leonisadobemuseum.org; Fri and Sun 1–4pm, Sat 10am–4pm), a two-story 1844 Monterey-style ranch house transformed by "King of Calabasas" Miguel Leonis into this charming home, fully restored and furnished with livestock and artifacts. Located on the same property is the **Plummer House** (serving as the **park visitor center**), a pretty Victorian cottage that was transported from Hollywood to avoid demolition.

Los Encinos State Historic Park ❼ (16756 Moorpark Street, Encino; tel: 818-784-4849; www.parks.ca.gov; Wed–Sun 10am–5pm), originally the site of a Native American village, later became a ranch belonging to the de la Ossa family, who planted vineyards and orchards, and raised cattle. Amid the five acres (2 hectares) of manicured lawns, duck ponds, and eucalyptus and citrus groves is the de la Ossa Adobe, built in 1849 and restored with period furnishings. A stone blacksmith shop and a two-story French provincial home, built by the ranch's second owners, are also located here.

Near the junction of Interstates 5 and 405 in Mission Hills is the historic and interesting **Mission San Fernando Rey de España** ❽ (tel: 818-361-0186; www.missionscalifornia.com; daily 9am–4.30pm), California's 17th mission, founded in 1797. Its history has been shaped by destruction in two earthquakes (1806 and 1971) and

reconstruction. The tour of the working, sleeping, and recreation areas, and an extensive collection of artifacts vividly recreate a sense of day-to-day early mission life.

Nearby, the **Andres Pico Adobe**, the oldest home in San Fernando and second-oldest in the Greater LA area, was built by Mission San Fernando Indians in 1834. After years of disuse, it was purchased and restored in 1930 by the curator of the Southwest Museum, housing the **San Fernando Valley Historical Society** (www.sfvhs.com). Just to the northeast are the very different **Nethercutt Museum** (Tue–Sat 9am–4.30pm) and **Nethercutt Collection** (15151 and 15200 Bledsoe Street, Sylmar; tel: 818-364-6464; www.nethercuttcollection.org; guided tours only Thu–Sat 10am or 1.30pm), two private facilities owned and operated by the Merle Norman Cosmetic Co. They offer the visitor a world-class and sizeable collection of antiques, vintage automobiles, rare musical instruments, and music boxes. Tours of the collection require reservations.

⊘ Where

A stunning scenic route is Mulholland Drive (called Mulholland Highway in its western section), which goes across the Santa Monica Mountains from the Hollywood Hills and almost to the ocean at Santa Monica. The drive offers – among other pleasures – a 360-degree view of Los Angeles. It also gives its name to the movie directed by David Lynch, who lived nearby and said of it: "You feel the history of Hollywood in that road."

Inside Mission San Fernando Rey de España.

⊘ HALLOWEEN HAUNT

For over 35 years, Knott's Berry Farm has presented the world's largest (and most famous) theme park Halloween event: the annual Halloween Haunt. From late September to Halloween night, Knott's Berry Farm becomes Knott's Scary Farm, treating fear-lovers to several spooky mazes, where you'll encounter murderous mutants, deadly arachnids, lurking vampires, cursed pirates, and the infamous Grendel.

In addition, you'll see irreverent comedy routines, magic shows, and "psychobilly" concerts. Some might find the experience corny, but it's definitely worth a look. Be aware that Halloween Haunt is a special ticket event (not covered by regular theme park admission and not recommended for children under 13).

Disney once said that Disneyland grew out of his search for a clean, safe, friendly park where he could take his own daughters.

One of Disney's early designers, John Hench, referred to Walt's knack for putting "little touches of humanity" in everything he did. Hench said that Mickey Mouse's appeal has something to do with his body shape – all circles, all round, harmless and non-threatening. In fact, because of a height restriction – you can't have Mickey towering too much over his fans – most of the besuited Mouse persons in Disneyland are actually girls.

There's still no successful way to avoid the crowds and the lengthy line-ups, especially in summertime. Obviously, it helps to get there as soon as the gates open and head straight for the most popular rides. To avoid backtracking, cover the park one "land" at a time, including the ever-pleasing and hugely ambitious worlds of Fantasyland, Adventureland, Frontierland, Critter Country, and jazzy New Orleans Square.

Head to Fantasyland and Mickey's Toontown to meet Disney characters, Mickey and Minnie, Goofy, and Donald Duck.

Andres Pico Adobe.

DISNEYLAND: THE MAGIC KINGDOM

Despite the great popularity of newer theme parks, there's nothing quite like the original **Disneyland** ❾ (1313 Harbor Boulevard, Anaheim; tel: 714-781-4000; www.disneyland.disney. go.com), first opened with the tagline "Magic Kingdom" in 1955. Walt

THE DISNEY LANDS

Main Street is the place to get information and maps (City Hall), exchange foreign currency and get money from an ATM, hire a stroller or wheelchair (just inside the main entrance), stash your surplus items in a locker (adjoining Disney Clothiers), and attend to your infant (Baby Center, near the Magic Castle).

Fantasyland is often a favorite for younger children, home to Sleeping Beauty's Castle and rides like the It's a Small World cruise, the 68-horse King Arthur Carrousel, Mad Tea Party teacups, and miniature circus train that tours Storybook Land. Some of the other rides in Fantasyland, such as Peter Pan's Flight, **Matterhorn**, Mr Toad's Wild Ride, **Snow White's Scary Adventures**, and Alice in Wonderland, seem to be aimed as much at adults. The first two are especially interesting, demonstrating how much illusion owes to darkness and luminous paint.

Fantasyland is also a key place to meet characters. Disney Princess Fantasy Faire offers little ones a chance to meet princesses like Snow White, Aurora, Cinderella, and Mulan. Over in Pixie Hollow, you can snap photos with Tinkerbell and her fairy friends. Then head over near the Pinocchio's Daring Journey ride to meet Rapunzel and Flynn Rider from Disney's Tangled.

Another spot youngsters enjoy is Mickey's Toontown, where you can explore Mickey's House, Minnie's House, Goofy's Playhouse, Donald's Boat, and the Chip 'n' Dale Treehouse.

Adventureland is home to the popular Indiana Jones Adventure, a ride into an ancient temple full of giant snakes and screaming mummies. For a tamer experience, the Jungle Cruise, Tarzan's Treehouse, and the Enchanted Tiki Room are fun options. The tiki room was first visualized as a restaurant, but grew into a major attraction. The audio-animatronics pioneered with the moving, speaking figure of Abraham Lincoln on Main Street culminated in the 225 talking, moving birds, flowers and figures of the **Enchanted Tiki Room**.

In Critter Country, paddle along the Rivers of America in a canoe, then cool off on Splash Mountain, a water

◔ Fact

After its 500-ton steel framework was in place, the 147ft (45-meter) Matterhorn – 1/100th the size of the real thing – was built from the top down. This was to stop the subsequent cement droppings spoiling the appearance of the slopes below.

Sleeping Beauty's Castle at Disneyland.

⊙ Tip

If you have a car (and very limited time), you could just squeeze Disneyland and a visit to the architecturally fascinating Christ Cathedral of Roman Catholic Diocese of Orange (formally Crystal Cathedral; 13280 Chapman Avenue, Garden Grove; tel: 714-971-2141; www.christcathedralcalifornia. org; Mon–Fri 10am– 3.00pm, Sat 9am–4pm) into the same day, and still have dinner while watching the jousting at Medieval Times.

flume ride that finishes with a five-story plunge.

Frontierland is home to the amusingly hokey Big Thunder Mountain Railroad, the Mark Twain Riverboat, an infrared shooting gallery, Pirate's Lair on Tom Sawyer Island, and a recreated 1880 ranch with a petting zoo. This is also where the pyrotechnic nighttime spectacular **Fantasmic!** takes place, for which crowds start jostling two hours' before it starts to get a good view. North of Frontierland there is a new land under construction: Star Wars: Galaxy's Edge (scheduled to open in 2019).

Pointing the way to Tomorrowland is Astro Orbitor, which has colorful rockets circling a series of moving planets. People pilot their own spaceships as they soar through an animated "astronomical model" of constellations. Tommorowland is also home to one of the park's most famous attractions: the Space Mountain roller coaster. After a thrilling turn on Space Mountain, hop on the Disneyland Railroad or Disneyland Monorail for a relaxing ride.

Theme park rides at Disneyland.

Try not to miss **New Orleans Square**, with its spooky **Haunted Mansion** and the nearby **Pirates of the Caribbean**. Talking about his cast of 64 humans and 55 animals in Pirates, sculptor Blaine Gibson explained: "In a ride system you have only a few seconds to say something about a figure through your art. So we exaggerate their features, especially their facial features, so they can be quickly and easily understood from a distance... we have to instantly communicate 'good guy' or 'bad guy.' We try to provide the illusion of life."

In addition to the Disneyland Park, you can visit **Disney's California Adventure**, a 55-acre (22-hectare) theme park with a 750-room luxury hotel and a huge shopping, dining, and entertainment center, aptly named the **Downtown Disney District**. Rides like Guardians of the Galaxy–Mission: BREAKOUT!, Radiator Springs Racers, and the Guardians of the Galaxy – Monsters After Dark are fun for older kids, along with the thrilling California Screamin' and Grizzly River Run. Little ones can take an It's Tough to Be a Bug! ride or play at Princess Dot Puddle Park.

Tickets can be bought for both parks, although you really need more than one day to visit them.

KNOTT'S BERRY FARM

A few miles north of Disneyland is the 160-acre **Knott's Berry Farm** ⑩ (8039 Beach Boulevard, Buena Park; tel: 714-220-5200; www.knotts.com; hours vary). A recreated 19th-century gold town, Knott's Berry Farm grew out of a roadside snack bar operated by farmer Walter Knott and his wife Cordelia, whose reputation spread far and wide for tasty chicken dinners and slabs of boysenberry pie (served on the couple's wedding china). The oldest theme park in the county, predating its bigger and much more famous rival by a few years, is just as interesting but a little funkier. The characters are more primitive than high-tech and the staff charm tourists with individual attention. The **Ghost Town** offers panning for gold, a stagecoach ride, a watery log ride, and stunt and vaudeville shows.

In the contemporary side of the park, the various other theme areas include stomach-dropping rides such as the 20-story-freefall Supreme Scream. Thrill-seekers will also enjoy GhostRider, Silver Bullet, Supreme Scream, Xcelerator, and the spinning coaster Sierra Sidewinder. Tributes to Southern California's beach culture include the 13-acre (5-hectare) water park with 22 slides, **Soak City**, and the surf-inspired dual roller coaster, Rip Tide. Meanwhile kids love the cartoon-themed **Camp Snoopy** with its miniature train and other rides. As a tribute to Spanish California, Knott's **Fiesta Village** entices visitors with mariachi bands, ferocious rides like Jaguar! and **Montezooma's Revenge**, as well as scrumptious and reasonably priced tacos, fajitas, and burritos.

You can continue the theme-park theme over dinner at **Medieval Times** in Buena Park (tel: 888-935-6878), where hundreds of enthusiastic customers dine every night, egging on pretend knights in jousting battles in a castle-like area while eating with their bare hands.

⏱ Fact

From the Sleeping Beauty Castle and the steam train to the Mark Twain Riverboat, most structures in Disneyland are scaled down from full size. Movie-set designers are experts at using tricks of scale to make buildings seem taller or further away. The first floors of the buildings on Main Street, for example, are 90 percent of full size, the second floor 80 percent and so on.

Scream-inducing ride at Knott's Berry Farm.

⏱ DISNEYLAND TIPS

Anaheim is best known for its amusement parks and similar attractions, of which Disneyland is by far the most famous and well attended. If you want to visit Disneyland when there are fewer visitors, come Tuesday to Thursday during mid-September through mid-November, mid-January through mid-March, or mid-April through mid-May.

To save time waiting in line, use Disneyland's free FASTPASS service (subject to availability). These passes save your place in line for Space Mountain, Big Thunder Mountain Railroad, and other popular attractions while you explore the rest of the park.

If you're traveling with children and have two or more adults in your party, you can use the rider swap program that lets you go on the ride while one adult waits with the child. You then "swap" to enable the other adult to enjoy the attraction as well.

If you don't want to drive, Metro Express Line bus 460 travels to Disneyland from Los Angeles, as does a train from Union Station. To make the trip more relaxed, you could stay in the Anaheim area. Pushing itself heavily as a convention destination, there's not a lot to see, but it will save traveling. Disneyland itself has pricey but amusing hotels located on its grounds, but there are cheaper motels on surrounding roads; most branches of major hotel chains operate free shuttle buses to the park.

Scenic
Route

22

SOUTH BAY AND THE ORANGE COAST

Pristine beaches, ecological preserves, and a
Surfing Walk of Fame are just a few of the
coastal attractions south of Los Angeles.

Driving down the coast from Los
Angeles towards San Diego takes
a little longer than whizzing down
the freeway, but the seaside route
along the Pacific Coast Highway
("the PCH") is much more beautiful
and interesting. Starting in the South
Bay neighborhood of Palos Verdes
(still part of Los Angeles County)
you explore a string of beach towns
– Long Beach, Seal Beach, Huntington Beach, Newport Beach, Laguna
Beach – before hitting Del Mar. Along
the way, Catalina Island and San Juan
Capistrano are delightful detours.

PALOS VERDES PENINSULA

The **Palos Verdes** peninsula is home
to magnificent seaside houses as
well as more humble natural attractions. Next to a lighthouse, the
Point Vicente Interpretive Center
❶ (31501 Palos Verdes Drive West;
tel: 310-377-5370; daily 10am–5pm)
includes exhibits focusing on the peninsula's natural and cultural history,
such as a relief map showing how
mountainous the peninsula's terrain is, an informative whale-watching video, and earphones to hear
the whales' mournful voices. Look
through telescopes to spot passing
whales (December to spring), then
pick up a leaflet that identifies plants

along the Botanic Trail, or picnic on
the grassy grounds. More nature
fun is found at **Abalone Cove** beach,
west of Narcissa Drive, which is an
ecological preserve perfect for diving
and exploring tidepools.

About two miles (3km) further on
is the wood-and-glass **Wayfarers
Chapel** (5755 Palos Verdes Drive; tel:
310-377-1650; www.wayfarerschapel.
org; visitors center daily 9am–
5pm, grounds are open from 9am),
designed by Frank Lloyd Wright's
son, Lloyd, whose inspiration is said

Main attractions
Queen Mary
Aquarium of the Pacific
Santa Catalina Island
Laguna Beach
San Juan Capistrano
  Mission

Map on page 252

*Posing on the Surfing Walk of Fame,
Huntington Beach.*

Avocados are grown along the coast from central to south California thanks to the soil type, amount of sunshine, and ocean breeze combining for ideal growing conditions.

to have been Northern California's majestic redwood trees. It was built in 1951 as a memorial to the 18th-century Swedish theologian Emanuel Swedenborg. In the peaceful gardens, songbirds warble and a fountain and stream gurgle. Services are held in the chapel every Sunday.

SAN PEDRO

Eastwards along the coast is **San Pedro**, headquarters of Southern California's fishing fleet, which once distinguished this town as a genuine fishing port. All the authentic old parts of what eons ago was a little fishing town are gone now, replaced by a pseudo construction called **Ports O'Call Village**. It is surprisingly imaginative: several blocks of saltbox-type, apparently weathered New England shops – all in appealing, matching styles. Harbor tours and fishing trips can be taken from here, as well as a classic sailing ship and the *Catalina Express* (tel: 800 613-1212; www.catalinaexpress.com), which sails to Santa Catalina Island.

A few miles south is San Pedro's **Cabrillo Beach ❷**, which has earned a reputation as one of the best places in the area to windsurf. Beginners especially favor the sheltered waters inside the harbor breakwater. Some visitors also relish the nearby Cabrillo Marine Aquarium (3720 Stephen M. White Drive; tel: 310-548-7562; www.cabrillomarineaquarium.org; Tue–Fri noon–5pm, Sat–Sun 10am–5pm) and elevated coastal trail. Palos Verdes Drive segues into 25th Street, from which a left turn on Gaffey (State Highway 110) and up to state Highway 47 over the **Vincent Thomas Bridge** takes you straight ahead through Long Beach on Ocean Boulevard.

Out in the bay take a close look at the palm-fringed island with the tall towers that are illuminated at night: it's actually one of four man-made islands created by a consortium of oil companies to hold (and conceal) all the working oil derricks that tap one of the richest offshore fields in the United States.

South Bay and Orange County

LONG BEACH

The most famous attraction in the town of **Long Beach** is the wonderful, historic *Queen Mary* ❸ (1126 Queens Highway; tel: 562-499-1739; www.queen mary.com), a retired ocean liner that made 1,001 trips across the Atlantic Ocean since it was launched in 1936. Today the Art Deco halls, restaurants, and lounges have been beautifully restored. Tours are available, as is dinner or a hotel room on the ship itself.

On the Rainbow Harbor across the water from the *Queen Mary* is the **Aquarium of the Pacific** ❹ (100 Aquarium Way; tel: 562-590-3100; www.aquarium ofpacific.org; daily 9am–6pm). One of the country's best, it houses 11,000 ocean animals representing more than 500 species, from mesmerizing jellyfish to leopard sharks and barracuda.

Art offerings include the local Long Beach Museum of Art (2300 East Ocean Boulevard; tel: 562-439-2119; www.lbma.org; Fri–Sun 11am–5pm, until 8pm Thu). Long Beach is also well known in particular for its video art and street murals.

One of the most attractive suburbs of Long Beach is **Naples**, with its winding streets, waterside houses, and one-hour **gondola tours** on boats that cruise elegantly along a series of canals.

SANTA CATALINA ISLAND

A temperate outcrop 26 miles (42km) off the coast, lovely **Santa Catalina Island** ❺ is home to rugged canyons and 54 miles (87km) of coastline. Two-thirds of the scenic island is protected, making it a quiet (and relatively car-free) weekend excursion, though if time is short, it can all be squeezed into one day.

Begin early in the day by taking the *Catalina Express* (tel: 800-613-1212; www.catalinaexpress.com) from Long Beach, zipping across to the charming capital of **Avalon** in one hour; with extreme luck you may even spot a whale en route. Ferries also run from San Pedro, Newport Beach, and Dana Point. The five-minute walk into town passes a couple of places that rent bicycles or the ubiquitous golf carts,

The Art Deco casino in Avalon, Santa Catalina Island, is a ballroom and movie theater; despite its name, no gambling takes place.

Retired ocean liner Queen Mary.

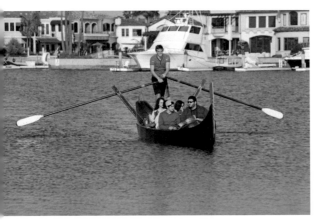

Gondola cruise in Naples, a suburb of Long Beach.

Navigating Avalon by golf cart, the main personal transportation on Santa Catalina Island.

in America to be built especially for the new talking pictures. Films are still screened nightly.

Water and island tours can be booked with companies on the pier. A 45-minute trip in a glass-bottomed boat from the **Pleasure Pier** traverses shallow waters filled with multi-colored fish (mostly olive or blue with the occasional orange garibaldi) darting in and out of a seaweed "garden." Fronds of kelp sway to the motion of the glass-bottomed boat, and at night little fish are replaced by nocturnal creatures, including "wimpy" lobsters that lack the formidable claws of their Maine cousins.

Inland motor tours often head up through the mountains to the island's airport, where historical pictures and a diorama featuring local animals are displayed. Apart from some flights to San Diego – which offer probably the most spectacular views of the island – the airport is used mostly by a freight company and a few private plane owners. A bus running from Avalon five times daily provides an

which are the main personal transportation on the island.

Head to the far end of the harbor to take in the **Casino on Avalon Bay**, the island's most recognizable landmark. It achieved national fame more than half a century ago with broadcasts of such famous bands as Count Basie and Kay Kyser playing in the Art Deco ballroom for as many as 6,000 dancers at a time. Built in 1929 at a cost of $2 million, the casino's ground-floor theater with a vintage pipe organ was the first

⊙ CATALINA ISLAND

Although "discovered" by Portuguese navigator Don Juan Rodríguez Cabrillo in 1542 and claimed for Spain 60 years later, Catalina was inhabited by Native Americans for thousands of years prior. But within two centuries of the Spaniards' arrival, the Native Americans had been virtually eliminated by Russian hunters searching for sea-otter pelts.

Descendants of General Phineas Banning, who operated the earliest legendary stagecoach routes across the West, once owned most of Catalina Island and began the process of turning it into a tourist resort, building the luxury Hotel St Catherine at Descanso Beach. Chewing-gum tycoon William Wrigley continued this development when he acquired the island after the great fire of 1915. He built the Hotel Atwater, an aviary, the Casino, and a mansion on Mount Ada (now an inn called Mt. Ada). The Wrigley family still owns about 11 percent of the island, having donated the remainder to the non-profit Island Conservancy.

Since the Conservancy took over, much of the damage has been repaired. Fauna such as bald eagle, fox, and wild boar have been protected and their numbers expanded. The Catalina gray fox is endemic to the island.

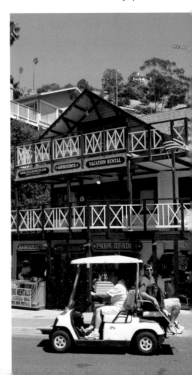

alternative way to get into the mountains from town.

Motor tours also stop at **El Rancho Escondido**, a ranch where Arabian horses are reared, before traversing the old stagecoach route across the island to various ancient Indian sites and secluded bays. The best parts of Catalina are these wilderness areas, popular with campers and hikers. You may even spot a couple of bison – descendants of a herd brought here (and then never taken away) when the movie of Zane Gray's book, *The Vanishing American*, was shot on the island in 1925. The house Grey once owned is now the **Zane Grey Pueblo Hotel**.

HUNTINGTON BEACH

In busy **Huntington Beach ➏**, slow down to avoid the surfers carrying their boards across the road to white-sand beaches fronting great waves. North and south of the 1,800-ft (540-meter) Huntington Pier is the three mile (5km) Huntington City Beach. It and the Huntington State Beach to the south have lifeguards, changing rooms, concessions, and parking. To the north, the Bolsa Chica State Beach is less crowded. Opposite the beach is a hotspot for bird-lovers: the Bolsa Chica Ecological Reserve, where hundreds of species including great blue herons have been spotted in the 1,180-acre (480-hectare) salt marsh.

Many of the communities around here dispute which most deserves the title "Surf City," but Huntington Beach may have the best case: the professional US Open surf competition is held here each July, a **Surfing Walk of Fame** commemorates legendary surfers on Main Street at the Pacific Coast Highway, and the International Surfing Museum (411 Olive Avenue; tel: 714-465-4350; www. surfingmuseum.org; Tue–Sun noon–5pm) displays classic surfboards and memorabilia.

NEWPORT BEACH

In chic **Newport Beach ➐**, the Balboa peninsula's six miles (10km) of sandy

Sailboats in Avalon's harbor.

Taking the Catalina Express ferry from Long Beach. The journey takes one hour and there are departures all year round.

Balboa Pavilion and Newport Harbor.

shore enclose Newport Harbor, home to 10,000 boats, many of them expensive yachts. On Main Street, it's hard to miss the **Balboa Pavilion**, built in 1906 as a railroad terminal, with its distinctive but totally unnecessary steeple. Behind it, you'll find fishing boats unloading their catch early in the morning.

Next to the pavilion is the ferry that makes the three-minute trip from Palm Street to **Balboa Island** ⑧. There you can gawk at million-dollar cottages and then shop and relax in cafés on Marine Avenue. Former homes of John Wayne and cowboy star Roy Rogers are on nearby islands. From **Balboa Pier**, you see kite flyers, frisbee-throwers, body-surfers, and sunbathers. Check out the diner at the end of the pier – the original branch of Ruby's – before finishing up at the **Balboa Fun Zone**, with its rides and video arcades, and the **Discovery Cube's Ocean Quest** (tel: 714-542-2823; www.oceanquestoc.org), which is great for kids. Almost a dozen luxury beachfront hotels have been built or

are under construction along the coast between here and San Diego.

South of Newport, **Corona del Mar** has gorgeous beaches, especially **Corona del Mar State Beach**. There are two reefs for snorkeling, plus volleyball courts, firepits, and restrooms on shore. En route to Laguna Beach, Crystal Cove State Park is a spot for beachgoers, tidepooling, hiking, and mountain biking.

LAGUNA BEACH AND DANA POINT

Ten miles south of Newport Beach, **Laguna Beach** ⑨ is another beautiful coastal community. This oceanside paradise has a creative streak. In the early 1900s, the California Plein Air (paintings created outside and not in a studio) art movement began here; today the Laguna Art Museum (307 Cliff Drive; tel: 949 494-8971; www.lagunaartmuseum.org; Mon–Tue and Fri–Sun 10am–5pm, Thu 11am–9pm) displays American art, fine art galleries and jewelry shops fill the streets, and the annual **Pageant of**

the **Masters** – first held in 1932 – presents tableaux of famous paintings with costumed participants each summer.

Before turning inland, the harbor at **Dana Point** is worth a stop to browse in the shops. Then it's off on Del Obispo Street to Camino Capistrano to visit a historic mission.

SAN JUAN CAPISTRANO

Nicknamed "The Jewel of the Mission" **San Juan Capistrano Mission** ⑩ (26801 Ortega Highway; tel: 949-234-1300; www.missionsjc.com; daily 9am–5pm) is seventh in the chain of 21 missions established by Franciscan padres in the 18th and 19th centuries (see page 34).

Father Junípero Serra founded several of the missions, this one included, and his statue stands beside the ruins of the Great Stone Church to the right as you enter. Behind the **Serra Chapel**, is the oldest still-in-use church in California. Pick up the free, annotated map, which points out what there is to see

here, from the bells to the left of the church to the location of the famous San Juan Capistrano swallows' nests, during their nesting season.

At the mission's far-left corner, where the tanning vats, metal furnaces, and tallow ovens can still be inspected, is the archeological field office, whose archaeologists still uncover old relics from time to time. The lovely gardens were added during the last century, but the main courtyard itself was always the

International Surfing Museum, Huntington Beach.

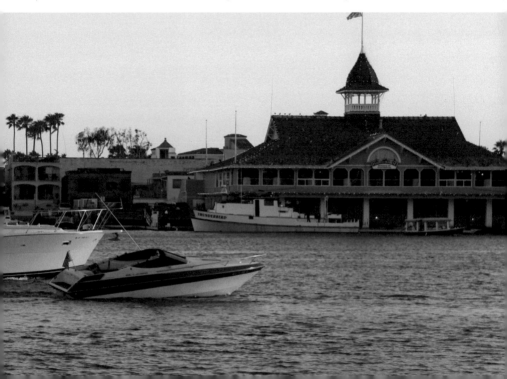

Visitors can snorkel, surf, dive, and spot marine life in tidepools at Laguna Beach, whose coast has been designated a Marine Protected Area (MPA).

central focus of the mission. It was also the site of rodeos in the old days, with eager spectators watching from the surrounding roofs, including that of the west wing, which now houses the **Mission Museum**.

SAN CLEMENTE TO RINCON SPRINGS

Just north of the controversial San Onofre Nuclear Generating Station is the town of **San Clemente**. Located 40 miles (65km) north in Yorba Linda, the **Nixon Presidential Library and Museum** (18001 Yorba Linda Boulevard; tel: 714-983-9120; www.nixon foundation.org; Mon–Sat 10am–5pm, Sun from 11am) chronicles the life and times of the former US president, who operated his western White House from San Clemente. San Clemente and Doheny state beaches allow camping for a small fee.

An interesting drive inland is along State Highway 76 (near Oceanside) to the village of **Pala**. The village is notable for the Mission San Antonio de Pala, an *asistancia* (extension

mission) built in 1816. Located on the Pala Indian Reservation, it is the only California mission still serving Indians and has celebrated its Corpus Christi Festival, with an open-air mass, dances, and games, on the first Sunday of every June since 1816.

The road continues southeast to **Rincon Springs**, a community to the north of Escondido on Road S6, and the gateway to **Palomar Mountain**. Rising 5,500ft (1,700 meters) above sea level and stretching for some 20 miles (32km), this is the home of the Hale Telescope and the Oschin Telescope, contained inside **Palomar Observatory** (Palomar Mountain, at the end of the S6 Road; tel: 760-742-2119; www.astro.caltech.edu/palomar; self-guided tours daily 9am–3pm, until 4pm in summer), which is owned and operated by the **California Institute of Technology**. Check the latest information before you set out as the observatory is closed in poor weather and hazardous travel conditions.

Off State Highway 76, you can catch Interstate 15 south towards San Diego.

⊙ SAN JUAN CAPISTRANO SWALLOWS

The famous cliff swallows of San Juan Capistrano historically arrived at the mission on or around March 19th, St Joseph's day, when they were greeted with a festival. "Scout swallows" tip off their return, arriving a few days before the rest of the flock. Come autumn, they would leave the mission on or near the Day of San Juan, October 23rd, flying 6,000 miles (10,000km) south to winter in Argentina.

Legend has it that the swallows first came to the mission seeking safety after a shopkeeper destroyed their gourd-shaped mud nests. Now their protection is guaranteed: the city prohibits destroying their nests, both in the church ruins and elsewhere in the Capistrano Valley.

While an innkeeper may have driven the swallows to the mission, they likely stayed because of the mission's location near two rivers, which provided plenty of insects for the swallows to feast on.

The swallows became truly famous after Leon Rene recorded "When the Swallows Come Back to Capistrano" in 1940. The hit song was also later recorded by Glenn Miller and Pat Boone.

Today, many of the swallows have relocated farther from town, a result of the area's development, which has reduced the number of insects in the area. Still, the town and Mission celebrate their return each year with a festival and Swallows Day Parade (www.swallowsparade.com).

Mormon Point in Death Valley.

THE DESERTS

California's deserts attract those seeking extremes: the striking rock formations of Joshua Tree National Park, a bouyant sea, and the desolate landscapes of the Mojave and Death Valley are some of the deserts' highlights.

California's deserts feature some of the state's most unusual and uniquely stunning landscapes. The 800,000-acre (300,000-hectare) Joshua Tree National Park is a Dr Seuss-like landscape of twisted trees, granite monoliths, and rugged canyons. The Anza-Borrego Desert State Park is renowned for its deluge of bright wildflowers every spring, and the buoyant Salton Sea for its ability to make everything float more easily. Colored sandstone towers and limestone spires punctuate the Mojave Desert, while Death Valley is home to the jagged Devil's Golf Course and an extinct volcano. Compared to all this desolation, the luxury spa resorts of Palm Springs are a veritable oasis, and make an easy entry into California's desert regions.

FROM LA TO PALM SPRINGS

The San Bernardino freeway, then the I-10, will bring you to Palm Springs (population 44,550) from Los Angles in just under three hours, but the Pomona Freeway (the continuation of the Santa Monica Freeway) is an alternative route, which takes you closer to the city of **Riverside ❶**.

Architect Charles Moore once observed that if you could see only one building in Southern California, downtown Riverside's **The Mission Inn Hotel**

and Spa (3649 Mission Inn Avenue; tel: 951-784-0300; www.missioninn.com; free 75-minute tours) should be it.

Opened in 1903, the grand hotel catered to Riverside's influx of wealthy residents and visitors: by the 1890s, Riverside had become the richest city per capita in the country. Albert Einstein, Henry Ford, Susan B. Anthony, Sarah Bernhardt, and Joseph Pulitzer are just a few of the dozens of celebrities who have visited the inn, political visitors have included former President Richard Nixon and Pat Nixon, who

Main attractions
Palm Springs Aerial
  Tramway
Joshua Tree National Park
Anza-Borrego Desert
  State Park
Salton Sea
Lake Havasu
Mount Whitney
Devil's Golf Course
Scotty's Castle

Map on page 262

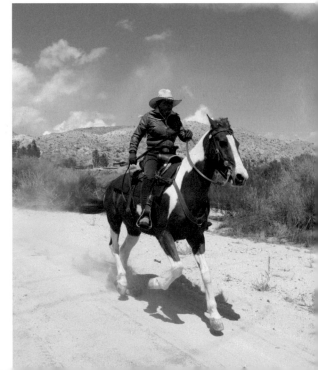

Riding at Cottonwood Canyon Ranch, near Palm Springs.

The Deserts

0   50 miles
0   50 km

N

NEVADA

ARIZONA

Deep Springs
Big Pine
Owens
Scotty's Castle 15
Death
Inyo
Ubehebe Crater
Amargosa Range
Beatty
Glendale 15
Amargosa Valley
Valley
Mt Whitney 12
14494
Lone Pine
Stovepipe Wells
Furnace Creek
190
Lake Mead
Keeler Ghost Town
Skidoo
National
Zabriskie Point 14
Death Valley Junction
Pahrump
Las Vegas
Olancha
Argus Range Wilderness
Devils Golf Course
Badwater Basin
-282
Dante's View
Spring Valley
Henderson
Telescope Peak 11049
Ballarat
Park
Shoshone
Chimney Peak Wilderness
Tecopa
Kingston Peak 7323
Ridgecrest
Trona
Searles Lake
Trona Pinnacles 11
Mojave National Preserve
Mountain Pass
Red Rock Canyon State Park
Randsburg 10
Johannesburg
Mojave 8
Kelso Dunes
Baker
Cima
Mojave National Preserve 9
Kingman
Bullhead City
California City
Desert
Kramer Junction
Calico Ghost Town
Kelso
Bakersfield
Mojave
Rosamond
Barstow
Mojave
San Bernardino
Needles
Lake Havasu City
Lancaster
Newbury Springs
Ludlow
40
Essex
Havasu National Wildlife Refuge 7
Palmdale
Vincent
Adelamo
Victorville
Apple Valley
Lucerne Valley
Amboy
Cadiz
Lake Havasu
San Gabriel Mtns
Hesperia
Landers
Vidal Junction
Los Angeles
Big Bear City
Big Bear Lake
Twentynine Palms
Rice
Parker Colorado River Tribes Res.
Pasadena
Ontario
Yucca Valley
Colorado
Santa Barbara
Los Angeles 1
Riverside
San Bernardino
Desert Hot Springs
Eagle Mountain
Phoenix
Long Beach
Anaheim
Santa Ana
Moreno Valley
Perris
Palm Springs 2
Palm Springs Aerial Tramway
Palm Springs 3
Joshua Tree National Park 4
Desert Center
Blyth
Huntington Beach
Orange
Hemet
Rancho Mirage
Indio
Coachella
Riverside
Mesa Verde
Newport Beach
Wildomar
Santa Rosa Mtns
Lake Cahuilla
Ripley
San Juan Capistrano
Temecula
Chocolate Mtns
Palo Verde
San Clemente
Bonsall
Pala
Pauma Ind Res.
Desert Shores
Salton Sea State Recreation Area 5
ARIZONA
Santa Cataline Island
Oceanside
Carlsbad
Vista
Pauma Valley
Salton Sea
Sonny Bono Salton Sea National Wildlife Refuge
Calipatria
Glamis
Encinitas
Escondido
Ramona
Poway
Anza-Borrego Desert State Park 6
Westmorland
Imperial
Santa Catalina
Santee
San Diego
Brawley
San Clemente Island
San Diego
El Cajon
Spring Valley
Imperial
El Centro
Chula Vista
Calexico
Yuma
Tijuana
Mexicali

MEXICO

held their wedding party in the hotel, and former President Ronald Reagan and Nancy Reagan, who chose it for their honeymoon.

The beautiful hotel, complete with gargoyles, flying buttresses, and spiral staircases, was reopened in 1992 after a seven-year renovation that preserved its Tiffany stained-glass windows, the gold-leaf altar from a 17th-century Mexican church, a 120-year-old Steinway piano, and the special chair built to accommodate one overweight visitor, former President William Howard Taft.

A few miles east of Riverside, State Highway 60 joins Interstate 10. Just beyond that, giant model dinosaurs tower 30ft (9 meters) above the highway at Cabazon truck stop. From this point, the hillsides become covered with row after row of state-of-the-art steel wind turbines for the generation of electric power.

PALM SPRINGS

From Interstate 10, turn onto State Highway 111 to enter the affluent town of **Palm Springs** ❷, where stressed-out Angelenos come on weekends to indulge in golf, spas, and pampering. **Indian Canyon Drive** and the aptly named **Palm Canyon Drive** are the parallel main streets around which the town is structured. Follow the latter to see the charming **Village Green Heritage Center** (tel: 760-323-8297; https://pshistorical-society.org), with its restored adobe, a handful of 1800s buildings, and a recreated general store from the 1930s.

Other cultural attractions include the **Palm Springs Art Museum** (101 Museum Drive; tel: 760-322-4800; www.psmuseum.org; Sun, Mon, Tue, Fri, Sat 10am–5pm, Thu noon–8pm), with its contemporary paintings and sculpture, Meso-American art, miniatures, and celebrity photographs.

Nature lovers will love the city's **Moorten Botanical Garden** (1701 South Palm Canyon Drive; tel: 760-327-6555; http://moortenbotanical garden.com; Thu–Tue 10am–4pm, in summer 9am–1pm). The attractive

⊘ Where

A half-hour southeast of Riverside, between Interstates 15 and 215, the Perris Valley airport is a lift-off point for hot-air balloonists, and, at Perris Valley Skydiving, (tel: (800) 832-8818; http://sky diveperris.com) would-be parachutists can take a training course that concludes with an actual jump. For people who can't decide, there's even an option to parachute out of a hot-air balloon.

Wedding party at Mission Inn.

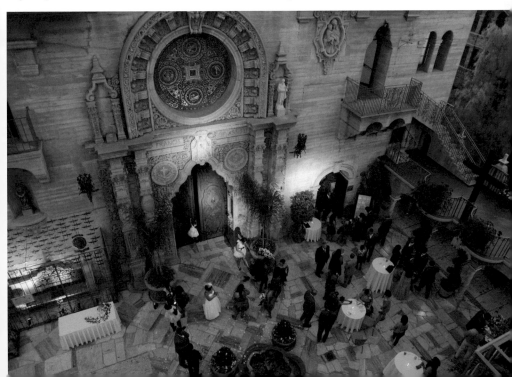

Awe-inspiring views at the top of the Palm Springs Aerial Tramway (at 8,500ft/2,600 meters) can be enjoyed along with either fine dining at Peaks Restaurant or cafeteria-style fare at the Pines Café. There's also a cocktail bar offering beverages and appetizers.

"living museum" established in 1938 is home to giant cacti, desert plants, flowers, and shaded nature trails.

If you're tired of cooling off in your hotel's pool, join the younger crowd at the seasonal **Wet'n'Wild** water park (1500 Gene Autry Trail; tel: 760-327-0499; www.wetnwildpalmsprings.com; check the website for opening hours) to enjoy water slides, a lazy river, and a wave pool.

COACHELLA VALLEY

Just west of the city is the **Palm Springs Aerial Tramway** ❸ (One Tramway Road; tel: 888-515-8726; www.pstramway.com; Mon–Fri 10am–9.45pm, Sat–Sun 8am–9.45pm), where an awesome 10-minute ride pulls you up the sheer cliffs of Chino Canyon to an 8,516ft (2,596meter) peak of the **San Jacinto Mountains**. The views are magnificent.

The 200-sq-mile (518-sq-km) Coachella Valley below is huge enough to accommodate 10 cities and a wildlife preserve, whose star is a rare lizard whose "fringe toes"

Palm Springs Aerial Tramway.

allow it to swim through the sand as readily as a fish in water.

As might be imagined, the area abounds in luxury resorts, many of whose guest registers are a litany of famous names. The **La Quinta Resort and Club** (tel: 760-564-4111; www.laquintaresort.com), for example, is where Frank Capra checked in to polish the movie script of *Lost Horizon* and Irving Berlin composed *White Christmas*, a song all the more poignant perhaps due to the hot sunshine outside. Renovations uncovered sketches on the lobby's high ceilings by artist Diego Rivera.

If you don't have time to explore the real thing, **The Living Desert** (47900 Portola Avenue, Palm Desert; tel: 760-346-5694; www.livingdesert.org) can give you a quick taste of the region's desert wilderness. Located 15 miles (24km) southeast of Palm Springs, the nature park is filled with eagles, irresistible exotic animals such as zebras, gazelles, and lovable meerkats, along with desert shrubs, flowers, and cacti.

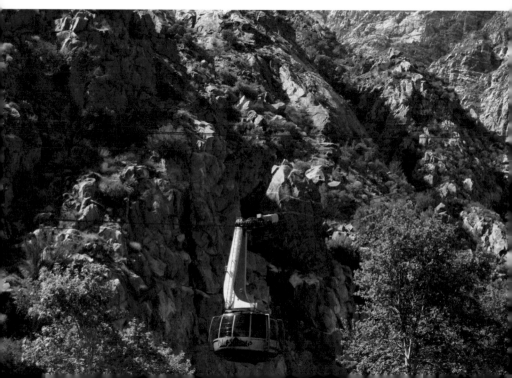

JOSHUA TREE NATIONAL PARK

Head north from Palm Springs on **Indian Canyon Drive** (which becomes Indian Avenue) to pass the city of **Desert Hot Springs** and eventually reach the **Joshua Tree National Park ❹** (tel: 760-367-5500; www.nps.gov). Established in 1936, the vast parkland is filled with strange rock formations, fascinating flora and fauna, and the tall, fibrous plants after which it is named (Mormon explorers named the plant in 1851). However, it's unlikely you'll see any of the mostly nocturnal animals – kangaroo rats, rattlesnakes – other than the occasional coyote and lizard, unless you stay overnight in one of the camping grounds.

The easiest way to visit this area, the similarly unspoiled Santa Rosa Mountains, and the Indian Canyons with their cool palm oases, is with one of the local adventure tour companies. Among the places they visit, **Indian Canyons** (tel: 760-416-7044; www.indian-canyons.com) are rich in flora and fauna. Hawks and bald eagles circle overhead; tiny kangaroo rats and fleet-footed bighorn sheep can occasionally be seen on the slopes. **Palm** and **Andreas canyons** have the largest stands of palm trees in the world.

INDIO AND THE SALTON SEA

The town of **Indio**, on Interstate 10 has been popular with tourists since 1921 when it began staging its annual National Date Festival (www.datefest.org). The week-long celebration in February includes an Arabian Nights pageant, and ostrich and camel racing. South of Indio and north of the Salton Sea is **Lake Cahuilla** (tel: 760-564-4712; www.rivcoparks.org). The lake is stocked with rainbow trout, striped bass and catfish. For non-anglers, there are hiking and equestrian trails, shady picnic spots, campsites, and a children's play area on the sandy beach – away from the fishermen.

The **Salton Sea ❺**, 35 miles (56km) long and 9 to 15 miles (14 to 24km) wide was, in fact, all a big mistake.

Wildflowers in Joshua Tree National Park. Depending on autumn and winter rainfall levels and spring temperatures, wildflowers may begin blooming in February, but March and April are usually the best months to see them.

Variety of cacti at Moorten Botanical Garden.

The Palms Oasis Trail in Joshua Tree National Park.

Hiking the Boy Scout Trail in Joshua Tree National Park.

In 1905 engineers attempted to divert some of the Colorado River to the Imperial Valley, but the river changed course and reflooded the ancient Salton Basin, 235ft (72 meters) below sea level. This formed a sea of 360 sq miles (932 sq km) with royal blue water filling the area where the Coachella and Imperial valleys merge. This human accident has resulted in an environmental mess today. Since the 1990s fish have died by the millions due to avian botulism in the location that was once referred to as the "California Riviera." Also, because the lake is receding, fine dust that is toxic to humans and crops is being released. Fortunately, funding has been secured to restore the lake that was once a playground for celebrities like Frank Sinatra and Jerry Lee Lewis as well as tourists from all over.

The Salton Sea is still a vital stopover point for over 420 species of birds and the Salton Sea State Recreation Area is an 18,000-acre (7,300-hectare) park with both developed and primitive campsites. There is a Bird Watch and Nature Trail (tel: 760-393-3059) and, 26 miles (42km) away on State Highway 86, an area where layers of marine fossils are visible along the base of the Santa Rosa Mountains.

ANZA-BORREGO DESERT STATE PARK

The 600,000-acre (200,000-hectare) **Anza-Borrego Desert State Park** ❻ (tel: 760-767-4205; www.parks. ca.gov) is the state's largest park. Its numerous canyons and gullies are easily accessible by car. Camping is permitted in the park, which is populated by jackrabbits, coyotes, kangaroo rats, and lizards, as well as more than 150 species of birds. The vegetation is equally varied, ranging from junipers and pines growing at the 5,000ft (1,500-meter) level to palm trees at sea level. A three-mile (5km) hike from Campfire Center to Palm Grove reveals plants used by the Cahuilla Indians for medicines, dyes, and food.

YUMA, ARIZONA, AND LAKE HAVASU

About 58 miles (93km) due east of the city of El Centro is **Yuma**, Arizona, a desert town built on the banks of the Colorado River where it enters Mexican territory. The Colorado forms the entire eastern border of Southern California from Mexico to Nevada. Several dams built across it have created reservoirs while also providing hydroelectric power for the metropolises of Los Angeles and San Diego.

Lake Havasu ❼ (tel: 928-855-4115), 46 miles (74km) long, and no more than three miles (5km) wide, is the reservoir trapped behind Parker Dam. Those who don't want to drink the water enjoy playing in it. Along Arizona State Highway 95 between Parker and Lake Havasu City are recreational-vehicle parks, marinas, and campgrounds with room for tens of thousands of visitors. Everyone, from water sportsmen and outboard boaters to yachtsmen, water skiers, and sailboarders, love the lake. There's fishing for bass, bluegills, and crappies. Small game populates the rugged southeastern (Arizona) shore of the lake that constitutes Lake Havasu State Park. Birds are everywhere, and the entire body of water is contained within the **Havasu National Wildlife Refuge** (tel: 760-326-3853).

Lake Havasu City, nonexistent as recently as the late 1960s, has exploded into a resort center of over 52,000 residents, and has become a popular vacation spot for collegiate types at spring break. Developed by the late millionaire Robert P. McCulloch Sr., its most famous landmark is the original **London Bridge**. (A popular story is that McCulloch thought he was buying the more decorative Tower Bridge.) The bridge was shipped in pieces to the US, then trucked to the "British town" the tycoon created at its feet.

THE MOJAVE DESERT

The **Mojave Desert** ❽ (named after a Southwestern native tribe, and pronounced "mo-hahv-ee") lies between US 395 and Interstate 40, adjoining the Nevada state border. Great, brightly colored columns of sandstone rise off the desert floor on either side of the highway: sculpted towers in the foothills of the eastern Sierras. The desert is relatively unexplored, despite its geological importance. On weekends, state rangers give guided nature walks and facilities include picnic tables and about 50 primitive campsites for tents and recreational vehicles. Visitors must bring their own food and water.

The gateway to the **Mojave Desert** is the small town of Mojave, at the junction of State Highways 14 and 58. From borax to the B-1 bomber, it has seen more history than places many times its size. Near Edwards Air Force Base, Mojave was part of the Antelope Valley aerospace boom, serving as a temporary community for the aerospace workers, as well as those employed in agriculture and

⊙ **Tip**

The popular and well-run Coachella Valley Music and Arts Festival (www. coachella.com), commonly called just "Coachella," is held each year across three days in April at Indio's Empire Polo Club, drawing big-name international acts and offering plenty of other entertainment for all ages.

Aerial view of Yuma.

railroads. The winter season is its busiest time, when weekend skiers, heading to and from Sierra slopes, pack the motels and roadside cafés.

East of Mojave, near the town of **Barstow**, paleontologists are still carrying on the work of the late Dr. Louis Leakey, the leader of a team of eminent scientists who believed they had found a prehistoric "tool factory" estimated to be some 200,000 years old. Visits to the so-called **Calico Early Man Site** (http://calicoarchaeology.com) have been suspended indefinitely. Nearby Barstow, a bustling desert town, is largely the suburb of a military community. Situated at the junction of Interstates 15 and 40, it has a five-mile (8km) stretch of motels, gas stations, and grocery stores that makes it a very good base for stocking up.

From **Barstow**, you can also explore the **Calico Ghost Town** (www.sbcounty.gov; daily 9am–5pm). The town of Calico was established by silver miners in the 1880s. Today, it is half history and half Hollywood;

the town was restored by LA's Walte Knott of Knott's Berry Farm fame Part authentic mining town, par theme park, it's fun to discover which is real and which is whimsy, and visitors can explore mining tunnels, rid the ore train, and browse in old-fashioned dry-goods shops.

Continuing east on Interstate 15 o 40 brings you to the 1.6 million-acr (650,000-hectare) **Mojave Nationa Preserve** ❾ (www.nps.gov/moja). The scenic Kelbaker Road, a 56-mile (90km) paved road, connects the town of Baker on the I-15 and Ludlow on the I-40. Kelso Depot, 34 miles (55km) south of Baker, is the park's main information center. A furthe seven miles (11km) from Baker ar the impressive Kelso Dunes, standing about 600ft (200 meters) high and covering 45 sq miles (120 s km). Other top attractions includ the 1,500ft (460-meter) -high Cima Dome (reach it via the paved Cima Road from the I-15), which passes through the world's largest, dense Joshua tree forests.

Beachfront hotel at Lake Havasu City, Arizona.

RED ROCK CANYON STATE PARK AND RANDSBURG

An alternative to heading east to explore the **Mojave National Preserve** is to head north. About 25 miles (40km) north of Mojave along Highway 14 is **Red Rock Canyon State Park** (tel: 661-946-6092; www.parks.ca.gov). Here, in the middle of the 19th century, prospectors discovered gold nuggets on the surface of dry stream beds, prompting a mini-boom that removed about $16 million worth of ore, including one 5lb (2.27kg) nugget.

Nearby is **Randsburg** 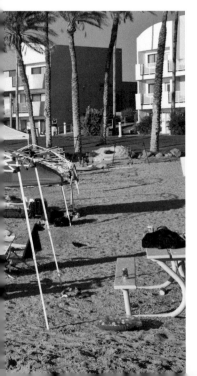, a 19th-century ghost town that is still home to a tiny community, about 20 miles (32km) east of Red Rock Canyon on US 395. Named after one of the gold towns of South Africa, Randsburg struck it rich three times between 1895 and 1947, first with gold, then with silver, and finally with tungsten. After its discovery late in the 19th century, the Yellow Aster mine yielded $20 million in gold before it was exhausted. Turn-of-the-20th

century Randsburg was as wild and wooly as any Western boomtown, with saloons and dance halls, scoundrels and rogues.

Among the ramshackle remains of the original wood-and-corrugated-iron buildings on Randsburg's main street today is the **Desert Museum** (http://randdesertmuseum.com; open weekends 10am–4pm and by special appointment), with its collection of mining and geological artifacts. Also open are the town saloon, dance hall, and barber shop, which have been quaintly converted into shops offering rocks, bottles, and mining curios. At the **Randsburg General Store**, wayfarers can sip a chocolate soda at the same swivel-chaired soda fountain that was hauled into town by mules over a century ago.

England's original London Bridge, at Lake Havasu City.

CHINA LAKE AND THE TRONA PINNACLES

China Lake is a dry basin near Ridgecrest off US 395. It is best known as the focus of the important China Lake Naval Air Warfare Center. Near

⊙ THE CAHUILLA TRIBE

The Cahuilla Indians survived in the hostile desert region not only because of their knowledge of desert plants and animals, but also because of the curing techniques of their shamans, or medicine men.

Among the Cahuilla, as with other Native Americans, shamans – "technicians of the sacred" – were believed to possess supernatural powers and mediated between the world of mortals and the world of spirits. Because they employed both plant remedies (which have enriched medicine ever since) and sacred power, they occupied a more prominent place in the community than doctors do in modern society. They gave advice on political decisions, cured diseases, and searched nature for signs from the spirit world.

The origin and meaning of the word Cahuilla is unknown: "master" (in both mental and physical strength) has been suggested. Their territory ranges from valleys as high as 5,000ft (1,500 meters) altitude, in the Santa Rosa Mountains, to the desert around the Salton Sea, 200ft (60 meters) below sea level. South of Palm Springs, the tribe still owns the five Indian Canyons in which their villages used to sit. There are still some traces of house foundations, ditches, and dams.

ALTERNATIVE ENERGY

California is at the forefront in researching and implementing alternative forms of energy.

In the 1970s, tax credits helped establish a new wind and solar industry. Wind turbines began snaking along California hills, particularly on the Altamont Pass near San Francisco, Tehachapi Pass near Bakersfield, and San Gorgonio Pass near Palm Springs.

The early experiments with solar energy in the Mojave Desert known as Solar Two (which closed in the late 1990s) used hundreds of giant mirrors to concentrate the sun's rays on a 300ft (90-meter) tower and heat, to a temperature of 1,050°F (566°C), a molten nitrate salt stored in an insulated tank. When needed, the molten salt – a yellowish syrup that retains heat better than water or oil – will convert water into the steam required to power a turbine generator.

Wind turbines near Palm Springs.

California's alternate energy industry really gained momentum after the deregulation of the electric utilities in 1998, after which the California Energy Commission launched a new Renewable Energy Program. Following a decade of legislation pushing for renewable energy laws, real change can now be seen. In 2009, 11.6 percent of California's electricity was coming from renewable resources such as wind, solar, geothermal, biomass, and small hydroelectric facilities; an additional 9.2 percent came from large hydro plants. Other energy sources are also being explored. California has the largest geothermal generating capacity in the country, biomass plants produced 2.1 percent of the state's electricity in 2007, and ocean energy projects are being explored.

MAKING IT LAW

In 2011, California Governor Jerry Brown signed into law the country's most ambitious renewable energy mandate: by the end of 2020, state utilities need to obtain one-third of their power from renewable energy sources such as solar panels and wind turbines. All three of the state's major investor-owned utilities – Southern California Edison, Pacific Gas and Electric, and Sempra's San Diego and Electric – currently will need to meet these goals or else pay hefty fines. The main hurdles may be in getting renewable projects built: development can be delayed, permits are hard to obtain, and legal opposition from local residents is expensive.

Some of the mature renewable energy sources, however, are getting cheaper. The Electric Power Research Institute reports that the cost of producing wind energy has decreased four-fold since 1980. On the solar front, over 30 large solar thermal power plants have been proposed in California's deserts.

The state is encouraging residents to participate in this renewable energy initiative as well: the California Energy Commission and the California Public Utilities Commission have teamed up to run the Go Solar California program, which encourages Californians to install solar energy systems on homes and businesses, through rebates and tax credits.

the main gate of the naval station is the small **Maturango Museum** (tel: 760-375 6900; https://maturango.org; daily 10am–5pm). The museum occasionally conducts field trips to study Native American rock inscriptions found nearby, possibly the best such collection in the state. As a result of the discoveries made at China Lake, some scientists are tempted to say that humans migrated from Asia at least 40,000 years ago, perhaps even 100,000 years ago.

Not far from China Lake, near the banks of the equally dry Searles Lake, are the **Trona Pinnacles** ⓫. This great pincushion of ancient limestone columns in the middle of the Mojave Desert is both rare and bizarre. The spooky stone spires are "national natural landmarks," probably the most outstanding examples of tufa formations in North America, and a challenging moonscape to explore for hikers and rock climbers. The Trona Pinnacles are situated on the west side of bleakly awesome **Searles Lake**, access to which is via State Highway 178 north from **Johannesburg**. Camping is

permitted at the Pinnacles. Ninety-four miles (151km) north of Johannesburg on US 395 is **Lone Pine**, a picturesque village that has been a popular location for Hollywood Westerns.

MOUNT WHITNEY

From here, **Mount Whitney** ⓬, at 14,494ft (4,418 meters) the highest peak in the continental United States, is accessible, although it's an 11-mile (18km) challenge from the end of Whitney Portal Road to reach the summit. After the climb, a good place for a break is **Keeler**, a ghost town about 10 miles (16km) from Lone Pine. About 50 miles (80km) to the east, beyond Towne Pass, State Highway 190 runs into the Panamint Mountains, some of whose rugged canyons bustled with people and activity in 1873.

The town of **Panamint**, now an abandoned ghost town, came into being when the robbers of a Wells Fargo express discovered silver while hiding out in **Surprise Canyon**. Persuading two state senators to make a deal with the express company in return for part ownership of the lode,

◎ **Tip**

The park's three visitor centers – Kelso Depot Visitor Center (tel: 760 252-6108; Thu–Mon 10am–5pm), Hole-in-the-Wall Visitor Center (tel: 760-252-6104 or 760-928-2572; Thu–Mon 9am–3pm), and the headquarters in Barstow (tel: 760-252-6100; Mon–Fri 8am–4pm) – provide information, maps, ranger-led talks, restrooms, and bookstores. Kelso Depot and Hole-in-the-Wall also have water and picnic areas.

View from Amboy Road, which runs through the landscape between Mojave National Preserve and Joshua Tree National Park.

◉ Tip

Native Americans have moved into the gaming business with enthusiasm. Tribes formed partnerships with MGM Mirage and Donald Trump that created lavish casinos in downtown Palm Springs and elsewhere, to rival those in Las Vegas. Las Vegas, of course, isn't too far: only a two-hour drive from the Mojave National Preserve, or less than five hours by car from Palm Springs.

they presided over an instant boomtown with stores, saloons, boarding houses, and banks, all along a main street that occupied the entire width of the narrow canyon. Within a year, the boom was over, but the canny miners cast their silver in the form of 700lb (318kg) cannon balls, a burden too heavy for robbers to carry away.

Indian Ranch Road, an unpaved track off the Trona–Wildrose road and which forks off up Surprise Canyon, continues down to **Ballarat**. Only crumbling adobe walls and ruined shacks remain here of what was once an important supply town for the miners, to which the stagecoach used to run all the way from Johannesburg.

Another deserted mining town, off Emigrant Canyon Road, is **Skidoo**. Its name was derived from the phrase "23 Skidoo," it having been 23 miles (37km) from Telescope Peak. Skidoo is famous for its "million-dollar slope," from which $1 million in gold ore was taken early in the 20th century: "it could be scraped out in wheelbarrows," boasted its former owner.

Devil's Golf Course, Death Valley.

But Skidoo has gone down in legend more than this as "the town that hanged its killer twice," after an incident in which a drunken saloon keeper killed a popular town banker. Skidoo's citizens were wary of what kind of justice might be administered from the nearest lawmen at Lone Pine, so they took it upon themselves to promptly hang the killer. The next day, when a reporter from the big-city *Los Angeles Herald* arrived, they dug up the body and hanged it again so the newsman could get a picture.

DEATH VALLEY

Death Valley National Park ⓭ (www.nationalparks.org) was first established as a national monument in 1933. Its namesake 120-mile long (193-km) valley is the result of a geological phenomenon. At least five million years ago, the deep gap between the Panamint and Funeral mountains was formed by earthquakes and the folding of the earth's crust. This created, technically, not a valley but what geologists tend to call a graben.

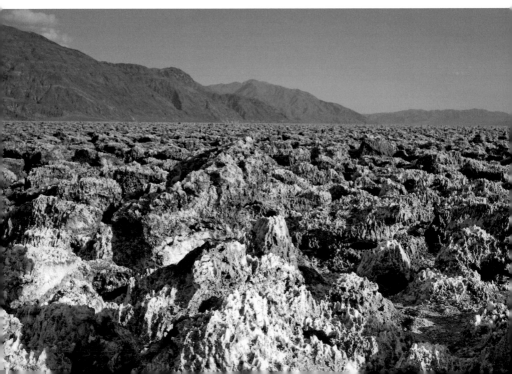

The environment is extremely harsh, yet about 900 different species of plant grow in the national park. In many ways, Death Valley's human population of 200 or so seems just as indomitable, enduring terrific heat and isolation. However, the growth of Las Vegas, Nevada, 140 miles (225km) away, inspired the development of the town of Pahrump. It's now only a 60-mile (97km) drive from Death Valley to the nearest big grocery store.

Today the valley's fearsome reputation seems to attract as many as it intimidates. Winter or summer, sightseers, hikers, and amateur naturalists come to scramble up the sand dunes near **Stovepipe Wells**. They also want to marvel at the views, study old mines and abandoned charcoal kilns, explore old ghost towns, and snap scores of pictures at sites such as humble **Badwater**, 282ft (86 meters) below sea level, the lowest spot in North America, and throughout the park.

Years ago, it was traditional for all concessions to close down in the summer, but the tourists kept on coming. Nowadays, in the town of **Furnace Creek,** the **Furnace Creek Ranch** and the nearby **Stovepipe Wells Village** complex stay open throughout the year, and neither is ever empty. Tour groups also arrive in the white-hot summer months from Las Vegas, albeit sheltered from the worst elements by desert-tough, air-conditioned vehicles.

Furnace Creek is a good focal point for a visit to Death Valley. Located not

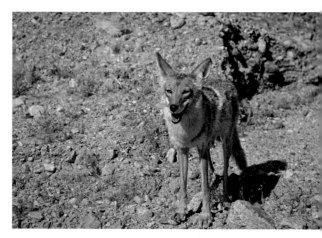

Coyote in Death Valley. Despite seeming like an unlikely environment for life to flourish, the National Park supports 51 species of native mammals, 36 reptile species, five amphibian species, and 346 species of birds.

⊘ SURVIVAL IN THE DESERT

The first settlers who wandered into Death Valley in 1849 found the name to be unfortunately true, but travel these days is infinitely easier and safer, with well-supervised roads and accommodations (including two inns and a luxury resort). Autumn through spring, the climate is ideal for exploring, with daytime temperatures in the 60s and 70s Fahrenheit (about 16–26°C), although it is chillier at night. Summer temperatures (May–Oct) are exceeded only in the Sahara: the July average daily high is 116°F (47°C). It commonly soars past 120°F (49°C), and once hit a national high of 134°F (57°C). It is quite literally life-threatening to remain under the desert sun for too long.

The vast Mojave covers roughly the combined area of the states of Massachusetts, Rhode Island, and Connecticut. It's easy to get lost and, with conventional vehicles, even to get stranded off the main roads. Take adequate provisions, and adequate precautions. Have your car checked out thoroughly before setting off, paying particular attention to the tires and any problems concerning overheating. Pack food, water, and sunscreen, for use even while in the car (do not make the journey in a convertible), and try to let someone know your route and expected arrival time. If you have car trouble, rangers suggest you wait where you are: do not wander off to look for help.

Rhyolite Ghost town, Death Valley, deserted in 1916.

Scotty's Castle.

far from Badwater, its **Visitor Center** (tel: 760-786 2331; admission charge for park) is open daily all year round. Although Furnace Creek Ranch's 18-hole golf course is said to be the lowest course on earth, nobody would hire a caddy for the valley's other "links," the so-called **Devil's Golf Course** , an otherworldly expanse of rugged salt crystals that point to the sky in jagged little edges. It lies between the former sites of the Eagle Borax mill, southwest of Badwater, and the Harmony Borax Works, just north of Furnace Creek, where the former workers' quarters were developed into a resort. At the **Harmony Borax Works**, an old cleanser-processing plant has been stabilized to show interested visitors the now very primitive 19th-century manufacturing methods.

Overlooking Badwater to the east is **Dante's View** (5,475ft/1,669 meters) and, in the west, **Telescope Peak**, the highest point in the Panamint Range (11,049ft/3,368 meters).

Among Death Valley's other natural beauty spots are **Zabriskie Point**, made famous by a 1960s movie and located southeast of Furnace Creek in the Black Mountains near interesting **Twenty Mule Team Canyon**, **Artists Drive**, and the **Golden Canyon**, with its vivid displays of color among old outcroppings; and empty **Ubehebe Crater**, an extinct volcano nearly 2,000 years old at the north end of the national park.

Near Ubehebe Crater is the 25-room Death Valley Ranch, also known as **Scotty's Castle** (tel: 760-786 2392; currently closed due to flood damaged and expected to reopen in 2020), a $2 million palace that is a facsimile of a Spanish-Mediterranean villa. Death Valley's biggest visitor attraction, Scotty's Castle is operated by the National Park Service, which runs hourly tours. Work on the castle began in 1926, at the foot of a natural spring-fed canyon at an elevation of 3,000ft (900 meters). About 2,000 hard-working men assembled the castle, completing it in 1931, all at the expense of a young, enthusiastic Chicago millionaire by the name of Albert Johnson.

⊘ SCOTTY'S CASTLE

Touring the grounds of Scotty's Castle, Death Valley's biggest visitor attraction, visitors might wonder how a villa came to be in the desert, and who Scotty was.

Its builder was Chicago millionaire Albert Johnson, who had been charmed into investing thousands of dollars in a fruitless search for gold by an affable roustabout named Walter Scott, popularly known as "Death Valley Scotty."

After years of waiting, Johnson's patience ran out, but not before he had grown so fond of Death Valley that he decided to build a summer retreat there.

The Chicago financier and his wife lived on and off at the castle for many years until his death in 1948. "Death Valley Scotty," the good-natured rogue, also lived nearby. The castle is currently closed due to flood damage and is expected to reopen in 2020.

SAN DIEGO

Beautiful beaches, a world-class zoo, museum-filled Balboa Park, and the trendy Gaslamp Quarter help attract families, surfers, and culture-hounds to sunny and relaxed San Diego, the state's second-largest city.

Home to 77 miles (124km) of beautiful Pacific coastline, the busy, elegant harbor town of San Diego is the state's birthplace. It was here, in what is now the historic Old Town, that a group of Europeans first settled in 1769; today the city has a population of more than 1.3 million, second only to Los Angeles.

Twenty-first-century **San Diego** ➊ is a vibrantly modern and evolving city, with a growing roster of cultural attractions in the 1200-acre (490-hectare) Balboa Park and a revitalized Gaslamp Quarter with a hip shopping and nightlife scene. Active travellers love the city for its surfing, diving, and hang-gliding opportunities, and families come to explore SeaWorld, nearby Legoland, and the world-class San Diego Zoo.

OLD TOWN

The six-block **Old Town** ➓ area (bounded by Juan, Twiggs, Congress, and Wallace streets) is where the town's original pueblo once stood. Now you'll find old adobes, restored Victorian homes, open-air stands, museums and galleries, and charming patio restaurants which offer fine dining. Mariachi groups entertain in the Bazaar del Mundo, a Spanish-style plaza flanked by craft shops and Mexican restaurants.

San Diego has numerous surf schools.

Of special historical interest are the **Thomas Whaley House Museum** (http://whaleyhouse.org) – possibly Southern California's first two-story brick home and one of America's allegedly most haunted houses – and the Robinson-Rose house. The latter once housed law and railroad offices, and now serves as the **Old Town State Historic Park Visitor Center** (4002 Wallace Street; tel: 619-220-5422; www.parks.ca.gov). Stop in to pick up detailed maps including the neighborhood's historic attractions.

Main attractions
Old Town
SeaWorld
Balboa Park
Timken Museum of Art
San Diego Zoo
Hotel del Coronado
La Jolla

Maps on pages 278, 281

PRESIDIO HILL

Up the hill from Old Town's historic center, **Presidio Hill** and its sprawling park are an historic oasis in a sea of traffic (Interstates 5 and 8 are just to the west and north). Here, Father Junípero Serra conducted a mass on July 16, 1769, dedicating first the Mission San Diego de Alcalá and then the military settlement that surrounded and protected it.

In 1774, the mission was moved from the hill to its present site in Mission Valley (10818 San Diego Mission Road; tel: 619-281-8449; www. missionsandiego.com; daily), where you can view original records in Father Serra's handwriting.

Take the curving road east of the Old Town to see, on the hillside, the elegant **Junípero Serra Museum** (2727 Presidio Drive; tel: 619-232-6203; www. sandiegohistory.org/serra_museum; Sep–Jun Sat–Sun 10am–4pm, Jun–Sep Fri–Mon 10am–5pm), which displays documents of early California life. It looks like a mission, but was actually built in 1929.

MISSION BAY AND SEAWORLD

The 4,600-acre (1,900-hectare) **Mission Bay** area combines parkland, beaches and inner lagoons with extensive outdoor leisure activities. Located here is the 189-acre (76-hectare) **SeaWorld** Ⓑ (500 SeaWorld Drive; tel: 619-222-4SEA; https://seaworld.com/san-diego; daily, hours vary by season), one of the world's largest marine parks, filled with aquariums, live-animal shows, and rides. The most famous animals in the park are the orca whales; experience their natural behavior up close and learn more about the life of these powerful predators from the informative displays. Other popular attractions are the bottlenose dolphin shows, sharks, polar bears, and 300 penguins. On a hot day the Shipwreck Rapids ride will cool you off.

South of the channel leading into Mission Bay is **Ocean Beach**. To the north of Mission Beach is **Pacific Beach**, where activities center around Crystal Pier and the area along Mission Boulevard and up Garnet Avenue, and where locals shop and dine. The beaches are a great draw most of the year, but there are wonderful beaches along most of this coast – 25 miles (40km) of them in an unbroken line between Del Mar and Oceanside.

DOWNTOWN SAN DIEGO

Towards the top end of the vast bay discovered by Cabrillo is downtown San Diego. A complex adjoining what was formerly the Santa Fe railroad station now consists of the 34-story **One America Plaza** tower, a hotel, and the downtown branch of the **San Diego Museum of Contemporary Art C** (1001 Kettner Boulevard; tel: 858-454 3541; www.mcasd.org; Thu–Sun 11am–5pm). This is a collection of world-class modern art, with rotating exhibitions and interesting programs. The museum's other branch has a delightful ocean-front setting at La Jolla, (currently closed for major renovation).

Along the Embarcadero just north of the station is the large **Maritime Museum D** (1492 North Harbor Drive; tel: 619-234-9153; https://sdmaritime. org; daily 9am–9pm), which encompasses six ships built prior to 1914. The USS Midway moored at Navy Pier in 2003 now serves as the **USS Midway Museum** (tel: 619-544-9600; www.midway.org; daily 10am–5pm).

Much of the harbor is centered around attractive **Seaport Village**, with its cafés and live entertainment. Adjoining this carefully landscaped "village" is the spiffy-looking **Convention Center**, right opposite **Gaslamp Quarter**, a several-block area of brick-paved sidewalks flanked by restored Victorian buildings now occupied by galleries, trendy boutiques, and cafés. This refurbished section, with a demonstrable appeal to artists and young entrepreneurs, has also become the breeding ground of a flourishing theater movement, as well as a popular destination for nightlife and shopping.

BALBOA PARK

Located at the northeast edge of town, the 1,400-acre (570-hectare)

⊙ Tip

San Diego has always been a big naval town, and taking a harbor cruise will confirm that there is still plenty of activity on the water. In winter, whale-watching tours start from the harbor. Among the Maritime Musuem's ships is the 1863 *Star of India*, one of the last steel-hulled merchant sailing ships still afloat.

Entering the city's Gaslamp Quarter.

Mission San Diego de Alcalá.

The Botanical Building in Balboa Park.

Balboa Park (www.balboapark.org) is the largest urban cultural park in the country. Many people take pleasure in just strolling or picnicking in the park (though note, it is not a place to visit after dark), but Balboa Park is really an activity "city" all on its own. Many of the city's museums are housed here in Moorish- and Spanish-style buildings, several of which date back to international expositions held here in 1915 and 1935. Other attractions include a science center, an arts center, several theaters, and the city's famous zoo.

To learn about space and aviation history, visit the **San Diego Air and Space Museum** (2001 Pan American Plaza; tel: 619-234-8291; www.sandiego airandspace.org; daily 10am–4.30pm), which houses artifacts and aircrafts, including the actual Apollo 9 command module, a replica of *The Spirit of St Louis* in which Charles Lindbergh crossed the Atlantic, and the only real GPS satellite on display in the world.

The **San Diego Museum of Art** (1450 El Prado; tel: 619-232-7931; www.sdmart.org; Mon–Tue, Thu and Sat 10am–5pm, Fri 10am–8pm; Sun noon–5pm) is the region's largest and oldest art museum. In addition to 19th- and 20th- century American art, the collection features fine examples of European and Asian art and growing collections of contemporary and Latin American work.

Just next door is the white marble **Timken Museum of Art** (1500 El Prado; tel: 619-239-5548; www.timken museum.org; Tue–Sat 10am–4.30pm, Sun noon–4.30pm). Considered one of the world's great small museums, its collection includes paintings by European old masters such as Rembrandt, Rubens, and Pieter Bruegel the Elder, as well as American paintings and Russian icons.

Other museums of note include the anthropology-focused **Museum of Man** (1350 El Prado; tel: 619-239-2001; www.museumofman.org; daily 10am–5pm) the **Mingei International Museum** (1439 El Prado; tel: 619-239-0003; www.mingei. org; Tue–Sun 10am–5pm), which showcases international folk art, craft, and design; and the **Natural History Museum** (1788 El Prado; tel: 619-232-3821; www.sdnhm.org; daily 10am–5pm).

Enthusiasts of all ages will get a kick out of the large **Model Railroad Museum** (tel: 619-696-0199; http://sdmrm.org; Tue–Fri 10am–4pm, Sat–Sun 11am–5pm) and a ride on the park's 1910 carousel or its miniature train. The **San Diego Automotive Museum** (2080 Pan American Plaza; http://sdautomuseum.org; daily 10am–5pm), which features over 80 historic cars and motorcycles, is also worth a visit.

Visit the park's centrally located **Visitors Center** (tel: 619-239-0512) for more information on all museums and to buy a passport offering cost-effective admission to 17 of the park's museums.

SAN DIEGO ZOO

Giant pandas, Bornean sun bears, jaguars, California condors, and the largest colony of koalas outside Australia can all be found on the western side of Balboa Park in the famous **San Diego Zoo** ⊕ (tel: 619-234-3153; http://zoo.sandiegozoo.org; daily 9am–5pm). One of the largest zoos in America, it houses over 3,500 rare and endangered animals representing more than 300 animal species. The zoo has a policy of eschewing cages in favor of moats wherever possible, in an attempt to recreate natural conditions. Admission to the zoo includes a Children's Zoo – with more than 30 kid-friendly animal exhibits and activities – and a ride on Skyfari, an aerial tramway from which you can admire all the uncaged elephants, lions, tigers, giraffes, and bears in their canyon habitats.

CORONADO

Coronado, with stately Victorian homes among the cottages and condos, is set on a peninsula and is the most popular and wealthiest of the string of communities surrounding the lower end of San Diego Bay. It is

Sculpture at the outpost of the San Diego Museum of Contemporary Art, La Jolla.

Elephants in an uncaged enclosure in San Diego Zoo.

Around San Diego

Oceanside
Carlsbad ★ Legoland
Los Angeles
San Marcos
San Diego Zoo Wild Animal Park ★
Escondido
Encinitas
Cardiff
Solana Beach
Del Mar
Torrey Pines State Natural Reserve ❸
San Diego – La Jolla Underwater Park Ecological Reserve
❷ La Jolla
Pacific Beach
SeaWorld ★
San Diego International Airport ✈ ❶
San Diego
Lake Hodges
Rancho Santa Fe
North City
Carmel Valley
Birch Aquarium at Scripps Institution of Oceanography ★
Linda Vista
Rancho Bernardo
Carmel Mountain
Mira Mesa
San Diego
Santee
La Mesa
Escondido
Ramona
Pine Valley
Spring Valley
National City
Coronado
San Diego Bay
Chula Vista
Imperial Beach
Tijuana
MEXICO

N
PACIFIC OCEAN

0   5 miles
0   5 km

Hotel del Coronado.

best known for the superlative **Hotel del Coronado ❶**, a perfect example of Victorian architecture (1888). A dozen presidents have stayed here since Thomas Edison personally installed the electric lighting; here Britain's future Edward VIII met his wife, the notorious Mrs Simpson, who lived in a bungalow on the grounds (the bungalow is still here); Charles Lindbergh dropped by for dinner before and after making the first trans-Atlantic flight; and author L. Frank Baum is said to have used it as an inspiration for *The Wizard of Oz*. Such milestones are memorialized in the **Museum of History and Art** (1100 Orange Avenue; tel: 619-437-8788; https://coronadohistory.org; daily 10am–4pm) right next door to the visitor center.

LA JOLLA, TORREY PINES, AND DEL MAR

The wealthy, charming town of **La Jolla ❷** is the home of the San Diego campus of the University of California, the highly regarded **Salk**

Desirable houses in La Jolla.

Institute, the cliff-top **Birch Aquarium at Scripps**, and an iconic outpost of the **San Diego Museum of Contemporary Art** (currently closed for renovation).

The San Diego-La Jolla Underwater Park Ecological Reserve is a popular destination for kayaking, diving, swimming, and snorkeling; snorkelers should head for the **La Jolla Caves**.

Heading up Interstate 5 toward Los Angeles, you can break up your journey from San Diego by stopping off for a walk through the groves of strangely twisted trees at **Torrey Pines State Reserve ❸** (www.calparks.org) and watch daredevil hang-gliders soar off the 300ft (90-meter) cliffs.

Another detour is **Del Mar**, a beautiful spot with a sweeping hillside view of the Pacific. The San Diego County Fair is held here in June and July, and the Del Mar National Horse Show (https://delmarnational.com) in the spring. The season begins in July, a week after the big fair ends, and continues to run until well into September.

ⵁ LEGOLAND

Just a 30-minute drive north of San Diego, Legoland is one of the best amusement parks for children under 13 in Southern California. There are more than 60 rides, shows, and attractions to choose from, with areas themed on pirates, medieval times, dinosaurs, 1920s Egypt, and miniature American landmarks. Kids and parents will both be amazed by the more than 22,000 Lego models in the park – from a brontosaurus named Bronte to a tiny rabbit in a magician's hat – created from over 57 million Lego bricks. There are also plenty of restaurants and shops, with everything geared to families. Strollers and wheelchairs can be rented on a first-come, first-served basis. (1 Legoland Drive, Carlsbad; tel: 760-918-5346; www.legoland.com.)

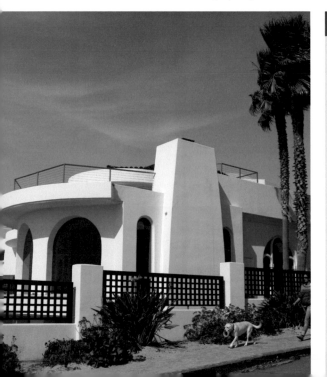

TIJUANA, MEXICO

Rancho Tía Juana (Aunt Jane's Ranch) became an international border town in the 1840s, following the Mexican–American War. Today it is arguably the 'most crossed border in the world.'

By the early 1900s, Tijuana was enticing countless North Americans with its diverse marketplaces, live bullfights, horse races, thermal baths, and other unique attractions. Today, Tijuana is fun, but can be dangerous, and visitors come as much for the nightclubs and duty-free bargains on jewelry, pottery, perfume, and fine art as they do for historic sites.

Crossing to and from San Diego into Baja California is relatively easy, but time-consuming. Be sure that you have valid passports, proper health coverage, and Mexican auto insurance. As you drive into Tijuana or cross the footbridge, you'll soon enter the tourist zone of Tijuana, which stretches along Avenida Revolución. There are tourist information offices at the border but the main Tourist Assistance Office is in the **Viva Tijuana Shopping Center**, located on Calle Vía de la Juventud.

The lovely beaches of **Rosarito** have provided the backdrop for movies like Titanic, Pearl Harbor, and Pirates of the Caribbean, and if you visit you'll understand why. Though it is a resort area that has become a popular retirement getaway for Americans, it is still a fun party place for the younger set due to the drinking age being 18 in Mexico. That said, keep your wits about you when you're out and about.

Avenida Revolución is lined with bars, nightclubs, crafts stores, and clothing and jewelry shops mixed up along with the traditional ponchos and leather sandals (for more shopping, visit the **Plaza Río Tijuana** shopping mall, the largest shopping center in northwestern Mexico). Behind the Plaza Revolución is the **Wax Museum** (daily 10am–6pm), whose eclectic subjects range from Madonna, Gandhi, Marilyn Monroe, and the Pope to Cortéz and an Aztec priest holding the bloody heart of a prostrate victim.

A few blocks down Revolución, past the former **Jai Alai Fronton** (an open-walled playing area for this sport that originated in Spain's Basque Country), turn left on 10th Street to head towards the river. The main street continues south, seguing onto the Boulevard Agua Caliente and running past the city's old **bullring**, most of its best hotels, Hipódromo Caliente Racetrack, and the Sports Arena where concerts and most big events take place.

The famous old **Hipódromo Caliente Racetrack** still has its marble floors, ornate decoration, mirrored elevators, and a lobby filled with sculptured cowboys, caged birds, and an incongruous pair of playful anteaters, but retains little of the glamour that once caused it to be regarded as the American Monte Carlo. In the days when the track's regular clientele included Charlie Chaplin, Jean Harlow, and heavyweight champion Jack Dempsey, fortunes were won and lost at dice, blackjack, and roulette.

Head eastwards along 10th Street, watching out for the giant globe (indicating a "world of culture") housing the concert hall and the 85ft (26-meter) -high **Omnitheater**. Adjoining is the ultra-modern **Tijuana Cultural Center**, whose historical survey embraces Olmec stone heads, Aztec charts showing the god of the hour, a meticulous model of the 16th-century Aztec capital, Tenochtitlan, plus skillfully embroidered Indian costumes, and is well worth a visit.

Traffic jams at the Tijuana border for those returning to California, with street vendors selling food.

Laguna Beach.

CALIFORNIA

TRAVEL TIPS

TRANSPORTATION

GETTING THERE

By air

San Francisco International Airport (SFO)
Tel: 650-821-8211 or 1-800-435-9736; www.flysfo.com.
The airport is 14 miles (23km) south of downtown San Francisco near the town of San Mateo. For public transportation to and from the city, Bay Area Rapid Transit (BART; www.bart.gov) provides a Metro rail service within the Bay Area and has a station at SFO and several within San Francisco. Take the SFO AirTrain to the Garage G/BART Station stop where you can buy your ticket and board. The one-way fare from SFO to downtown San Francisco is $9.65. SamTrans (tel: 800-660-4287; www.samtrans.com) operates a 24-hour public bus service to San Mateo County and parts of San Francisco (buses KX, 292, 397 and 398 stop at the airport terminals). Caltrain Commuter Rail (www.caltrain.com) runs trains between San Francisco and San Jose on weekdays until 10pm (take BART to Millbrae station to connect with Caltrain). The taxi fare from SFO to downtown San Francisco is approximately $50. Several private shuttles, including BayPorter Express (tel: 1-877-467-1800 (toll free Bay Area); www.bayporter.com) can also be booked in advance or upon arrival.

Oakland International Airport
Tel: 510-563-3300; www.oaklandairport.com.
Much smaller and less crowded than SFO, Oakland Airport is well-served by public transportation and much closer to East Bay destinations. The airport's BART station is just across from Terminal 1 and a short walk from Terminal 2. There are several bus lines run by AC

Santa Fe train station in San Diego.

Transit (www.actransit.org) connecting the airport with Oakland downtown and other destinations in the area. As with SFO, private shuttles can also be booked.

Los Angeles International Airport (LAX)
Tel: 310-646-5252; www.lawa.org.
LAX is one of the world's busiest airports, handling the majority of the state's international, domestic, and regional air traffic. There are information booths just outside the terminal for the Metro (the Metropolitan Transportation Authority; www.metro.net) and buses (tel: 323-466 3876). A free, frequent shuttle bus "C" connects LAX with Metro's Green Line Light Rail. The LAX FlyAway bus service (www.flylax.com/flyaway) provides frequent non-stop transportation between LAX and Van Nuys Bus Terminal, Union Station in downtown Los Angeles, and Westwood/UCLA. You can also arrange for door-to-door shuttle van service, rental cars, and taxicabs (about $40–50 from LAX to the city center).

⊘ Airlines

Numerous major airlines fly regularly into California, including:
Air France, www.airfrance.com
Alaska Airlines, www.alaskaair.com
American Airlines, www.aa.com
British Airways, www.britishairways.com
Delta Airlines, www.delta.com
jetBlue, www.jetblue.com
KLM, www.klm.com
Southwest, www.southwest.com
United, www.united.com
Virgin Atlantic, www.virginatlantic.com

Palm Springs International Airport
www.palmspringsca.gov.
San Diego International Airport (Lindbergh Field)
Tel: 619-400-2404; www.san.org.
Flights arrive from most major American cities. Transportation information: tel: 619-400-2404.
In addition to the international airports listed above, there are smaller, regional airports in several locations throughout California, including Palmdale, Ontario, Burbank, Fresno, Sacramento, San Jose, Van Nuys, and Orange County. Shuttle flights are usually available at all of the larger air terminals.

By rail

Amtrak
Tel: 1-800-872-7245; www.amtrak.com.
Amtrak is the major rail passenger carrier in the US. Though the system is little used by Californians, it can be a pleasant way to get around the state, provided you are not in a hurry. The California Zephyr is the main rail line into Northern California connecting Chicago with San Francisco. In California, the

Zephyr stops, among other places, at Colfax, Roseville, Sacramento, Davis and Martinez.

Amtrak also offers several major rail lines in Southern California. The Sunset Limited from New Orleans stops at North Palm Springs, Ontario, and Pomona before it reaches Los Angeles. The Pacific Surfliner links San Diego to Los Angeles and on to Santa Barbara and San Luis Obispo, while the San Joaquins runs between Sacramento and Bakersfield, with stops at Stockton, Modesto, Merced, and Fresno.

The state is tied together by the Coast Starlight, which travels north from Los Angeles all the way to Seattle, stopping at Van Nuys, Simi Valley, Oxnard, Santa Barbara, San Luis Obispo, Paso Robles, San Jose, Oakland (from here, there's a bus transfer to San Francisco before the route continues), Emeryville, Martinez, Davis, Sacramento, Chico, Redding, and across the Oregon border. Amtrak offers some local services also.

By bus

Greyhound Lines
Tel: 800-231-2222; www.greyhound.com.
The national bus line, Greyhound Lines, as well as a number of smaller charter companies, provide an impressive network of ground travel throughout California, offering daily service to major towns and cities. Routes and schedules are subject to change; it is a good idea

to check all arrangements with local stations, in advance. San Francisco, Oakland, Los Angeles, San Diego, and other large towns all have municipal bus systems.

By road

The principal **north–south** byways in California are listed below:
Interstate 5 (the Golden State and Santa Ana freeways), which covers the distance from Canada to Mexico via Seattle, Sacramento, Los Angeles, and San Diego.
Interstate 15, which transits San Bernardino and San Diego after a long passage from Montana's Canadian border, via Salt Lake City and Las Vegas.
US 101 (the Ventura and Hollywood freeways), which proceeds south down the Pacific coast from Washington state, crosses San Francisco's Golden Gate Bridge, and ends in downtown Los Angeles.
State Highway 1, which hugs the coast from south of Los Angeles to San Francisco and further north.
The principal **east–west** byways in California are:
Interstate 8, which departs from Interstate 10 at Casa Grande, Arizona, and ends in San Diego.
Interstate 10 (the San Bernardino and Santa Monica freeways), which begins on the east coast in Jacksonville, Florida, and continues through New Orleans, Houston, El Paso, Tucson, and Phoenix before cutting through Los Angeles, then ending at the coast in Santa Monica.

Interstate 40, which connects Knoxville, Tennessee, with Barstow, California, via Memphis, Oklahoma City, and Albuquerque.

GETTING AROUND

Public transportation

San Francisco
San Francisco is served by an excellent public transportation system. The city's Muni network (tel: 415-701-2311 or 311 (within San Francisco); www.sfmta.com; runs 6am–late, with some night service) of buses, street cars, and historic cable cars makes getting around a snap. Bus fare for adults is $2.50, which is paid in exact change upon boarding the front of the bus. Riders paying cash are given a transfer slip, and can ride other buses for several hours by just flashing this piece of paper to the bus driver. The "owl" late-night service runs every 30 minutes from midnight–5am. There are numerous discounts and passes on offer. For details consult www.sfmta.com/getting-around/muni/fares.

The Bay Area Rapid Transit (known locally as BART) subway system (tel: 415-989-2278; www.bart.gov; runs Mon–Fri 4am–midnight, Sat 6am–midnight and Sun 8am–midnight) connects San Francisco with the East Bay via a tunnel that goes under the bay. BART is one of the most efficient and modern rail lines in the United States and serves 45 stations in

Cable car in San Francisco.

three counties, from San Francisco to Millbrae and throughout the East Bay. Its stations provide maps that clearly explain routes and fares, and nearby ticketing machines allow passengers to purchase tickets.

Oakland and Berkeley are serviced by East Bay Transit (tel: 510-891-4777, www.actransit.org)

Caltrain (tel: 1-800-660-4287; www.caltrain.com) runs passengers between San Francisco and San Jose, with several stops along the peninsula. This rail service operates from the terminal at Fourth and King streets in San Francisco.

Many locals use ferries to get to and from work, but for visitors they provide a great scenic and environmental alternative to driving. Departing from Fisherman's Wharf or the Ferry Building, they travel to Angel Island and throughout the North and East Bay areas:

Blue and Gold Fleet, Pier 41 Marina Terminal, The Embarcadero at Beach St; tel: 415-705-8200; www.blueandgoldfleet.com.

Golden Gate Ferry, Ferry Building, The Embarcadeo at Market St; tel: 415-455-2000 or 511 (toll free); www.goldengateferry.com.

Los Angeles

The main public transportation option in Los Angeles is the Los Angeles County Metropolitan Transportation Authority bus company (tel: 323-466-3876; www.mta.net), which everyone calls the Metro. The MTA oversees the city's surprisingly comprehensive bus system, as well as the newer Metro and light rail system.

The Napa and Sonoma Valleys are perfectly suited for scenic, day-long road trips.

The popular Red Line operates between Downtown, North Hollywood, and Universal City; the Purple line overlaps part of it. The Blue Line operates between Downtown and Long Beach. The Green Line runs all the way to Redondo Beach, crossing the Blue Line just north of Compton. The Gold Line, travels between Downtown and Pasadena, and the Expo Line goes out to Culver City.

A basic fare is $1.75, and a day pass (which is valid until 3am the next day) costs $7. Drivers do not have change, so carry the exact fare. A $25 seven-day pass for Metro bus and rail lines is also available – check sale locations at www.mta.net, where you can also plan your route with schedules and maps.

San Diego

The public transportation service here is the San Diego Metropolitan Transit System (tel: 619-233-3004; www.sdmts.com), which offers bus and trolley routes throughout the San Diego area, from Old Town to Mission Beach and Mission Valley. One-way bus tickets are $2.25, trolley tickets are $2.50; an all-day pass for either is $5. Without the all-day pass, no transfers are allowed without purchasing a new ticket. Purchase your ticket before boarding the trolley from the ticket vending machines at each station.

The system also provides access to other towns in and around San Diego County, including Coronado, Del Mar, Escondido, Oceanside, Borrego Springs, and Tecate. For tickets, monthly passes, and general and route information, contact the

Transit store (1255 Imperial Avenue; tel: 619-234-1060).

A handy tool for public transportation in California is NextBus (www.nextbus.com). Also available as a mobile phone application, this service provides real-time arrival information for publication transportation so you can find out whether your bus is coming in 5 minutes or 35.

Private transportation

Driver's license and insurance

Drivers are required to carry a valid license at all times. California visitors may drive for up to 12 months with a non-California driver's license. Visitors can also obtain an International Driving Permit (IDP) from international automobile associations.

Be sure to keep these and a certificate proving you have liability insurance with you at all times because you will be required to show them to any law enforcement officers who stop your car. It is illegal to drive without these items.

Laws for safety

Belts and child seats: California law requires that every passenger wear a seat belt. Youth or infant seats are required for babies and small children under 60lbs or 6 years of age.

Cell phones: It is illegal in California to talk on a cell phone while driving unless you are able to listen and talk hands-free.

Emergency vehicles: When a fire truck, ambulance, or police vehicle approaches from either direction with flashing lights and/or a siren, you must immediately pull over to the side of the road.

Helmets: State law requires all motorcycle riders to wear helmets.

Hitchhiking: Hitchhiking is illegal on all highways and Interstates and on many secondary roads as well. Because traffic is sparse in some regions, it can also be quite difficult. In California, as elsewhere in the United States, hitchhiking can be dangerous and unpredictable. However, if you do decide to hitch, it is best to do it from an exit ramp (if legal) or a highway rest stop, rather than on the road itself. For long distances, it is advisable to make a sign clearly stating your destination. To find the safest situations, try checking ride services and college campus bulletin boards for posted rideshares.

Roadside assistance: The Highway Patrol cruises the state's highways, not just monitoring speed limits but also looking for drivers in trouble. If you have any emergency that won't allow you to continue the trip, signal your distress by raising the hood. Motorists are often advised that they are safer staying in the car with the doors locked until a patrol car stops to help, rather than leaving it and trying to hitchhike.

Motoring advisories

If you plan on driving any distance, it's a good idea to join the American Automobile Association (tel: 1-800-222-4357; www.aaa.com). In addition to emergency road service, AAA offers maps, guidebooks, and insurance. There are reciprocal arrangements with many international AAA organizations, such as those in Great Britain, Germany, and Australia.

Parking

Parking meters accept coins, and sometimes credit cards. Parking meters do not need to be fed on Sundays or major holidays. When you're looking for a parking space, note the color of the curb, which corresponds to the following limitations:

No color: No specific limitations; follow guidelines on nearby signs or meters.

White: You may stop only long enough to pick up or drop off passengers.

Green: You may park for a limited time; look for a sign nearby with the time limit, or a time limit painted on the curb.

Yellow: Stop no longer than the time posted to load or unload passengers or freight; drivers of non-commercial vehicles usually must stay in the car.

Red: No stopping or parking.

Blue: Parking is permitted only for a disabled person who displays a special placard or license plate.

Rules of the road

Some roads are for one-way traffic only and are identified by a black and white sign with an arrow pointing in the permitted direction of travel. At an intersection with a four-way red stop sign, motorists must

⊘ Renting a car

National car-rental companies are located at all airports and large towns. The best rates are usually available by booking in advance. In most cases, you must be at least 21 years old to rent a car (often 25), and you must have a valid driver's license and at least one major credit card. Foreign travelers may need to produce an international driver's license or a license from their home country. Be sure to take out collision and liability insurance, which may not always be included in the base price of the rental. It is also a good idea to inquire about an unlimited-mileage package, especially on a long trip, if not already included:

given the vast area of California, the extra mileage costs can add up quickly.

Alamo: Tel: 1-844-354-6962; www.alamo.com
Avis: Tel: 1-800-352-7900; www.avis.com
Budget: Tel: 1-800-218-7992; www.budget.com
Dollar: Tel: 1-800-800-5252; www.dollar.com
Enterprise: Tel: 1-855-266-9565; www.enterprise.com
Hertz: Tel: 1-800-654-3131; www.hertz.com
National: Tel: 1-844-382-6323; www.nationalcar.com
Thrifty: Tel: 1-800-847-4389; www.thrifty.com

completely stop and then proceed across the intersection following the order in which they arrived at the stop. If you arrive at the same time, the person to the right has the right of way, but usually one person just waves on another.

In California, it is legal to make a **right turn** on a red light after making a full stop, unless signs indicate otherwise.

Speed limits for roads and highways are posted on white signs to the right, as are all other **road signs**. Unless otherwise indicated, the speed limit is 65mph (105kmh) on freeways, 55mph (88kmh) on two-lane highways, 25mph (40kmh) near schools and in residential or business districts.

Watch for white signs warning that you will be in a different "Speed Zone Ahead." Be prepared to slow to the lower speed you will soon see posted on upcoming white signs. Some very small towns are notorious for catching and fining drivers who have not slowed down quickly enough from the highway speed to the (much lower) in-town speed limit

Taxis

Taxis are an easy, though expensive, way to get about major cities. They hover around popular tourist or nightlife spots, but in out-of-the-way locations it's best to call a radio-dispatched taxi. Your fare will be displayed on the meter and will include a flag-drop charge plus a per-mile and/or a per-hour charge.

Fares follow standard rules by city, listed below. A 10 percent tip, rounding up to the next dollar, is standard.

Taxi alternatives — mobile app ride request companies

Often less expensive that taxis are companies that can be accessed through apps. These mobile app companies are extremely popular, reliable, and easy to use. An account needs to be set up using a credit card and the app must be downloaded to a smart phone in order to request service. Most offer rideshare possibilities that further cut down on transportation costs.

Some of the best known companies are:

Uber: www.uber.com
Lyft: www.lyft.com
Flywheel: www.flywheel.com

San Francisco

Standard charges are $3.50 for the first one-fifth mile or flag, $0.55 each additional one-fifth mile or fraction thereof, $0.55 each minute of waiting or traffic time delay, plus a $4 airport surcharge.

Flywheel Taxi: Tel: 415-970-1370
Green Cab: Tel: 415-626-4733
CityWide Taxi: Tel: 415-643-9500
Yellow Cab: Tel: 415-333-3333

All cabs authorized by the city (look for the metal "license plate" on the dashboard, and the driver's ID, visible from the back seat are obligated to let you pay by credit card, though they will often complain that their machine is "broken" as they prefer cash to avoid paying a

Sharing the road in Marin County.

surcharge to the credit card companies. For a list of these companies, see www.sfmta.com.

Los Angeles

Look for the Official City of Los Angeles Taxicab Seal before boarding – this means the taxi driver is insured, well trained, and authorized by the city to operate. Fare is $2.85 for the first 1/9 mile or flag, $0.30 for each additional 1/9 mile ($2.70 per mile), and 0.30 for each 37 seconds waiting ($29.19 per hour).

For taxi cab companies and the areas each serves, go to www.taxicabsla.org.

San Diego

Standard charges are $2.80 for the first 1/6 mile, $2.60 for each additional mile, and $24.00 per hour of waiting time.

Traveling in deserts and mountains

A word of caution for desert travelers: the single most important precaution you can take is to tell someone your destination, route, and expected time of arrival. Be sure to check tires carefully before setting out; heat builds pressure, so have tires at slightly below normal air pressure. The desert's arid climate makes carrying extra water – for passengers as well as for vehicles – essential. Carry at least 1 gallon (4 liters) per person. Keep an eye on the gas gauge; it's a good idea to have more than you think you need. Remember, if you should have car trouble or become lost, do not strike out on foot. A car, visible from the air and presumably on a road, is easier to spot than a person on their own, and it affords shelter

from the weather. Just be patient and wait to be found.

Mountain drivers are advised to be equally vigilant. Winter storms in the Sierras occasionally close major roads, and at times chains are required for tires. For 24-hour information on road conditions throughout the state, call tel: 1-800-427-7623. Remember to phone ahead for road conditions before you depart.

Traveling to Mexico

Since March 1, 2010, all US citizens – including children – have been required to present a valid passport or passport card for travel into Mexico, as are all other nationalities (along with their Green Card, if they have one, for re-entry to the US.)

US citizens do not require a visa or a tourist card for tourist stays of

---

⊘ Tours via car

Seagull signs in blue and white mark San Francisco's 49-Mile Scenic Drive, a name which says it all. A free map from the San Francisco Visitor Center at Powell and Market streets details the route.

Drivers who seek to explore old US Route 66 in the south of the state can get a free map from the LA Visitors Center (6801 Hollywood Blvd; tel: 323-467-6412) which charts 29 points of interest along 62 miles (100km) of the historic road.

The 17-Mile Drive in Pebble Beach (charge except for bicycles) is another beautiful ride (motorcycles prohibited).

---

72 hours or less within the 12–19-mile (20–30km) "border zone". US citizens traveling as tourists beyond this zone, or entering Mexico by air, must pay a fee to obtain a tourist card, also known as an FMM, available from Mexican consulates, Mexican border crossing points, Mexican tourism offices, airports within the border zone, and most airlines serving Mexico. Proof of nationality must accompany the visa.

Mexican law requires that any non-Mexican citizen under the age of 18 departing Mexico must carry notarized written permission from any parent or guardian not traveling with the child to or from Mexico. This permission must include the name of the parent, the name of the child, the name of anyone traveling with the child, and the notarized signature(s) of the absent parent(s).

US insurance is not valid in Mexico and it is definitely a wise move to obtain short-term insurance, obtainable at innumerable sales offices just north of the border.

Crossing into Mexico can be relatively easy. There are three major crossings: at busy **San Ysidro**, 18 miles (29km) south of downtown San Diego, which is the gateway to Tijuana; at **Tecate** off State Highway 94, where there is rarely a wait, although the border does tend to close early in the evening; and at **Mexicali** (which is also Baja's capital), a dreary industrial city situated opposite the California town of Calexico, about 90 miles (145km) to the east.

Because driving in Tijuana for those unfamiliar with the city (and the Spanish language) can be troublesome, many drivers park in San Diego's San Ysidro, crossing into Tijuana via the elevated pedestrian walkway. Avoid leaving your car in the parking places of merchants as it will be towed away by police.

There's an all-day secure lot off the "Last Exit US parking" ramp – turn right at the stop sign to the Tijuana side. Cheap taxis and buses are also available.

The return to California can be a bit more tense than the entry into Mexico, as US Border Patrol officers take far more interest in who's coming into the country (hence those passports and Green Cards). Waiting several hours to cross back into the US is not uncommon.

Accommodations

California offers the complete spectrum of accommodation, from elegant European-style hotels to inexpensive motels that can be rented by the week.

In San Francisco, the most expensive hotels are generally located in Nob Hill, the Financial District, and Union Square. These grand hotels are particularly well suited to the international traveler, and many are attractive landmarks in their own right. In Los Angeles, the most expensive are situated Downtown and in Beverly Hills, with the best access to shopping and public transportation.

The concierge at most upscale hotels will arrange theater tickets, tours, limousines with bilingual drivers, and airline reservations.

There are also a large number of smaller hotels and hotel chains, which usually offer all of the essential comforts without the high prices of the grand hotels. California is also well endowed with cheap hostels and campgrounds.

Admission charges

Most large museums have reasonably moderate entrance fees – typically $7 to $15 for the first visit. Smaller art galleries tend to be free. Special exhibitions usually cost extra, but many museums have free general admission on certain days each month or once a week in the evenings. These free days are always indicated on the museum's website. Some attractions, like LA's Getty Center, are always free. Plays, concerts, and sporting events are often expensive, as are theme park tickets. You can sometimes get free tickets to live TV shows, especially sit-coms, if you call in advance.

Age restrictions

In California, the legal age to consume alcohol and marijuana is 21. The legal age for driving is 16.

Budgeting for your trip

San Francisco and Los Angeles tend to be more expensive than other parts of California, although exclusive resorts for skiing or spa holidays are more expensive still. If you're looking for a hotel room with an acceptable minimum level of comfort, cleanliness, and facilities, a reasonable starting point for the price of a double room is $85 in budget-class hotels; upping your budget from there to at least $150 will make a significant difference in quality. For between $150 and $300 a whole range of hotels opens up, from bland but functional business traveler places to hip little boutique hotels. Beyond this, and certainly beyond $350, you're moving into deluxe territory; though you don't really arrive at "discreet hideaway for celebrities" status until $700 and above.

Food costs range from $3 to $10 for a perfectly acceptable hot dog, burrito or Asian delicacy, to $50 for a two- or three-course meal at a cute California-cuisine type restaurant. Expect to pay $100-plus at a fine restaurant. A glass of house wine is usually under $10, a beer around $6.

Getting around by public transportation can cost as little as $3–5 a day, with bus tickets $2.50 in San Francisco, $1.75 in Los Angeles, and $2.50 in San Diego. Car rentals cost $40 or more per day. A taxi to or from the airport can cost $50 in San Francisco and Los Angeles.

Children

Home to Disneyland, the San Diego Zoo, the Monterey Bay Aquarium and other kid-friendly attractions, the Golden State is a great place to bring kids, and a popular destination for family vacations. Playgrounds are plentiful, and children pay a reduced fee for admission to museums, other attractions, and on public transportation.

Children's menus are common (some restaurants even provide crayons), although young children rarely make an appearance at fancy restaurants. From beginning kids' ski lessons in Tahoe to nature walks in Yosemite, offering programs specifically for kids is the norm. Childcare is not usually offered by hotels, but reputable baby-sitting services can be recommended by hotel concierges. It's best to call in advance to arrange this.

The official website of the California State Tourism Commission, www.visitcalifornia.com, has a separate link for families.

Climate

When to visit

Northern California: San Francisco's climate is typical of the Northern California coast. Daytime temperatures average in the mid-50s Fahrenheit (12–14° C) and drop as much as 10°F (6°C) at night. Average temperatures are significantly higher in the South Bay and inland valleys. In fact, in the Sacramento

CLIMATE CHART
Los Angeles

Maximum temperature
Minimum temperature
— *Rainfall*

Ocean Beach, San Diego.

CLIMATE CHART
San Francisco

Maximum temperature
Minimum temperature
— *Rainfall*

CLIMATE CHART
Lake Tahoe

Maximum temperature
Minimum temperature
— *Rainfall*

and San Joaquin valleys, summer temperatures often reach the 90s°F (32–37°C). Summers tend to be warm and dry. Winters are generally rainy; temperatures rarely go below freezing along the coast.

Do note that San Francisco can be chilly and foggy during the summer months, even though the sun might be shining just over the bridge in the Bay Area. If you plan to visit the city itself, wait until the fall, when the weather is often perfect.

Southern California: This is one of the few places in the world where you can ski in the morning and surf in the afternoon. It is not uncommon for the temperature to vary by 30–40°F (17–22°C) as you travel from mountains to deserts to the beach. The change of seasons is not as dramatic as it is elsewhere. The winters are mild, with a rainy season that lasts from January through March. In the summer months, the humidity is usually low, so discomfort is rare. The famous LA smog is at its worst in August and September.

What to wear

Northern California: With the exception of the finer restaurants, jackets, ties, and formal dresses are unnecessary. San Francisco is famous for its fog and breezy hilltops, so bring along a sweater or jacket, even if it is warm when you first step out.

Southern California: Dress in Southern California is casual – designer jeans and handbags are quite common – and few restaurants require jackets and ties for men. Unless you are visiting the mountains, heavy clothing is unnecessary. Wool sweaters or lightweight overcoats are sufficient for winter evenings, and a light jacket is adequate for summer evenings. Expect rain in winter and springtime.

Crime and safety

Like urban centers anywhere, California's cities have dangerous neighborhoods. Common sense is an effective weapon. Do not walk alone at night. Keep a careful eye on belongings. Lock valuable possessions in a safe. Never leave your car unlocked. Never leave children by themselves.

If you are driving, never pick up anyone you don't know. Always be wary of who is around you. If you have trouble on the road, stay in the car and lock the doors, turn on your hazard lights and leave the hood up in order to increase visibility and alert police cars.

Hotels usually warn that they do not guarantee the safety of belongings left in the rooms. If you have any valuables, you may want to lock them in the hotel safe.

Customs regulations

Whether or not there is anything to declare, all people entering the country must fill out a US Customs form (usually provided on the airplane) and go through US Customs. This can be a time-consuming process, but, in order to speed things up, be prepared to open your luggage for inspection and try to keep the following restrictions in mind:

There is no limit to the amount of money you can bring in with you. If the amount exceeds $10,000, however, you must fill out a report.

Anything you have for your own personal use may be brought in duty- and tax-free.

Adults are allowed to bring in one quart (1 liter) of alcohol for personal use; 100 cigars or 4.4lbs of tobacco or 200 cigarettes; and $100 worth of gifts.

Agricultural items – including fruits, plants, and vegetables - may not be brought into the US.

Dogs, cats, and other animals may be brought into the country with certain restrictions. For details, contact the US consulate nearest you or write to the Department of Agriculture.

Automobiles may be driven into the US if they are for the personal use of the visitor, family, and guests.

For a full list of prohibited or restricted items, see: www.cbp.gov/travel/international-visitors.

US Customs & Border Protection, 1300 Pennsylvania Avenue NW; Washington, DC 20229; tel: 1-877-227-5511; www.cbp.gov.

Disabled travelers

California has legislation requiring public buildings and most public transportation to be accessible to the disabled. There are also some special concessions: all Greyhound buses are equipped with a wheelchair lift and offer priority seating to disabled persons (tel: 1-800-752-4841) and the railway system, Amtrak, offers discounted tickets and accessible rooms. For more information, visit www.greyhound.com or www.amtrak.com.

Eating out

California is a food-lover's delight, and has the statistics to prove it. San Francisco alone has more than 3,000 restaurants and bars, said to be more per capita than anywhere else in the nation. It has also been estimated that Southern Californians dine out on average two or three times a week, therefore it is no surprise that California has a reputation for fine food.

There is an endless variety of cuisines to try, from classic American and "California Cuisine," to all manner of ethnic food. From Europe you'll find Italian trattorias, French bistros, German beer halls, and Mediterranean eateries with hookah lounges. From Asia you can taste curries from India, Vietnamese pho, Korean BBQ (especially in Los Angeles), sushi,

and dim sum, plus Americanized fusion fare from several regions. From nearby Central America, California has whole-heartedly adopted Mexican dishes, including the now-ubiquitous burritos, quesadillas, and tacos al pastor, especially in San Diego and in San Francisco's Mission District. South America is represented in the state as well, from Brazilian steakhouses to Peruvian restaurants serving savory lomo saltado and fresh ceviche. In short, California offers one of the most diverse dinner menus in the world. Of course, the drink menu has the best local wine in the country, too.

Electricity

The standard electric current in the United States is 110 volts, and outlets are generally for flat-blade, two-prong plugs. Foreign appliances usually require a converter and an adaptor plug. Many hotel bathrooms have plugs for electric shavers that work on either current.

Embassies and consulates

Australia: 575 Market St, San Francisco. Tel: 415-644-3620; http://usa.embassy.gov.au
Also: 2029 Century Park E, Suite 3150, Los Angeles. Tel: 310-229 2300
Canada: 580 California St, 14th Floor, San Francisco. Tel: 415-834-3180; http://international.gc.ca
Also: 550 S. Hope St, Los Angeles. Tel: 213-346 2700

Great Britain: 1 Sansome St, Suite 850, San Francisco. Tel: 415-617-1300; www.gov.uk
Also: 2029 Century Park East, Suite 1350, Los Angeles. Tel: 310-789 0031
Ireland: 100 Pine St, San Francisco. Tel: 415-392-4214; www.dfa.ie
New Zealand: 2425 Olympic Blvd, Suite 600E, Santa Monica (Los Angeles). Tel: 310-566 6555; www.mfat.govt.nz
South Africa: 6300 Wilshire Blvd, Suite 600, Los Angeles. Tel: 323-651-0902; www.dirco.gov.za

Emergency

In the case of an emergency, dial 911 from any telephone for the police, fire department, or ambulance service.

Etiquette

People usually address each other in friendly, rather than formal, terms. Mr. and Ms. are used in business and formal settings if the person is a superior. Mrs. is rarely heard or used. When meeting someone, a handshake is expected. Occasionally, the European kiss on the cheeks is seen, but the "air kiss," as it is often called, is not common. If you are invited to someone's home, a bottle of wine, a box of candy, or a small personal token is thoughtful. Flowers are less popular. Discussing politics can lead to nasty arguments. It's best to avoid the topic, although you may be asked how things are viewed in your country. Gender etiquette can be a minefield. The best

Police take a break at San Francisco's Golden Gate Park.

advice is to treat everyone with the same level of respect that you want for yourself.

Festivals and events

Here are just a few of the most popular festivals and events in California.

January

Tournament of Roses Parade and Rose Bowl Football Game, Pasadena
Tel: 626-449-4100
www.tournamentofroses.com
Kick off **New Year's Day** alongside 100,000 happy spectators at this massive, float-filled parade in Pasadena.

February

AT&T Pebble Beach National Pro-Am Golf Tournament, Pebble Beach
www.attpbgolf.com
First hosted in 1937 by Bing Crosby in Santa Fe, the high-profile Pro-Am is now held in scenic Pebble Beach. There, celebrities and professional golfers team up on the links to raise money for hundreds of non-profits.
Chinese New Year
Fireworks, parades with dancing dragons, and Miss Chinatown pageants mark the start of the Chinese New Year. Especially large celebrations are held in San Francisco, Los Angeles, and San Diego. Visit each city's visitor center for more information.
Clam Chowder Cook-Off, Santa Cruz
Tel: 831-423-5590
http://beachboardwalk.com/Clam-Chowder-Cook-Off
A fundraiser for the City of Santa Cruz Parks and Recreation Department, this 30-year-old cook-off event draws individuals and restaurants – who whip up their best Boston- and Manhattan-style chowders – plus the public who gets to taste them!
Riverside County Fair & National Date Festival, Indio
Tel: 760-863-8247
www.datefest.org
Over 60 years old, this festival delights crowds with live music, hypnotist shows, sea lions, camel and ostrich races, and a nightly Arabian-themed pageant.

Sex Tour, San Francisco Zoo, San Francisco
Tel: 415-753-7080
www.sfzoo.org
If you're looking for something unique, the San Francisco Zoo heats up on Valentine's Day with a guided tour focused on animals' mating and courtship habits.

March

Academy Awards, Los Angeles
www.oscars.com
"And the Oscar goes to..." Before the rest of the country watches the Oscars on television, those in Los Angeles can brave the crowds and see the stars walk the red carpet live.
North Lake Tahoe Snow Festival, Tahoe
Tel: 530-583-7167
www.tahoesnowfestival.com
Held either in late February or early March, these 10 fun-filled days offer special on-snow events, parties, and parades.
Return of the Swallows, San Juan Capistrano
www.swallowsparade.com
Celebrate the mid-March return of the swallows to San Juan Capistrano on St Joseph's Day (March 19) with the Fiesta de las Golondrinas and Swallows' Day Parade, the country's biggest non-motorized parade.
Saint Patrick's Day
Don something green and drink to the luck of the Irish on March 17th. Parades and celebrations are held around the state, including in San Francisco, Los Angeles, and San Diego.

April

Cherry Blossom Festival, San Francisco
Tel: 415-563-2313
www.sfcherryblossom.org
A 45-year-old Japantown tradition, the Cherry Blossom Festival is a celebration of Japanese heritage and traditions – including martial arts, music, and dance – that draws 200,000 people each year.
Coachella Valley Music Festival, Indio
www.coachella.com
Now one of the country's biggest music festivals, Coachella lures urbanites to the desert for three days of alternative rock, hip hop, and electronic music, plus large sculptural art.

Doo Dah Parade, Pasadena
Tel: 626-590-1134
www.pasadenadoodahparade.info
In the mood for a crazy frolic? This outrageous parade is full of off-beat floats and eccentric performers.
San Francisco International Film Festival, San Francisco
Tel: 415-561-5000
www.sffs.org
The country's longest-running film festival showcases more than 175 films from around the world.

May

Cinco de Mayo
With music and margaritas, Los Angeles, San Diego, Santa Barbara, and San Francisco all commemorate Mexico's May 5, 1863, victory over the French.
Jumping Frog Jubilee, Angels Camp
Tel: 209-736-2561
www.frogtown.org
Channel Mark Twain and watch amphibians hop to a prize, then have fun at the rodeo and county fair.
Kinetic Grand Championship, Arcata to Ferndale, Humboldt County
Tel: 707-733786-38413443
www.kineticgrandchampionship.com
Transportation meets art at this three-day race; participants ride human-powered sculptures over a 38-mile (61km) course.
Sacramento Music Festival, Sacramento
Tel: 916-444-2004
www.sacjazz.com
Once known as the Jazz Jubilee, this festival now features a full range of music: jazz, swing, blues, zydeco, rockabilly, bluegrass, Latin music, and more.
Zazzle Zappos Alaska Airlines Bay to Breakers, San Francisco
Tel: (415) 231-3130415-864-3432
www.zapposbaytobreakers.com
Thousands of costume-clad runners converge in San Francisco to for an entertaining 12km dash from Ferry Building to Ocean Beach.

June

Ojai Music Festival, Ojai
Tel: 805-646-2094
www.ojaifestival.org
Drawing an eclectic group of performers, this music celebration features everything from bluegrass to rockabilly to classical.
Playboy Jazz Festival, Los Angeles
Tel: 323-450-1173
www.playboyjazzfestival.com

At the Hollywood Bowl, this long-time jazz fest now features both classic styles (New Orleans, swing, bebop) and jazz-rock fusions.
San Francisco Pride
San Francisco
Tel: 415-864-5889
www.sfpride.org
Over 40 years old, this huge LGBTQ celebration includes a two-day festival culminating with a Sunday morning parade.
Temecula Valley Balloon and Wine Festival
Tel: 951-676-6713
www.tvbwf.com
Wine-tasting, live music, and balloon launches comprise this community affair, launched in 1983 by commercial air pilot and avid balloonist Walt Darren.

July
Comic-Con International, San Diego
Tel: 619-491-2475
www.comic-con.org
The largest comic book and popular arts convention in the world.
Fourth of July
Fireworks explode throughout the state, celebrating America's Independence Day.
Gilroy Garlic Festival, Gilroy
Tel: 408-842-1625.
www.gilroygarlicfestival.com
Everything from traditional garlic fries to the more innovative garlic ice cream can be tasted at this celebration of Gilroy's major industry.
Pageant of the Masters, Laguna Beach
Tel: 949-497-6582
www.foapom.com
This long-standing festival wows audience with its tableaux vivants ("living pictures") – incredibly faithful live depictions of classical and contemporary artworks, complete with intricate sets.

August
California State Fair, Sacramento
Tel: 916-263-3247
www.castatefair.org
This 18-day state fair features competitions in livestock, wine and beer, and cheese; dozens of rides, and tons of food, music, and live entertainment.
Nisei Week, Little Tokyo, Los Angeles
Tel: 213-687-7193
www.niseiweek.org
One of the country's oldest Japanese-American festivals, Nisei

Week includes a karate tournament, gyoza-eating competition, parade, and numerous other sport competitions.
Old Spanish Days Fiesta, Santa Barbara
Tel: 805-962-8101
www.oldspanishdays-fiesta.org
Take your pick from folk dancing, a market, a carnival, a rodeo, and a parade.

September
Monterey Jazz Festival, Monterey
Tel: 831-373-3366
www.montereyjazzfestival.org
Co-founded by Jimmy Lyons and Ralph J. Gleason in 1958, this is the world's longest-running jazz festival. Among other renowned performers, it has presented Louis Armstrong, Billie Holiday, Dave Brubeck, Miles Davis, Diana Krall, Wynton Marsalis, and Terence Blanchard.
Sausalito Art Festival, Sausalito
Tel: 415-331-3757
www.sausalitoartfestival.org
Over 250 artists converge in Sausalito on Labor Day weekend, showcasing everything from ceramics and sculpture to photography, watercolor, glass, and mixed media.

October
Art and Pumpkin Festival, Half Moon Bay
Tel: 650-726-9652
www.miramarevents.com
At the World Pumpkin Capital you'll find gigantic pumpkins, a Haunted House, harvest-inspired crafts, pie-eating and costume contests, an enormous jack-o-lantern, and pumpkin ale.
California Avocado Festival, Carpinteria
Tel: 805-684-0038
www.avofest.com
Described as "three days of peace, love, and guacamole," this eco-friendly festival features music, recipe contests, and the world's largest vat of guacamole.
Fleet Week, San Diego and San Francisco
Tel: 619-858-1545, 650-599-5057
www.fleetweeksandiego.org
Contests, air shows, and ship tours are all held in honor of the US military.
Hardly Strictly Bluegrass Festival, San Francisco
www.hardlystrictlybluegrass.com

Conceived and patronized by late philanthropist Warren Hellman in 2001, this free, annual music festival held every first weekend of October in Golden Gate Park draws crowds in the hundreds of thousands.

November
Death Valley '49ers Encampment, Death Valley
www.deathvalley49ers.org
Fiddlers contest, art shows, and a trek through the hot, hot valley.
Dia de los Muertos Festival, Los Angeles
Tel: 323-469-1181
www.ladayofthedead.com
The Mexican Day of the Dead is celebrated with processions, masks, face-painting, and other rituals that pay homage to the dearly departed.

December
Parade of Lights
http://sdparadeoflights.org
Beautifully illuminated boats parade through Southern California harbors, including Newport Beach and San Diego; call the local tourist bureaus for information.

H

Health and medical care

There is nothing cheap about being sick in the United States. It is essential to have adequate medical insurance and to carry an identification card or policy number at all times.

In the event that you need medical assistance, consult the local *Yellow Pages* for the physician or pharmacist nearest you. In large cities, there is usually a physician referral service number listed. If you need immediate attention, go to a hospital emergency room.

Some medicines that are available over the counter in your home country may require a prescription in the US. Walgreens drugstores (pharmacies) have 24-hour locations in major cities.

Hospitals

San Francisco: some of the larger hospitals with 24-hour emergency services are:
California Pacific Medical Center, with buildings at 3700 California St,

3898 California St, 2333 Buchanan St, and at Castro and Deboce streets; tel: 415-600-6000.
Saint Francis Memorial Hospital, 900 Hyde St (Downtown); tel: 415-353-6000.
San Francisco General Hospital, 1001 Potrero Ave; tel: 415-206-8000.
UCSF Medical Center, 505 Parnassus Ave (Richmond); tel: 415-476-1000.
Los Angeles: some of the most central hospitals are:
California Hospital Medical Center, 1401 S. Grand Avenue (Downtown); tel: 213-748-2411.
Cedars-Sinai Medical Center, 8700 Beverly Boulevard (Beverly Hills); tel: 310-423-3277.
LAC+USC Medical Center, 2051 Marengo Street; tel: 323-409-1000.
Saint John's Health Center, 2121 Santa Monica Blvd. (Santa Monica); tel: 310-829-5511.
UCLA Medical Center, 757 Westwood Plaza; tel: 310-825-2111.

Internet

You should be able to find internet cafés in all major cities and larger towns, but they are not nearly as commonplace as in Europe. Most public libraries have free terminals, and **FedEx Office,** a national chain (www.fedexoffice.com), rents out space on terminals, scanners, and printers by the minute or by the hour. The company has many locations throughout the state.

If you've brought your own laptop computer, nearly all cafés in cities now offer free wireless connections.

Most hotels offer high-speed internet connections in their guestrooms and common areas, although it's not always free. Even modest hotels tend to have at least one computer for the use of guests.

LGBTQ travelers

San Francisco is one of the world's most welcoming places for gay men and lesbians. The best sources for up-to-date information

on new clubs, shows, films, events, and gay news are the free newspapers, notably the *Bay Times* and the *Bay Area Reporter (BAR;* www. ebar.com*)* found in cafés or street-corner boxes. **The Center**, at 1800 Market Street, has become a vital nexus for the LGBTQ community and has numerous flyers and listings for events. **The Women's Building,** www.womensbuilding.org, houses various non-profit organizations and you'll find newspapers, bulletin board postings, and information here too. The on-line newspaper *Bay Guardian* (www.sfbg.com) and *SF Weekly* (www.sfweekly.com*),* have useful listings and information as well.

In Los Angeles, **West Hollywood** contains Southern California's largest homosexual population, and sponsors LA's annual Gay Pride Parade. Visit www.visitwesthollywood.com for more information. Also check out the website www.oneinstitute.org for details about the **ONE National Gay & Lesbian Archives** (909 W. Adams Boulevard; tel: 213-821-2771), the world's largest research library on lesbian, gay, bisexual, and transgendered issues.

Lost luggage

File claims for damaged or missing luggage before leaving the airport. For queries and complaints, contact the Federal Aviation Administration Consumer Hotline (tel: 1-866-835-5322, www.faa.gov) or the Aviation Consumer Protection Division (tel: 202-366-4000; www.transportation.gov/airconsumer).

Maps

In San Francisco, if you find yourself confused and without a map, look for a Muni bus shelter, which often has a detailed map of the city, including a close-up map of Downtown. Visitor centers also provide free maps. Some corner shops and gas stations also sell maps.

Tourists can receive a variety of Los Angeles maps from **Metro (Los Angeles County Metropolitan Transportation Authority)** and

individual visitor bureaus. In addition, the **AAA** has various branches in the area, offering assorted street maps of LA plus maps of California and Mexico. It's worth joining if you plan to drive within Los Angeles, because the cost of being towed away once by traffic wardens could be less than the annual membership fee.

Insight Flexi Map: San Francisco and *Insight Flexi Map: Los Angeles* are laminated, easy-to-fold maps that combine detailed cartography with pictures and essential information.

Media

Television & radio

Television and radio are invaluable sources of up-to-the-minute information about weather, road conditions, and current events. Television and radio listings are published in local newspapers. Sunday papers usually have a detailed weekly guide to events and activities.

Newspapers, magazines, and websites

San Francisco's major daily newspaper is the *San Francisco Chronicle* (www.sfchronicle.com). The weekend edition of the *Chronicle* includes special sections, such as "Datebook," which highlights the area's sports, entertainment, and cultural events. Other papers in Northern California include the *Sacramento Bee,* the *San Jose Mercury-News,* and the *San Francisco Bay Guardian.*

The websites www.7x7.com and www. sanfranmag.com keep up to date with events and activities.

The *Los Angeles Times* (www. latimes.com) is one of the most widely read papers in the country. There are several editions, and there is probably no better local entertainment section than the *Times'* Sunday "Calendar" section. Other large daily papers are San Fernando Valley's *The Daily News, The San Diego Union-Tribune,* and the *Orange County Register.*

Los Angeles Magazine, Palm Springs Life, San Diego, Santa Barbara, and *Orange Coast* are monthly regional magazines that carry feature articles on Southern California culture, as well as listings of restaurants and current events.

The website www.la.com describes area attractions, spas, hotels, eateries, clubs, and shops, and lists most local events.

Some of the free local weekly newspapers, available in cafés and newspaper boxes on the street, are excellent sources of up-to-the-minute information on what's going on in a particular town. Check out the *LA Weekly* in Los Angeles, the *East Bay Express* in the East Bay, the *San Francisco Bay Guardian,* and *SF Weekly* in San Francisco.

Money

Cash: Most banks belong to a network of ATMs (automatic teller machines) which dispense cash 24 hours a day.
Credit cards: Not all credit cards are accepted at all places, but most places accept either **Visa**, **American Express** or **MasterCard**. Major credit cards can also be used to withdraw cash from atms. (Look for an ATM that uses one of the banking networks indicated on the back of your credit card, such as Plus, Cirrus, or Interlink.) Most likely there will be a charge.
Traveler's Checks: With the popularity of ATMs, credit cards, and debit cards, traveler's checks are becoming less and less common. Still, banks, stores, restaurants, and hotels generally accept US dollar-denominated traveler's checks. If yours are in foreign denominations, they must be changed to dollars. Banks readily cash large traveler's checks, although be sure to take along your passport. When lost or stolen, most traveler's checks can be replaced; record the checks' serial numbers in a separate place to facilitate refunds of lost or stolen checks.

Opening hours

Standard business hours are 9am–5pm weekdays. Most department stores open at 10am and many stores, especially those in shopping malls, stay open until 9pm. San Francisco, Los Angeles, and San Diego have a number of 24-hour restaurants. A few supermarkets and convenience stores

are also open around the clock. Bank hours usually run from 9am to 5pm, although some stay open until 6pm. Some branch offices keep Saturday morning hours. However, most banks are equipped with 24-hour automated tellers on the outside of their buildings, and, if you have an ATM card, you can use these machines for simple transactions at your convenience. Be careful at night.

Keep in mind that, during public holidays, post offices, banks, government offices, and many private businesses are closed.

Postal services

Post offices open between 9am and usually close at 6pm, Monday–Friday. Many are also open for a few hours on Saturday morning. Post offices are closed all day on Sunday. If you don't know where you will be staying in any particular town, you can receive mail by having it addressed to General Delivery at the main post office in that town. You must pick up General Delivery mail in person and show proper identification.

You can buy stamps in most convenience stores, although you may

Nearly all city cafés offer free Wi-Fi.

have to buy a book of stamps. You can also buy them at post offices.

Public holidays

National US holidays are:
New Year's Day (January 1)
Martin Luther King Jr. Day (3rd Monday in January)
Presidents' Day (3rd Monday in February)
Memorial Day (Last Monday in May)
Independence Day (July 4)
Labor Day (1st Monday in September)
Columbus Day (2nd Monday in October)
Veteran's Day (November 11)
Thanksgiving (4th Thursday in November)
Christmas Day (December 25)

Religious services

There is no official religion in the US or California. The majority of Americans identify themselves as Protestant or Catholic. Non-Christian religions (including Judaism, Islam, Buddhism, and Hinduism) collectively make up about 5 percent of the adult population. In keeping with the state's open-minded culture, Californians

Students at the University of California, Berkeley.

are generally very tolerant of diverse religions.

Senior travelers

Senior citizens (65 and older) are entitled to many benefits, including reduced rates on public transportation and for entrance to museums. Seniors who want to be students should contact Elderhostels (tel: 1-800-454-5768, www.roadscholar.org) for information on places that provide both accommodation and classes. The Bay Area has a number of Elderhostel locations.

Shopping

California is a true shoppers paradise. From exclusive boutiques on Rodeo Drive in Los Angeles to large malls in the San Fernando Valley, the state is ready to satisfy all tastes and suit every pocket. Besides the glitzy designer outlets, California also has its fair share of small town art galleries and quirky craft shops while the Wine Country and farmers' markets brim with world-class vintages and artisan food products.

Smoking

California's famed tolerance is not extended to smokers. State law bans smoking in bars, clubs, restaurants, within 25ft (7.5 meters) of playgrounds or sandboxes, and within 20ft (6 meters) of all public buildings.

In San Francisco, smoking is also prohibited in all city-owned parks, plazas, and public sports facilities. Even some public beaches in Southern California have made cigarettes illegal; look for signs on the sand to see if you can light up. You may find it difficult to reserve a smoking room in a hotel, so be sure to check at the time of booking, and be prepared to shop around.

Student travelers

With a current school ID, a student traveler can take advantage of discounts at some museums, movie theaters, and public transportation. Check out colleges in the summer for dormitory accommodation.

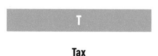

Tax

Depending on which county you are in, the sales tax in California ranges from 6.5 to 10.25 percent (Compton enjoys the most expensive rate). The average combined rate across the state is 8.15 percent. The sales tax will be added to your bill at shops and restaurants. When calculating a tip at restaurants, calculate a tip on the pre-tax total.

In most California cities, there is a hotel room tax of anywhere from 8 to 14 percent (with both San Francisco and Los Angeles at the 14 percent mark).

Telephones and faxes

Telephones: with the growing popularity of cell phones, coin-operated telephones are not as common as before, but can usually be found in hotels, gas stations, and often in lighted booths on street corners.

Local US phone numbers are seven-digit numbers. When you're placing a long-distance call, you must first dial "1" and then the three-digit area code of the place you are calling, and then the seven-digit local number. Make use of toll-free numbers when possible (toll-free telephone numbers within the US are indicated by 1-800, 855, 866, 877 or 888). When making personal calls, take advantage of lower long-distance rates after 7pm on weekdays and during weekends. Helpful dialing information:

US calls outside your area code: Dial 1 + area code + local number.

International Calls: Dial 011 + country code + number.

Directly inquiries: Dial 411 for information assistance, which can provide telephone listings.

Operator: If you are having problems, dial "0" for assistance with local calls; or 00 for international calls.

Cell phones: To use your GSM cellular phone in the US, contact your service provider before you leave to set up international roaming. Depending on the length of your stay, it may be cheaper to buy a US-issue phone or SIM card.

Fax machines: Although email and cell phones have replaced the need for many faxes, machines can be found in most hotels and motels, and at FedEx Office locations.

Time zone

California is on Pacific Standard Time (PST), which is two hours earlier than Chicago, three hours earlier than New York and eight hours earlier than Greenwich Mean Time. During Daylight Savings time, which occurs from the second Sunday of March to the first Sunday of November, the clocks are rolled forward one hour and PST becomes only seven hours earlier than GMT.

Tipping

Just as in other parts of the country, service personnel in California rely on tips for a large part of their income. In most cases, 18–20 percent is the going rate for waiters and bartenders and 10–15 percent for taxi drivers. The accepted rate for baggage handlers at airports and hotels is around $1 per bag. The rule of thumb is to leave a minimum tip of one or two dollars per night stayed in the room for housekeeping staff. A doorman expects to be tipped at least $1 for unloading your car or for other services.

Tourist information

General information on visiting the Golden State is available from:
California Tourism,
555 Capitol Mall Suite 1100, Sacramento, CA 95814
Tel: 1-916-444-4429
www.visitcalifornia.com
Anaheim/Orange County Visitor and Convention Bureau
2099 S. State College Blvd. Suite 600, Anaheim
Tel: 714-765-8888
www.visitanaheim.org
Berkeley Convention and Visitors Bureau
2030 Adison St, #102 Berkeley
Tel: 510-549-7040
www.visitberkeley.com
Beverly Hills Conference and Visitors Bureau
9400 South Santa Monica Blvd, #102, Beverly Hills
Tel: 310-248-1015
www.lovebeverlyhills.com
Buena Park Convention and Visitors Office
6601 Beach Blvd, Suite 200, Buena Park
Tel: 800-541-3953

www.buenapark.com
Catalina Island Chamber of Commerce
1 Green Pleasure Pier, Avalon
Tel: 310-510-1520
www.catalinachamber.com
Hollywood Visitor Information Center
6801 Hollywood Blvd at Hollywood and Highland
Tel: 323-467-6412
www.discoverlosangeles.com
Lake Tahoe Incline Village and Crystal Bay Visitors' Bureau,
969 Tahoe Blvd, Incline Village, NV 89451
Tel: 1-800-468-2463
www.gotahoenorth.com
South Lake Tahoe Visitors Center
3066 Lake Tahoe Blvd, South Lake Tahoe
Tel: 530-541-5255
www.tahoesouth.com
Long Beach Area Convention and Visitors Bureau
301 East Ocean Blvd #1900, Long Beach
Tel: 562-436-3645
www.visitlongbeach.com
Los Angeles Area Chamber of Commerce,
350 South Bixel St.
Tel: 213-580-7500
https://lachamber.com
Los Angeles Official Visitor Center
6801 Hollywood Blvd
Tel: 323-467-6412
www.discoverlosangeles.com
Monterey Visitors Center
401 Camino El Estero, Monterey
Tel: 888-221-1010
www.seemonterey.com
Napa Valley Welcome Center
600 Main Street, Napa
Tel: 707-251-5895

https://donapa.com/visitor-center
Palm Springs Desert Resort Communities Convention and Visitors Authority
70100 State Highway 111, #100, Rancho Mirage
Tel: 760-770-9000, 1-800-967-3767
www.visitgreaterpalmsprings.com
Sacramento Visitors Bureau
1608 I St, Sacramento
Tel: 1-916 226 5783
www.visitsacramento.co
San Diego Visitor Information Center
996-B N. Harbor Drive, San Diego
Tel: 619-291-4903
www.sandiego.org
San Francisco Visitor Information Center
900 Market St, San Francisco
Tel: 415-391-2000
www.sftravel.com
San Jose Convention and Visitors' Bureau
408 Almaden Blvd, San Jose
Tel: 408-792-4511
www.sanjose.org
San Luis Obispo County Visitor and Conference Bureau
811 E1 Capitan Way, Suite 200, San Luis Obispo
Tel: 805-541-8000
www.visitsanluisobispocounty.com
Santa Barbara Conference and Visitors Bureau
I Garden Street, Santa Barbara
Tel: 805-965-3021
www.santabarbaraca.com
Santa Cruz County Conference and Visitors Council
303 Water St, Santa Cruz
Tel: 831-425-1234
www.santacruzca.org
Sonoma County Tourism Bureau
3637 Westwind Blvd. Santa Rosa
Tel: 707-522-5800
www.sonomacounty.com
Sonoma County Tourism
400 Aviation Blvd, Suite 500, Santa Rosa
Tel: 800-576-6662
www.sonomacounty.com
Ventura Visitors Center
101 South California St, Ventura
Tel: 805-648-2075
https://visitventuraca.com
Mariposa County (Yosemite) Visitors Center
5158 State Highway 140
Tel: 866 425 3366
www.yosemite.com
Tour operators and travel agents
Adventure Bus
Tel: 1-909-633-7225
www.adventurebus.com

San Francisco Convention and Visitors' Bureau.

Inexpensive transportation through much of California, departing from Salt Lake City and Las Vegas. Destinations include Yellowstone and the southwestern national parks, plus other trips, stopping at scenic spots en route.
Architours
Tel: 323-294-5821
www.architours.com
Various Los Angeles tours visit works by Frank Lloyd Wright and Richard Neutra, as well as restaurants and other facilities of architectural merit.
foot!
Tel: 415-793-5378
www.foottours.com
Fun, informative, interactive walking tours that allow for personal and memorable experiences. Guides are professional comedians who share their love and knowledge of San Francisco with you.
Mangia! North Beach – History, Food, and Culture Tours
e-mail: gaw@sbcglobal.net
Learn about the Italian heritage of the neighborhood, taste truffles and focaccia, and enjoy a three-course lunch with SF Chronicle food columnist GraceAnn Walden. Named one of the 100 best things about San Francisco by Gourmet magazine. Reservations necessary.
Old Town Trolley Tours
Tel: 1-888-910-8687
www.trolleytours.com
Vibrant green-and-orange trolleys, driven by spirited conductors, take visitors to San Diego's most popular sites, including Old Town, the San Diego Harbor Seaport Village, Petco Park, the Gaslamp Quarter, the Hotel del Coronado, the San Diego Zoo, and Balboa Park.
San Francisco City Guides
Tel: 415-557-4266
www.sfcityguides.org
Nearly 70 free architectural and history tours by trained volunteers are offered all year long. Tours cover topics from the murals of the Mission to the mansions of Pacific Heights, and everything in between.
Starline Tours
Tel: 1-800-959-3131
www.starlinetours.com
An assortment of LA sightseeing tours, from movie stars' homes to the delights of Disneyland.
Victorian Home Walk
Tel: 415-252-9485
www.victorianhomewalk.com

Go where buses can't. Learn about San Francisco architecture and history from long-time residents. Most days at 11am a tour leaves from the old lobby of the Westin St Francis on Powell and Geary in Union Square. No reservations required.
Warner Bros. Studios V.I.P. Tour
Tel: 1-877-492-8689
www.wbstudiotour.com
For two colorful hours, small groups of movie lovers can ride through this famous Burbank lot, visiting such classic sets as the Walton family home and Errol Flynn's Sherwood Forest as well as sound stages and post-production labs.
Wok Wiz Walking
Tel: 650-355-9657
www.wokwiz.com
SF's Chinatown history, culture, and folklore are presented from an insider's view of the largest Chinatown outside of China. The daily tour includes a seven-course dim-sum lunch. Reservations required.

Useful addresses

California has 16 Welcome Centers situated throughout the state to assist visitors. The centers provide maps, brochures, and helpful on-the-spot advice. For more information and precise driving directions, go to: www.visitcalifornia.com.
Anderson (Shasta Cascade), 1699 Highway 273, south of Redding on I-5. Tel: 530-365-1180.
Auburn (Gold Country), 1103 High Street. Tel: 530-887-2111.
Barstow (Deserts), 2796 Tanger Way, Suite 100. Tel: 760-253-4782.
Buena Park, 6601 Beach Blvd. Tel: 1-800-541-3953.
El Dorado Hills, 2085 Vine St Ste 105. Tel: 916-358-3700.
Mammoth Lakes, 2510 Highway 203/ Main Street. Tel: 760-924-5500.
Merced (Central Valley), 710 W. 16th St, Suite A. Tel: 209-724-8104.
Oceanside (San Diego), 928 North Coast Highway. Tel: 760-721-1101.
Oxnard (Central Coast), 2786 Seaglass Way, Space 5105. Tel: 805-988-0717.
Pismo Beach (Central Coast), 333 Five Cities Drive, Suite 100, in the Prime Outlets. Tel: 805-773-7924.
Salinas, 1213 N Davis Rd. Tel: 831-757-8687.

San Francisco, Pier 39, Building P. Tel: 415-981-1280.
Santa Rosa (North Coast), 9 Fourth St, Downtown. Tel: 1-800-404-7673.
Truckee, 10065 Donner Pass Rd. Tel: 530-587-8808.
Yucca Valley (Deserts), 56711 Twentynine Palms Highway. Tel: 760-365-5464.

Visas and passports

Foreign travelers to the US must have a passport, and, depending on where they are arriving from, a visa or a health record. However, in an effort to attract more tourists, the US initiated the Visa Waiver Program (VWP) for those coming on vacation for a maximum of 90 days. With several dozen countries participating, the program allows travelers to enter the US with only a machine-readable passport.

The terrorist attacks of September 11, 2001 have caused an increase in security measures taken by the Department of Homeland Security. It now requires all VWP participants to apply with the Electronic System for Travel Authorization (ESTA). Done online, authorization does not take much time and can be done at any time before entry into the US; try to apply as early as possible to minimize complications.

To check your eligibility for the Visa Waiver Program, and for complete and up-to-date travel entry requirements, visit the US State Department website, https://travel.state.gov.

If a visitor loses their visa while in the country, a new one may be obtained from the embassy of the visitor's home country. Extensions are granted by various service centers of the Bureau of Citizenship and Immigration Services (tel: 1-800 375-5283; www.uscis.gov).

Weights and measures

The US uses the imperial system for measurement, Fahrenheit for temperature, and mile for distance.

GENERAL

Back Roads to the California Coast: Scenic Byways and Highways to the Edge of the Golden State, by Earl Thollander and Herb McGrew. A guide for meandering through the state on 15 scenic back-road drives.

Cruel Justice: Three Strikes and the Politics of Crime in America's Golden State, by Joe Domanick. A deep look at how the "three strikes" law came to be, and its wide-ranging impact.

A Guide to Architecture in Los Angeles and Southern California, by Gebhard and Winter. Considered a must-have guide to Los Angeles architecture by scholars and enthusiasts alike.

Los Angeles A–Z: An Encyclopedia of City & Country, by Dale & Leonard Pitt. A one-volume encyclopedia packed with information on everything from native trees and who the Black Dahlia was to Engine House #18 and O.J. Simpson.

My California: Journeys by Great Writers. Several dozen great writers – including Pico Iyer, Michael Chabon, and Thomas Steinbeck – share stories to benefit the California Arts Council.

Tales of the City, by Armistead Maupin. Originally a serial in the San Francisco Chronicle, Maupin's novel stitches together the lives of residents of the fictitious Barbary Lane, told with delightful candor.

A Very Good Year: The Journey of a California Wine from Vine to Table, by Mike Weiss. Award-winning journalist spent nearly two years with a Sonoma County winemaker to vividly chronicle all that goes into the process of winemaking.

PEOPLE AND PLACES

Baseball in San Diego: From Padres to Petco, by Bill Swank. A look at San Diego's love affair with the Padres, from 1936 to the present.

Hollywood Interrupted: Insanity Chic in Babylon – The Case Against Celebrity, by Andrew Breitbart and Mark Ebner. A journey into the entertainment industry's underbelly, complete with medications, meltdowns, and how the media plays along.

The Los Angeles Watts Towers, by Bud and Arloa Goldstone. How

Simon Rodia's creation came into being, plus the history of the Watts neighborhood.

The Mayor of Castro Street: The Life and Times of Harvey Milk, by Randy Shilts. Quintessential biography of the first openly gay man elected to office in America, from his triumphant election and ground-breaking championing of gay rights, to his tragic assassination and the subsequent rioting upon the sentence of his killer.

Movie Star Homes: The Famous to the Forgotten, by Judy Artunian. Nearly 400 entries on homes of celebrities from Gloria Swanson to Buster Keaton.

⏻ Send us your thoughts

We do our best to ensure the information in our books is as accurate and up-to-date as possible. The books are updated on a regular basis using local contacts, who painstakingly add, amend and correct as required. However, some details (such as telephone numbers and opening times) are liable to change, and we are ultimately reliant on our readers to put us in the picture.

We welcome your feedback, especially your experience of using the book "on the road". Maybe you came across a great bar or new attraction we missed.

We will acknowledge all contributions, and we'll offer an Insight Guide to the best letters received.

Please write to us at:
Insight Guides
PO Box 7910
London SE1 1WE

Or email us at:
hello@insightguides.com

Stairway Walks of San Francisco, by Adah Bakalinksky. A delightful guide to 27 urban hikes up and down some of the city's 350 stairways.

GEOGRAPHY AND NATURAL HISTORY

California Wildlife Reviewing Guide, by Jeanne L. Clarke. Explores 150 of the state's top sites for wildlife viewing, including maps, access information, and nearly 100 color photos.

Day Hiker's Guide to California State Parks, by John Mckinney. Over 150 day hikes in California, from Lake Tahoe to Anza-Borrego.

Introduction to Air in California, by David Carle. Part natural history guide, part intriguing assessment of how humans have changed California's air.

HISTORY

Agrarian Dreams: The Paradox of Organic Farming in California, by Julie Guthman. Guthman casts doubt on the success of organic farming.

The California Gold Rush and the Coming of the Civil War, by Leonard L. Richards. An award-winning historian reveals how the Gold Rush in California spurred contention between Northern industrialists and slave-owning Southerners.

The Golden Game: The Story of California Baseball, by Kevin Nelson. From the 1850s to recent times, how California baseball came to be, and its impact.

The Times We Had: Life with William Randolph Hearst, by Marion Davies. The mistress of one of America's richest men, Davies chronicles the glittering life she led at Hearst Castle and in Los Angeles.

CREDITS

PHOTO CREDITS

Abraham Nowitz/Apa Publications 116
Alamy 14/15, 36, 46, 48, 52, 53, 55, 56, 59, 76, 77, 79, 81, 83, 93BL, 202/203, 208B
Bigstock.com 32R, 136, 147, 151, 164, 183B, 191, 199, 247
Corbis 41, 50, 51, 201ML
CTTC 281B
Daniella Nowitz/Apa Publications 6MR, 8T, 29, 68, 109, 110, 111, 112, 117, 119T, 119B, 121, 122, 123, 126/127T, 126BR
David Dunai/Apa Publications 6BR, 7TR, 7ML, 7ML, 7TL, 9B, 10, 11, 18, 19T, 19B, 20, 21, 22, 23, 24, 26/27, 28, 33, 34BC, 35BR, 35BL, 35TR, 63, 66, 67, 70BR, 70/71T, 70BL, 71ML, 71BR, 71TR, 71BL, 73, 75, 82, 86L, 86R, 87, 88, 91, 103T, 103B, 128, 129, 131B, 131T, 132, 133, 140, 141, 143, 144B, 144T, 145, 146T, 146B, 149, 150, 152/153, 155T, 155B, 156, 157, 158, 159, 160, 161B, 161T, 162B, 162T, 163, 165, 166, 167, 169B, 169T, 170, 171,

172, 173, 174, 175, 176, 177T, 177B, 178, 179, 180, 181, 192, 193, 195, 196, 197, 204, 205T, 206, 207, 208T, 209, 210T, 211, 212, 213T, 216, 217, 218, 219, 220, 221T, 221B, 222T, 222B, 223, 225, 226, 227T, 227B, 228, 230, 231T, 231B, 232, 233, 234, 235, 236/237T, 237BR, 237BL, 238, 239, 242, 243T, 243B, 244, 245, 246B, 249, 250, 251, 252, 253B, 253T, 254T, 254B, 255, 256/257B, 256T, 257, 258, 259, 261, 263, 264/265, 265B, 265T, 266T, 270, 276, 277, 279, 280T, 280B, 281T, 282T, 282B, 284, 286B, 286T, 288, 290, 290/291, 292
Dreamstime 7BR, 9T, 34/35T, 34BR, 39, 90, 154, 188T, 198, 200/201T, 200BR, 201BR, 201BL, 210B, 246T, 248, 267
Gene Blevins/ZUMA Wire/REX/ Shutterstock 93ML
Getty Images 12/13, 16/17, 25, 30, 31, 32L, 38, 62, 64/65, 72, 78, 80, 85, 92/93T, 92BR, 92BL, 93BR, 93TR, 96/97, 98/99, 106, 237ML, 237TR

Giovanni Simeone/4Corners Images 1
iStock 4, 74, 84, 94/95, 139, 184, 205B, 236BL, 283, 287, 301
Library of Congress 42, 43, 44, 49, 54, 57, 127BL, 200MR
Martyn Goddard/Apa Publications 6ML, 6ML, 7MR, 89, 183T, 185B, 185T, 187B, 187T, 188B, 189, 190T, 190B, 260, 266B, 271, 272/273, 273, 274B, 274T, 275
National Archives and Records Administration 45
Photoshot 47
Public domain 37, 40
Richard Nowitz/Apa Publications 8B, 69, 102, 107, 108B, 108T, 113, 114, 120, 124, 125, 126BL, 127ML, 127TR, 135, 137, 138, 268/269, 269, 293, 297, 298, 299
San Francisco Public Library/San Francisco History Center 127BR
Scala Archives 201TR
Sonoma Tourism Bureau 148/149
SuperStock 213B, 236BR
TopFoto 58, 60, 61

COVER CREDITS

Front cover: View over Half Dome, Yosemite National Park *Francesco Carovillano/4Corners Images*
Back cover: Hollywood Walk of Fame *David Dunai/Apa Publications*
Front flap: (from top) Golden Gate Bridge *Richard Nowitz/Apa*

Publications; Vineyard in Sonoma *Sonoma Tourism Bureau*; Rodeo Drive *iStock*; Dune buggy at Pismo Beach *David Dunai/Apa Publications*
Back flap: Highway 1, Big Sur *David Dunai/Apa Publications*

INSIGHT GUIDE CREDITS

Distribution
UK, Ireland and Europe
Apa Publications (UK) Ltd;
sales@insightguides.com
United States and Canada
Ingram Publisher Services;
ips@ingramcontent.com
Australia and New Zealand
Woodslane; info@woodslane.com.au
Southeast Asia
Apa Publications (SN) Pte;
singaporeoffice@insightguides.com
Worldwide
Apa Publications (UK) Ltd;
sales@insightguides.com
Special Sales, Content Licensing and CoPublishing
Insight Guides can be purchased in bulk quantities at discounted prices. We can create special editions, personalised jackets and corporate imprints tailored to your needs.
sales@insightguides.com
www.insightguides.biz

Printed in China by CTPS

All Rights Reserved
© 2018 Apa Digital (CH) AG and
Apa Publications (UK) Ltd

First Edition 1984
Ninth Edition 2018

Every effort has been made to provide accurate information in this publication, but changes are inevitable. The publisher cannot be responsible for any resulting loss, inconvenience or injury. We would appreciate it if readers would call our attention to any errors or outdated information. We also welcome your suggestions; please contact us at:
hello@insightguides.com

www.insightguides.com

Editor: Sian Marsh
Author: Barbara Rockwell
Head of DTP and Pre-Press:
Rebeka Davies
Update Production: Apa Digital
Picture Editor: Tom Smyth
Cartography: original cartography
Phoenix Mapping, updated by Carte

CONTRIBUTORS

This, the ninth edition of Insight Guides California, was commissioned by **Carine Tracanelli** and edited by **Sian Marsh**.
The guide was updated by **Lisa Dion**, a Californian native, and **Maciej Zglinicki**. This update built on previous work by **Barbara Rockwell**, a writer, editor, and life-long California resident. From backpacking in Yosemite's high country and houseboating on Lake Shasta to discovering hidden staircases in San Francisco and little-known wines in Napa, she never tires of getting to know the state better. She regularly contributes to California guidebooks.
The photos were taken by **David Dunai**. **John King** proofread the book, and it was indexed by **Penny Phenix**.

ABOUT INSIGHT GUIDES

Insight Guides have more than 45 years' experience of publishing high-quality, visual travel guides. We produce 400 full-colour titles, in both print and digital form, covering more than 200 destinations across the globe, in a variety of formats to meet your different needs.
Insight Guides are written by local authors, whose expertise is evident in the extensive historical and cultural background features. Each destination is carefully researched by regional experts to ensure our guides provide the very latest information. All the reviews in **Insight Guides** are independent; we strive to maintain an impartial view. Our reviews are carefully selected to guide you to the best places to eat, go out and shop, so you can be confident that when we say a place is special, we really mean it.

Legend

City maps

Freeway/Highway/Motorway
Divided Highway
Main Roads
Minor Roads
Pedestrian Roads
Steps
Footpath
Railway
Funicular Railway
Cable Car
Tunnel
City Wall
Important Building
Built Up Area
Other Land
Transport Hub
Park
Pedestrian Area
Bus Station
Tourist Information
Main Post Office
Cathedral/Church
Mosque
Synagogue
Statue/Monument
Beach
Airport

Regional maps

Freeway/Highway/Motorway (with junction)
Freeway/Highway/Motorway (under construction)
Divided Highway
Main Road
Secondary Road
Minor Road
Track
Footpath
International Boundary
State/Province Boundary
National Park/Reserve
Marine Park
Ferry Route
Marshland/Swamp
Glacier   Salt Lake
Airport/Airfield
Ancient Site
Border Control
Cable Car
Castle/Castle Ruins
Cave
Chateau/Stately Home
Church/Church Ruins
Crater
Lighthouse
Mountain Peak
Place of Interest
Viewpoint

INDEX

MAIN REFERENCES ARE IN BOLD TYPE

INSIGHT ⊙ GUIDES

OFF THE SHELF

Since 1970, INSIGHT GUIDES has provided a unique perspective on the world's best travel destinations by using specially commissioned photography and illuminating text written by local authors.

Whether you're planning a city break, a walking tour or the journey of a lifetime, our superb range of guidebooks and phrasebooks will inspire you to discover more about your chosen destination.

INSIGHT GUIDES

offer a unique combination of stunning photos, absorbing narrative and detailed maps, providing all the inspiration and information you need.

PHRASEBOOKS & DICTIONARIES

help users to feel at home, when away. Pocket-sized with a free app to download, they go where you do.

CITY GUIDES

pack hundreds of great photos into a smaller format with detailed practical information, so you can navigate the world's top cities with confidence.

EXPLORE GUIDES

feature easy-to-follow walks and itineraries in the world's most exciting destinations, with our choice of the best places to eat and drink along the way.

POCKET GUIDES

combine concise information on where to go and what to do in a handy compact format, ideal on the ground. Includes a full-colour, fold-out map.

EXPERIENCE GUIDES

feature offbeat perspectives and secret gems for experienced travellers, with a collection of over 100 ideas for a memorable stay in a city.

www.insightguides.com